VEGETABLE PLEASURES

Colin Spencer has written nine novels, two books of non-fiction and had six plays produced. He has also written for film and television. For the last thirteen years he has had a regular food column in the *Guardian* and has published a dozen cookery books. He lives in Suffolk with the writer and journalist, Claire Clifton, where they are happy recluses in a two-acre garden, cultivating flowers, herbs and oriental vegetables, when not writing books and articles. At the moment he is passionately pursuing a *History of Vegetarianism*, to be published by Fourth Estate in 1993.

Inscribed for
Doreen & Les
with best wishes

Colin

VEGETABLE PLEASURES

COLIN SPENCER

FOURTH ESTATE · London

First published in Great Britain in 1992 by
Fourth Estate Limited
289 Westbourne Grove
London W11 2QA

Copyright © 1992 by Colin Spencer

The right of Colin Spencer to be identified as the author of this
work has been asserted by him in accordance with the Copyright,
Designs and Patents Act 1988.

A catalogue record for this book is available from the British Library

ISBN 1-85702-016-2

All rights reserved. No part of this publication may be reproduced,
transmitted, or stored in a retrieval system, in any form or by any
means, without permission in writing from Fourth Estate Limited.

Typeset by York House Typographic Ltd, London W7
Printed in Great Britain at the University Press, Cambridge

CONTENTS

B

C

E

F

G

H

I

L

M

V

W

Y

INTRODUCTION

For the last twelve years I have written a food column for the *Guardian*: this book is based on a selection of those articles and their recipes, covering the years from 1982 to 1991. I have long believed that the greatest threat to our environment is the pollution from intensive factory farming. This concern colours the choice of foods within these pages and it also embraces my own particular longings about what we eat, our relationship with the land, and our kinship with other animals.

It has become clear within the time I have been writing these articles that many people share these longings. We aspire to a concept of food which has all but vanished. We have a hatred of agribusiness with all that entails: the technology and the chemistry that treats living things, whether animals or the soil itself, like figures on a profit sheet. 'We can look on these animals – pork and bacon pigs, veal calves, beef cattle, fat lambs and table poultry – as machines to produce meat' – so wrote G. Boatfield in *Farm Livestock*, published in 1980, encapsulating a feeling which was driving intensive farming into ever greater productivity and profit.

As the American writer and environmentalist Wendell Berry has pointed out, the word 'agriculture' means *cultivation* of the land, and cultivation embodies the concepts of both culture and cult. We have all but lost our mystic reverence for the land, the mother that feeds us, because we have been deafened by the noise of the machines that have been raping her. Yet we are not Luddites, we do not want to get rid of technology, we know we cannot go back, we also know that past farming techniques were in many ways as cruel and barbaric to the animals as today's factory farming. No, what we want is for us to master the machines and for compassion towards the land and the animals to be the arbiter and judge of what is to be done and how we are to be fed.

It is far from being impossible, it is merely that everything in the modern food supply has to be altered so radically; up to now the food industry and the government have been resolute in seeing no necessity for it. But these monoliths are not the only enemies of such changes. We have as a society certain ideas about food which come from embedded traditions. These remain entrenched in our minds and, like many rigid ideas,

1

they limit experience and inflict needless suffering. Let me cite the two most obvious ones, which are generally linked together, 'meat is a necessary part of a balanced diet, while a vegetarian diet is dull', the inference being that no real gourmet or 'foodie' could be a vegetarian and be treated with respect by his colleagues.

Our whole culture places great significance on meat eating – celebrations, whether a wedding breakfast in Cheam or the Lord Mayor's banquet, revolve around the killing, roasting and serving up of the garnished dead bodies of numerous creatures and it is thought acceptable, right and proper that such food should be served. For our minds are trained to think of it as 'food' and not once living, pulsating flesh with blood coursing through its veins, cousins of the human family in the evolutionary scale.

However, different notions are now creeping into our conscious-ness, for most butchers now do not exhibit whole carcasses or poultry with heads and feet, nor do chefs serve dishes which resemble the living animal. They know that people do not want to be reminded; the flesh has to be cut from the carcass and refashioned into other shapes, while the flavour of blood and muscle is altered, drowned or fused with spices, herbs and fruits. There is, of course, among the carnivores who celebrate meat eating as a gustatory experience, a longing for the natural taste of meat and blood, exemplified in an enthusiasm for boudin noir, pink beef and underdone game. But this, I suspect, belongs more to feelings compounded of the backlash to vegetarianism, the denial that factory intensive farming is the biggest polluter of the green revolution and notions of what is trendy eating today.

Alas, there is much snobbery associated with food, and in these pages this is a windmill I have tried to pierce, but sadly my lance, like the Don's, does nothing but whirl in its sails. In one article I tried to explain how much I hate elitist food, but since that piece was written it has become much worse. The star chef tortures his ingredients, like circus animals trained in unnatural antics, as much as the chefs of ancient Rome or the medieval courts; food is prized solely for its entertainment value – its looks, its taste, its beauty and sensuous appeal, its fusion with everything else at and around the table is controlled to amuse and satisfy the diner and to justify its exorbitant price. There is no leading chef who has bothered to concern him- or herself with the deeper issues of our food supply today. Why, for example, do so many serve veal and foie gras? Two foods produced by pushing the animals to the very limit of a pathological disease: if the veal calf or the goose or duck were not slaughtered when it is, it would die from terminal illness created by the way we have fed and kept it. These practices are no different from those of the past that we affect to abhor, like sewing up the guts of living poultry, nailing geese to the floor and whipping calves and pigs to death with knotted ropes in the belief it made the flesh more tender. The absurdity of white veal is that if the calves are reared free-range and given a natural diet complete with the iron they need, their flesh cooks darker but has more flavour. There is simply a fashion for white veal which refuses to go away; it stemmed from Italy, where it still flourishes.

However, food as snobbery does not affect the majority of people, who by necessity see food only as survival and a routine pleasure. I have tried, over the years, to put food into the context of poverty and malnutrition both in the Third World and at home. What we eat today affects everyone else in the world, for we are all part of a chain of trade and commerce, and what we choose to buy and eat is highly significant to everyone else's happiness, health and livelihood. For we can help to erase poverty and malnutrition throughout the world; not to accept this notion, and find out how, strikes me as both irresponsible and inhumane. Halting the export of protein grains from Third World countries to feed livestock in the US and Europe, so that the poorer countries have more to feed their own malnourished peoples, means cutting down on our meat consumption – either giving it up altogether or eating it just once or twice a year, or at the most once a month. EEC policy is way behind on this issue, still paying out taxpayers' money to farmers as subsidies for unsold meat which goes into cold storage and adds to a vast beef mountain.

What the majority of people eat at home is over-refined and over-processed food of low nutritional content with too much sugar, salt, saturated fats and refined carbohydrates, a diet which we know promotes obesity, cancers, heart disorders and other afflictions. This diet is, of course, heavily advertised, geared towards a so-called modern lifestyle. It is the market where the chip is monarch and the earthy spud a lowly worker. The recent COMA (Committee on Medical Aspects of Food Policy) report stresses the importance of a diet high in fresh fruit and vegetables; what it does not point out is that a vegetarian diet is, of course, much cheaper to sustain and that the majority of people would be far better off if they cooked only natural ingredients and eschewed all packet, processed and convenience foods.

A further report from the World Health Organisation suggests three simple rules to observe.

1   We should consume half of our daily food as complex carbohydrates – grains, cereals, bread, potatoes, pasta and rice.
2   We should eat plenty of vegetables and fruit, cooked or raw, each day.
3   We should be very wary of eating saturated fat, that is meat and dairy products, both of which should form a minuscule part of the diet. Some vegetable fats, such as palm and coconut oil, are also saturated.

I have not included in this book all the articles which campaigned for greater humanity in the rearing of livestock. They have been omitted because, over the years, the facts of the animals' plight change and articles lose much of their force with constant updating. Public awareness has grown in the years I have been writing for the *Guardian*, so that now a much greater number of consumers know about the barbarities of modern farming – the laying hen crammed in its cage, the sow tethered in a concrete stall, the calf deprived of its natural diet for the sake of 'white veal'. The consumer has the right to such information in order to make a choice. However, such a choice is not only based upon humane concern for the plight of the livestock, for we know that free-range creatures, living as near as possible to a wild state and foraging for natural foodstuffs, have greater flavour and texture than any animal confined in a housing unit without exercise on a high-protein diet.

Although I discuss the use of meat and fish in regional cooking in this book, the recipes contain no protein of animal origin, other than eggs and dairy produce, and there is now a growing belief that a healthier and more interesting diet can be enjoyed without it altogether.

Note: Unless otherwise stated, all recipes serve four people. The imperial/metric conversions are approximate only; never switch between the two when following a recipe.

A P H R O D I S I A C S

St Valentine's Dinner for Two Celeriac Remoulade • Mayonnaise •
Cabbage and Walnut Mould • Porcini Sauce • Crémets d'Angers •
Mostarda

A P P L E S I N K E N T A N D L A N G U E D O C

Blue Cheese Apple Salad • Apple and Walnut Salad • Chilled Apple
Soup • Apple Sauce

A R T I C H O K E S I N B R I T T A N Y

Anginares à la Polita • Anginares me Koukia • Anginares Avgolemono •
Artichoke and Potato Salad

A S P A R A G U S

Asparagus Timbales • Asparagus Soufflé

A V O C A D O S I N I S R A E L

Hot Stuffed Avocado • Avocado and Butter Bean Salad • Apple and
Avocado Salad • Avocado and Spinach Salad • Iced Guacamole Soup .
Spiced Sweetcorn and Avocado • Avocado Flan • Two Pear Salad • Hot
Avocado with Cheshire Cheese

APHRODISIACS

Do aphrodisiac foods exist? There has been a fervent belief in them throughout recorded time, and almost every type of food – fish, vegetable, spice and meat – has at some time been attributed the power of providing erotic stimuli and working miracles on those parts that spin the world upon its axis. And some very odd objects have been pressed into the service of love: dried frog, brain of doves, deer sperm, milk of chameleon and genitalia of hedgehog are but a few. Science has not yet been attracted to this fascinating area of human experience to discover whether certain foods cause any actual physiological change or whether it is merely all in the mind. Even today, people still place huge trust in the power of the oyster, and I remember Derek Malcolm, the *Guardian* film critic, telling me of the effect that ginseng root had upon him. Not the tea, he emphasised, the root. Powdered rhinoceros horn fetches an outrageous price, as in the East it is still believed to be one of the most effective aphrodisiacs. Yet no one so far has identified a particular chemical agent in any of those foods which could have an effect upon the genito-urinary tract.

When it comes to the crunch, is that all we are talking about? An itch in the crotch? What about all those ideas we hear so much about? Sex in the head? The alignment of pheromones? The body scents which we all secrete, those chemical pongs fusing with lovers in mid-air, signalling the unity of those two physical masses they have just exuded from? Well yes, all that has to be there, but if, after all that, there was no itch in the crotch . . . oh, what frustration.

Yes, I fear the obsession with aphrodisiacs throughout history has come from men and they have been middle-aged, or even older, God forbid. And trying to regain lost youth and virility, wouldn't you know. Nothing else would explain the ingredients in the recipes – alligator's penis indeed. And that, by far, is not the oddest. But it does illustrate that the magical ingredients have to be expensive and exotic, which means Joe Bloggs cannot buy them, so reflecting that the man who can is rich and powerful. Sex, after all, in men's eyes is all about domination and how much you can impress and generally steamroller the poor bird.

Delving into the fascinating mystery of aphrodisiac foods one finds that they divide up into sections, beginning with those, like fish, which are high in protein and would just nourish a chap – 'build you up' as one's mother was wont to say. The more expensive the better: carp, lobster, crayfish and, of course, caviare, roe and eggs of all kinds, for those are also the source of life. Then there is beef and other meats cooked pink, so that there is plenty of red blood. The belief that eating steak makes a man of you is still prevalent, with the inverse implication that vegetarians cannot be horny.

The second section refers to the Doctrine of Signatures. This simply means that if a food looks remotely akin to the phallus or the vagina it has to somehow strengthen the power of the consumer's pudenda. Again, wouldn't you know that it is the chaps that come out on the top, for there are far more phallic-shaped vegetables – carrots, cucumbers, aubergines, etc. – than ever there are pomegranates, oysters or broad beans squinted at sideways? The Doctrine of Signatures is not in the least logical; why should men consume large amounts of oysters when they are supposed to stimulate the female? As like strengthens like. Oyster consumption should be the inverse of machismo – but it ain't. Whilst all broad beans do, with all the other pulses, is provide flatulence, although in the medieval period that was thought to provoke lust in itself. Many an abbot penned a letter starting 'a windy stomach promoteth lust'. I doubt whether any contemporary observer has noticed this phenomenon.

With the Doctrine goes the eating of the genitals of other animals, not raw, thankfully; there are numerous recipes which include the genitals of dogs, bulls, deer or, rather easier, the inclusion of an old rooster. The older the better, as it was thought the randy old cock's experienced prowess would always be beneficial. Recently, *Petits Propos Culinaires* printed a Yemenite recipe for penis from an ox or bull – directions were given for scalding 500 g of penis and then boiling it for ten minutes, after which it is removed, sliced, mixed with tomato, onion, garlic and coriander, and then cooked slowly for two hours. No aphrodisiac connection was made by the writer,* yet it is difficult to believe that this dish was eaten with as much insouciance as boiled beef and carrots.

The third section of foods are ideological. Fish again comes into it since Venus, the goddess of love, was born of the sea. But apples,

* It appears in a book *Yemenite and Sabra Cookery* by Naomi and Shimon Tzabar.

according to Scandinavian myth, were the food of gods, as was garlic and honey in the *Kama Sutra*.

Fourthly, there are the aromas, perfumes and spices to lull the beloved into a receptive and seductive mood. These can also be added to food and liquors or made up into potions and taken last thing at night. In old age Louis XIV drank distilled spirits, sugar and orange water as a restorative to vigour. A crude orange eau-de-vie, in fact. The citrus fruits, because of their astringent heady aroma, were often used as part of the arsenal of seduction, but so were basil, camphor, chocolate, cinnamon, civet, cumin, dill and fennel. Ambergris has been eternally popular, its pedigree beguiling in itself, for it is a waxy substance secreted from the sperm whale, found floating in tropical seas, used in cooking until recently but still used in perfumes. Its smell is indescribably marvellous, and, like the taste of caviare, is somehow beyond all words. Madame du Barry, it is said, used ambergris to retain the affection of Louis XV.

We also have a home-grown aphrodisiac, the root of sea holly, *Eryngium maritimum*, a handsome thistle-like plant with silver-blue leaves which grows on our beaches. The eryngo root was notorious. Falstaff in *The Merry Wives of Windsor* calls for kissing comforts and eryngos, while John Dryden talks of 'lewd dancing at a midnight ball/for hot eryngos and fat oysters call'. It was not only the phallic shape but the size of the eryngo that impressed – the root can be six foot long. These were dug up, parboiled, then peeled before slicing and cooked in syrup. Eryngo flourished and still does on the shingle coastline of East Anglia, and Colchester became a centre of candied eryngo. An apothecary named Burton started the business in the sixteenth century and it lasted three hundred years, for eryngo candy was still eaten in the Victorian age, though the freshly dug root must have been veiled from the eyes of Victorian matrons much as piano legs were covered.

As sexual arousal is such a rich combination of so many complex notions, any food that appears to increase our sexual pleasure automatically becomes an aphrodisiac. However, there are two substances known to us which are scientifically proven to excite sexual arousal and both are dangerous: cantharides and yohimbine. They work by irritating the genito-urinary tract. The former, notorious as Spanish fly, has been used for centuries to stimulate male livestock in breeding. The Marquis de Sade stuffed it in chocolates and dispensed it at tea parties as a prelude to wild orgies later in the evening. Yohimbine is a substance derived from the yohimbe tree and has been used in Central Africa since recorded time as a sexual stimulus. The bark is boiled in water and the liquor reduced, then drunk. A West Indian recipe mixes it with a puréed aubergine, pepper-corns, chillies, pimentos and vanilla. The bark contains strychnine, so as an antidote to impotency it is on the lines of kill or cure. A closer look at cantharides, too, is bound to be distinctly off-putting. It is an irritating substance found in the blister-beetle; the European species is *Lytta vesica-toria*. The substance was used in the East medicinally to burn off warts, it is toxic and contact with it produces a blister some eight hours later. Imagine what it does to your inside. Indeed, it can cause kidney damage, severe gastro-enteritis, blood in the urine and death. Priapism is merely men-tioned as a symptom.

I doubt whether Paula Wolfert knew of the more serious conse-quences when she mentioned cantharides as an ingredient in a recipe in her book on Moroccan cuisine. But you can still buy cantharides often mixed with other spices in the souks in Morocco. It shows up as fragments of iridescent blue-green, the broken wing of the beetle. The lethal dose is 0.3 g.

Better by far to stick to the Doctrine of Signatures and sculpt a few vegetable side dishes. More powerful too are all the subtle psychological aspects of consuming a perfect meal in the most beguiling context, with the right colours, candle light, music and perfume. Why not celebrate love on St Valentine's Day with a dinner *à deux* which includes some legendary aphrodisiac foods? Not just hand-whittled carrots and a dozen oysters; use aromatic spices like ginger, caraway, musk, tamarind, oregano and sage. And in such a meal texture should not be forgotten: a silk-like sauce or creamy centre upon the lips can lull the spirit into sensuality. Last year I cooked a meal for my own particular love which was heart-shaped – every course. The meal was vegetarian, for it seemed to me that no creature should end its brief existence for a celebration of love. We began with a celeriac remoulade with an aioli mayonnaise, washed down with pink champagne. For the main course there was a cabbage and walnut mould with a sauce made from porcini. The aroma of this dried fungus is a little like fresh truffles and is sensational. To refresh the palate we then enjoyed a salad of rocket leaves; this plant was banned in the Middle Ages as promoting lust, but thankfully monastery gardens continued to grow it. We drank an Australian shiraz, dark and infinitely fruity. For dessert there was a classic cream cheese mould with a hot home-made mostarda. I give the recipes below.

St Valentine's Dinner for Two

Celeriac Remoulade

3 TABLESPOONS HAZELNUT OIL
2 OZ/50 G PIECE GINGER ROOT, PEELED AND SLICED THINLY
4 CLOVES GARLIC, 3 SLICED AND 1 CRUSHED
1 GREEN CHILLI, CHOPPED
1 SMALL CELERIAC
JUICE FROM TWO LIMES
SEA SALT AND FRESHLY GROUND BLACK PEPPER
HOME-MADE MAYONNAISE (SEE BELOW)
RADICCHIO LEAVES
PARSLEY AND CHIVES

Method

Heat the hazelnut oil and fry the ginger root, sliced garlic and chilli until they are crisp – a few minutes. Leave to cool. Grate the celeriac and lightly salt it, place in a colander and leave for 1 hour, then press all the moisture from it and place in a bowl, pour over the lime juice and the oil with its spices, add some black pepper and toss well. Leave covered for another hour. Make an aioli mayonnaise by adding 1 crushed clove of garlic to a home-made mayonnaise. Arrange a few red radicchio leaves on two plates and spoon the celeriac over the leaves in a small mound, sprinkle with a little chopped parsley and chives. Serve with the mayonnaise.

Mayonnaise

1 EGG YOLK
PINCH MUSTARD POWDER
½ PINT/275 ML OLIVE OIL
1 TABLESPOON WHITE WINE VINEGAR OR LEMON JUICE
SEA SALT AND FRESHLY GROUND BLACK PEPPER

Method

Mix the egg yolk with the mustard powder to form a paste and begin adding the olive oil drop by drop, stirring with a wooden spoon or whisking all the time. As the yolk amalgamates with the oil, the oil can be poured more liberally. The trick is to keep on stirring and beating until all the oil is absorbed. When it is really thick, it can be thinned by adding the wine vinegar or lemon juice, but keep stirring or beating. Finally add the salt and pepper to taste. The egg yolk will take another ½ pint/275 ml of oil if you wish. Harold McGee, in his 1991 Badoit Lecture, 'Curious Cookery: Some Kitchen Experiments and Speculations', to the Guild of Food Writers, estimated that a single yolk can emulsify 100 cups of oil, which readers will probably agree is rather too much for domestic use.

CABBAGE AND WALNUT MOULD

I LARGE SAVOY CABBAGE
2 TABLESPOONS OLIVE OIL
2 CLOVES GARLIC, CRUSHED
¼ OZ/8 G BROKEN WALNUTS
6 OZ/170 G FETA CHEESE, CRUMBLED
2 EGGS, BEATEN
SEA SALT AND FRESHLY GROUND BLACK PEPPER

METHOD

Take off the outside leaves (cut out and throw away the thick spines) and blanch them. Slice the rest of the cabbage and stir fry it in the olive oil and garlic for a moment, so that it is reduced in bulk but still crunchy. Throw it into a bowl and add the walnuts, feta cheese and beaten eggs, mix thoroughly and add seasoning. Now butter a soufflé dish and line the bottom and sides with the blanched cabbage leaves, leaving enough to go over the centre. Pour the mixture in and fold over the leaves. Cover with some greaseproof paper and place in a preheated oven 400 F/ 220 C/gas mark 6 for ½ hour or until it has risen. Take out and leave to settle for 5–10 minutes, then unmould while it is still warm and serve straight away. Serve with the porcini sauce.

PORCINI SAUCE

¼ OZ/8 G DRIED PORCINI OR OTHER DRIED FUNGI
I OZ/25 G BUTTER
5 FL OZ/150 ML DRY WHITE WINE
I FL OZ/25 ML BRANDY
2 TABLESPOONS DOUBLE CREAM
SEA SALT AND FRESHLY GROUND BLACK PEPPER

METHOD

Place porcini or fungi in a bowl and pour boiling water over to cover, leave for an hour. Melt butter in a pan and add the drained fungi and the water, simmer for 5 minutes, then add the white wine and continue to cook for another 5 minutes until the sauce is reduced by a half. Now mix in the brandy and cream, seasoning a little. Stir the sauce well, then serve.

CRÉMETS D'ANGERS

These are heart-shaped moulds of cream cheese. The moulds in which they are made must have small drainage holes in them. Line the two moulds with cheesecloth and make them two days before you are going to eat them.

IO OZ/275 G CRÈME FRAÎCHE OR I PINT/570 ML DOUBLE CREAM
MIXED WITH 5 OZ/150 G CREAM CHEESE
4 EGG WHITES

METHOD

Beat the egg whites until they are stiff, then beat the crème fraîche until it will hold soft peaks, mix the two together and pile into the moulds. Leave in the refrigerator to drain for two days. Serve with a mostarda. You can buy this mixture of dried and preserved fruits in a mustard and sweet syrup, or you can make your own.

One year my partner, Claire Clifton, who is American, returned from Florida with a recipe with the unlikely title of many-fruited mustard. This in turn had been inspired by mostarda. Claire once again varied it and came up with the following recipe.

Mostarda

4 OZ/100 G DRY MUSTARD
½ PINT/300 ML WATER
4 OZ/100 G EACH OF SULTANAS, DRIED APRICOTS, GLACÉ CHERRIES, DRIED FIGS
2 OZ/50 G DRIED APPLE RINGS
6 PIECES STEM GINGER
6 FL OZ/175 ML VINEGAR (NOT MALT)
4 OZ/100 G LIGHT OR DARK BROWN SUGAR
1 TEASPOON SEA SALT

Method

Combine mustard and water in a bowl, stirring until smooth. Leave to stand for at least an hour – the longer the better. Measure out the fruit, chop roughly and set aside. Heat the vinegar and sugar in a heavy saucepan and cook over a moderate heat until it begins to thicken. Add the fruit, mustard and salt and stir until it boils. Continue to cook until it is quite thick. Cool, pot in clean jars, cover and label. It will keep indefinitely.

Apples in Kent and Languedoc

I was once a judge in Britain's Most Eatable Apple Contest, held down in Marden at the Fruit and Vegetable Show. We tasted a slice from forty-three different apples and marked them for eye appeal, aroma, flavour, texture and juice content. Nearly all of the entries looked superb, the kind that would grace any sideboard. One of the troubles in the trade is that the fruit is often bought for its aesthetic beauty and lies around for too long and then declines into pock-marked pap.

Few of the entries smelt of much at all, and the flavour of most was too bland, though the texture and juice content were always good. Entries were numbered and there was no conferring among the judges. Yet we were unanimous. The winning apple was Elstar. It is a cross between Golden Delicious and an Ingrid Marie. It is a red-flushed fruit with a honey glow and flavour. I particularly liked its sharpness because it had a slight lemon flavour. It was the nicest apple I have tasted for years. The apple we chose was grown by David Banfield of Kirkins Farm, Horsmonden, Kent.

The French have begun to grow Elstar. Let us hope that in years to come they do not monopolise the market.

It was with great relief that I discovered that French apples do not begin and end with Golden Delicious. In Languedoc I met and tasted the queen of them all – Reine des Reinettes, a suntanned, rosy apple with something of the flavour of a Cox's Orange Pippin, but even more delicious. Sadly, these apples are not commercial. We were told that English importers will not order them, for they cost three times the amount of a Golden Delicious.

They are more expensive because one hectare will yield only twenty tons of fruit, compared with fifty tons of Golden Delicious. Like peaches, the Reines need four to five separate pickings, while the Golden Delicious ripen at the same time and are all picked on the same day.

At a research station where they compute the trials of every possible effect of exposure to the sun, pruning and thinning, irrigation and protection from pests, they grow 300 different varieties of apple. The French were suitably modest, mentioning that at a research centre in Faversham, Kent, they grow five to six thousand types of apple.

In the Languedoc they introduce 100 different varieties of apple each year. Only one or two of these will be of some interest in the future. We were shown graphs which plotted in the apple the rise in sugar and the decline in acidity, pinpointing the best day on which a variety should be picked. The graph named 5 November for the Granny Smiths.

After biting into various apples to judge their quality, we were given lunch to show how the Golden Delicious could be cooked and served in different ways. I'm not complaining about a trip to the south of France to look at the French apple industry, but a lunch of ten courses, followed by a dinner of twelve courses, each course with apple in it, could be a trial to the most flexible of palates. On such occasions, it is a relief to be a non-meat eater: it lets you off at least two courses.

However, because the French are French and can turn a sliced apple prettily, some of their ways were beguiling enough. I was particularly keen on the *amuse-gueule* – palate ticklers which I still thought of, in my plebeian British manner, as amused girls. One could have had a whole meal of amused girls. We had small cabbage parcels, like dolmades, filled with apple, vegetables and salmon; tiny croquettes made from salt cod (brandade de morue) and vegetables; minute kebabs of apple, pepper and ham; and just pieces of apple cut as small as dice and deep fried.

It was the salads which I enjoyed most. Raw apple very thinly sliced with celery in a creamy chive dressing, mixed with very slightly cooked vegetables cut into julienne strips, was particularly good. But a galette of grated potato and apple, a hot apple soufflé served with a ripe Camembert, and a Calvados sorbet, were all very fine. Whilst some of the drinks served before the meal might become addictive: for instance, a Muscat de Lunel and Tavel rosé given a murky brilliance by the addition of a vin de noix – walnut macerated in white wine.

I now cook more with apples. But I had to leave it for a few weeks – until my stomach's memory of the apple marathon had become nostalgia.

There is a healthy tradition of apple dishes in Britain, many of them ingenious and imaginative, but they seem to stay within the pages of the recipe books. Apples are either baked with custard or made into a watery purée and eaten with roast pork. Mind you, medieval mixtures of fish or meat with apples, dried fruits, honey and mixed spices encased in flour and water crusts do not much appeal, but they don't have to.

One of the things that hinders us from cooking with apples is the way we have divided them up into eaters and cookers. The Bramley, for instance, will quickly subside into a fluffy purée and is perfect for sauces and soups, but the eating apples should be cooked too. These keep their shape and are delicious as a garnish for fish and game. There is an excellent Norman sauce for which the apple slices are coated in flour and fried in butter. When they are taken from the pan, cider is added and with the juices makes a sauce for fish. It is easy and quick to make and looks splendid as a garnish too, fanned out on a plate around the fish.

Cooking apples will reduce to a purée in a soup, whether hot or chilled. Eliza Acton gives a recipe for apples cooked in beef broth with some pearl barley or rice, flavoured with a little ginger and saffron. An apple and chestnut soup is a traditional and particularly delicious autumn combination, the apple lightening the earthy heaviness of the chestnuts.

In a summer when the postman delivers the letters wearing a sou'wester and a wet-suit, you are not likely to serve a chilled apple soup, delightful though chilled fruit soups of any kind are.

Apples go well with cabbage in a salad, but they are also good with nuts, celery, kohlrabi, carrot and courgette. Sliced with the first three, and grated with the last. There is never much point in adding anything to a beetroot salad as it stains purple and the beetroot flavour dominates.

BLUE CHEESE APPLE SALAD

1 LB/455 G COX'S ORANGE PIPPINS
2 HEADS OF CHICORY
2 OZ/50 G GOOD CRUMBLY BLUE CHEESE
    (SUCH AS ROQUEFORT OR FOURME D'AMBERT)
4 TABLESPOONS OLIVE OIL
1 TABLESPOON WINE VINEGAR
SEA SALT AND FRESHLY GROUND BLACK PEPPER

METHOD

Make the dressing, by crumbling or dicing the blue cheese into the olive oil and wine vinegar. Mix well and taste for seasoning. Without peeling the apples, slice them neatly into a bowl. Add the dressing and mix thoroughly so that all the slices are well coated. Take the leaves from the chicory and fan them out on a platter. Heap the apple slices in their dressing in the centre and serve.

APPLE AND WALNUT SALAD

I LB/455 G EATING APPLES
4 TABLESPOONS WALNUT OIL
I TABLESPOON WINE VINEGAR
2 CLOVES GARLIC, CRUSHED
I TABLESPOON SOUR CREAM
SEA SALT AND FRESHLY GROUND BLACK PEPPER
I LARGE COS LETTUCE
2 OZ/50 G WALNUTS

METHOD

Without peeling the apples slice them neatly into a bowl. In another bowl mix the walnut oil, vinegar, garlic, sour cream and seasoning. Pour this over the apples and mix thoroughly. Put the leaves from the cos lettuce in a large salad bowl, chop the walnuts and sprinkle them over the leaves. Just before serving add the apple slices in their dressing and toss well at table.

CHILLED APPLE SOUP

2 OZ/50 G BUTTER
I½ LB/675 G COOKING APPLES
I TABLESPOON FRESHLY GROUND CORIANDER
2 PINTS/1100 ML CELERY OR VEGETABLE STOCK
½ TEASPOON SEA SALT
FRESHLY GROUND BLACK PEPPER
½ PINT/285 ML SINGLE CREAM

METHOD

Melt the butter in a pan, grate the unpeeled apples into the butter and cook for a few minutes. Add the freshly ground coriander and the seasoning. Pour on the stock and simmer for 10 minutes. Let the soup cool then pour into the blender jar and liquidise. Taste and check the seasoning. Pour the cream into the soup and cool before serving.

APPLE SAUCE

- 2 OZ/50 G BUTTER
- I LB/455 G COOKING APPLES
- I ONION, CHOPPED FINELY
- 2 CLOVES GARLIC, CRUSHED
- SEA SALT AND FRESHLY GROUND BLACK PEPPER
- ½ PINT/285 ML DRY CIDER
- I OZ/25 G FLOUR OR 2 EGG YOLKS

METHOD

Melt half the butter in a pan and slice the unpeeled apples into it. Add the onion and the garlic and cook for a few minutes. Season then add the cider. Continue to cook for another five minutes. Pour into a blender jar and liquidise to a smooth purée. Melt the rest of the butter in a pan and add the flour to make a roux, cook for a moment and then add the apple purée. Heat gently and stir well until the sauce thickens. Simmer till cooked. Alternatively the sauce could be thickened with two egg yolks instead of the flour. Don't allow it to boil. This will make a thin sauce excellent with fish.

ARTICHOKES IN BRITTANY

A group of English tourists strolling in Brittany stared in puzzlement at a field of artichokes. The erect thistle-like globes, bottle green in the sun, framed by their large serrated leaves, resemble the formal design of a medieval tapestry. The English debated what kind of vegetable this could possibly be and eventually agreed it was a type of cabbage.

This area of coast from Finistère to Côtes du Nord has been growing globe artichokes for 400 years; they now produce about 90,000 tonnes, exporting to the UK only 475 tonnes, yet that is four times the amount it was ten years ago. The type grown is Camus de Bretagne, enormous and round. They can be poached for thirty minutes, left to cool and the interior leaves and choke extracted leaving the base and a circle of leaves. This provides a receptable or cup for a walnut vinaigrette or a stuffing.

I was intrigued to know if Brittany Prince could export to us the baby artichokes harvested earlier in the year. I pointed out that one could buy these in Spain and Italy, and that after trimming the whole raw artichoke was fried in oil and garlic then eaten whole. The French were insistent that the Camus de Bretagne variety could not be eaten in this way. So, in an experimental mood, I picked a few baby artichokes, took them back to England and stir-fried them for a few minutes – and amazingly delicious they were too.

The French refuse to take any suggestions from the British on these matters; there is a kind of national pride over food which is tantamount to arrogance. Though the Brittany coast is the source of magnificent fruits de mer, excellent local cheeses and delicate crêpes you will have to forgo vegetables, for the French now overcook them. Whole cauliflowers are boiled for forty-five minutes, while the florets are boiled for ten or else made into fritters smelling of stale cabbage. For them, the thought of vegetables having a brief cooking time and being al dente is a strange, alien idea of the barbarian English.

We were told that a full moon turns a field of white cauliflowers creamy yellow. But they taste best when they are that colour, we cried. No, no, the French housewife will not buy a creamy cauliflower, it must be bleached white. Nor will the French housewife buy new potatoes with the skin on; new potatoes are sold peeled and washed, thus losing much of the vitamin content. At any meal, there is hardly a salad or fresh green vegetable in sight.

So if Brittany Prince refuse to send us baby artichokes early in the spring, perhaps someone from Spain or Italy will?

Globe artichokes from Brittany are in the shops from June, complete with a printed collar around the stem that tells you how to prepare and cook them. It seems the French now serve them with the central bud and choke removed and the sauce poured into the central cavity.

Begin by slicing the top third of the leaves away. You will need a sharp, heavy knife, especially on these very large Brittany artichokes where the outside leaves tend to be tipped with brown and are solid fibre.

Boil them for up to forty-five minutes in salted water with a squeeze of lemon juice, or in a pressure cooker for ten minutes. When they are cool and well drained, twist the inner cone of leaves and lift out. Throw these inner leaves away, and then dig out the hairy choke with a teaspoon. The artichoke bottom lies beneath, a succulent bed of flesh – pour the sauce on to it, chill and serve.

It is usual to serve a strong, garlicky vinaigrette, but a couple of tablespoons of sour cream worked into the sauce goes down a treat. Or you can go to town with a strong lemony hollandaise or a mayonnaise flavoured with basil, garlic or mint. One of the classic combinations is artichoke and broad bean, and in its simplest form the cavity is filled with a broad bean purée made with a little lemon juice or wine vinegar, olive oil and flavoured with a suspicion of summer savory.

Some of the most mouth-watering recipes use only the bottoms or the tiny young hearts – the leaves are thrown away. The three here come from Greece.

You can of course always use a tin of artichoke bottoms, but let no one kid you that it is at all the same thing – especially as you would have to make up a stock from a vegetable stock cube and so far they do not come in artichoke flavour (though high-quality stock cubes for vegetarians are now readily available). Also in Brittany now they have begun to freeze the bottoms and these will be on sale soon.

ANGINARES À LA POLITA

6 GLOBE ARTICHOKES OR 14 OZ/396 G TIN ARTICHOKE BOTTOMS
JUICE OF 1 LEMON
2 LARGE ONIONS
3 SMALL CARROTS
½ LB/225 G SMALL NEW POTATOES
¼ PINT/145 ML OLIVE OIL
2 TABLESPOONS FRESH DILL
½ PINT/285 ML ARTICHOKE STOCK
  (THE WATER THE ARTICHOKES HAVE COOKED IN)
SEA SALT AND FRESHLY GROUND BLACK PEPPER

METHOD

Take all the leaves away from each artichoke, pull out the centre and cut away the choke. Trim the stalks so that you have 6 artichoke bottoms. Place these in a bowl of cold water with the lemon juice while you prepare the vegetables. If using a tin, just drain the bottoms carefully.

Slice the onions and carrots, wash and scrape the potatoes. Pour the olive oil into a pan and add the onions, carrots and dill, cook for about 3 minutes, then add the potatoes and artichoke bottoms, the stock and seasoning. Simmer over a low heat for about 40 minutes.

ANGINARES ME KOUKIA

6 GLOBE ARTICHOKES OR ONE 14 OZ/396 G TIN ARTICHOKE BOTTOMS
JUICE OF 2 LEMONS
2 LB/910 G FRESH BROAD BEANS
1 LARGE ONION
5 CLOVES GARLIC, CRUSHED
¼ PINT/145 ML OLIVE OIL
¾ PINT/425 ML ARTICHOKE STOCK
  (THE WATER THE ARTICHOKES HAVE COOKED IN)
2 TABLESPOONS CHOPPED DILL
SEA SALT AND FRESHLY GROUND BLACK PEPPER

METHOD

Prepare the globe artichokes as for the above recipe. Or open the tin and drain. Shell the broad beans and slice the onion. Heat the oil in a pan and cook the onion and garlic for a few minutes, add the rest of the ingredients and simmer for 45 minutes.

ANGINARES AVGOLEMONO

6 GLOBE ARTICHOKES OR ONE 14 OZ/396 G TIN ARTICHOKE BOTTOMS
JUICE OF 2 LEMONS
1 ONION
3 SMALL CARROTS
2 OZ/50 G BUTTER
3 CLOVES GARLIC, CRUSHED
½ PINT/285 ML ARTICHOKE STOCK
   (THE WATER THE ARTICHOKES HAVE COOKED IN)
2 TABLESPOONS CHOPPED DILL
SEA SALT AND FRESHLY GROUND BLACK PEPPER
3 EGG YOLKS
5 SPRING ONIONS, CHOPPED

METHOD

Prepare the artichokes as for the above recipes. Or open the tin and drain. Chop the onions and carrots. Melt the butter in a saucepan, add the sliced onion and garlic, cook for a few minutes then add the stock and the remaining lemon juice. Throw in the carrots and artichoke bottoms with the chopped dill and seasoning. Cook for about 30 minutes. Take the pan away from the heat and let it cool a little. Then stir the yolks of the eggs into the sauce, place back on the heat and let the sauce thicken. Stir in the chopped spring onions and allow the dish to cool. Delicious cold as a first course.

Artichokes and potatoes go particularly well together.

ARTICHOKE AND POTATO SALAD

2 TABLESPOONS WALNUT OIL

I DESSERT SPOON WINE VINEGAR

SEA SALT AND FRESHLY GROUND BLACK PEPPER

2 LB/900 G NEW POTATOES

14 OZ/396 G TIN OF ARTICHOKE BOTTOMS

12 BLACK OLIVES, STONED

3 TABLESPOONS CHOPPED FRESH MINT

I TABLESPOON SOUR CREAM

I TABLESPOON HOME–MADE MAYONNAISE

METHOD

Mix the oil, vinegar, salt and pepper together in a large bowl. Cook the new potatoes until tender, drain them well, dice them and add to the vinaigrette while still warm. Toss them well. Drain the artichoke bottoms and dice those. Add to the bowl with the olives, mix and sprinkle in the chopped mint. Lastly, mix the sour cream with the mayonnaise and stir that into the salad.

ASPARAGUS

May is the month when all tastebuds are in a state of trembling anticipation, for this is when the asparagus season begins. The first green shoots are above the ground sheathed in their tiny scales, tempting the gourmet with vivid recollections of their unique flavour. But we do not have to wait long: once above the earth the spear grows fast, ready to be cut at six inches high in a couple of days. No vegetable is quite so delicious, containing in its mineral flavour a vestige of both sea and earth, yet being the essence of a vegetable spring. It has been a top favourite since ancient times, exciting comment and celebration from emperors and poets alike.

It is one of those few plants that like salt, so it tends to grow and flourish near the sea. The wild variety (*Asparagus aphyllus*) still grows around the Mediterranean on that dry rocky coastline and is still gathered as a local speciality. Bunches of very spindly green stalks appear in the markets, and as it is strong and can be rather bitter, the plant is often mixed with other vegetables. In Spain I once ate it mixed in with chopped pimento and scrambled eggs – the bland creaminess of the eggs coated the strong savoury astringency beautifully.

It is at the end of March when this prickly spined plant, Patience Gray tells us in *Honey from a Weed* (Prospect Books), 'springs out of dry walls in deserted places and ramps about the limestone maquis'. It grows in wildernesses around Rome and over the foothills of the Pyrenees. When boiled for five minutes the colour changes from bronze to brilliant green.

Asparagus has always been expensive, for it occupies the ground where it grows for a good twenty years so that the ground cannot be used for anything else. It takes four years to establish an asparagus bed (though you can now buy crowns which are ready to harvest in a year) and though it will live for fifteen years or more, the harvest of the spears lasts for just that brief but glorious six-week interval in the spring. Expensive to harvest too. No machine can do it; each spear has to be cut beneath the surface and handled gently so that no harm comes to the tip. There is a particular asparagus knife used for this purpose, unobtainable in the UK, of course, but on the off chance I once entered a seed merchant's in Florence and haltingly asked for an '*asparago coltello*'. Only to be astonished when he instantly produced a long chisel with a sharp curved hook on the end. A formidable instrument but very efficient.

The first gardener to help asparagus along by sowing it above a hot bed – a trench filled with manure – is said to have been Jean de la Quintinie, Louis XIV's gardener at Versailles, for the Sun King was inordinately fond of the vegetable and la Quintinie managed to supply the King with spears from December. But then was there anyone who was not mad for this vegetable? Julius Caesar first tasted asparagus in Lombardy, eating it with melted butter. The Emperor Augustus coined a phrase, 'velocius quam asparagi coquantur', meaning to cook it faster than you can say Jack Robinson. Pliny recorded three spears so fat that together they weighed a pound.

There are three types of cultivated asparagus: white, purple and green. All three are grown and enjoyed in France, though other countries tend to have their particular favourite – Spain mostly cultivates white, much of the harvest being canned. The white asparagus never sees the light, the furrows in the fields are piled up (like potato cultivation) in rows, there is not a plant to be seen. I asked a Spanish farmer how on earth anyone finds the asparagus to harvest it. With great pleasure he showed me the hair cracks along the mound, evidence of that thrusting spear below. When the crack was seen the knife went in following the spear down and slicing six inches below. For me, alas, the white has little flavour and its blanched aspect does not much appeal. The purple variety is allowed to grow an inch or two above ground before it is cut and has more flavour than the white, but it is the green which we go for in Britain, and, unquestionably, this is the finest. When the asparagus is thin and pencil-like it is called sprue and this is frequently used in Italy, often with the addition of grated Parmesan, which fuses well with the flavour of asparagus.

Because of its shape and its method of consumption, asparagus has always been considered an aphrodisiac. The Emperor Augustus, though, would hardly have approved of the method of cooking recommended in an Arab love manual, where the asparagus is first boiled, then fried in fat, then covered in egg yolk. A daily dish, it was said, would keep the virile member alert night and day. As it is such a seasonal vegetable a daily dish is impossible, and I doubt whether tinned asparagus would have the same effect. But both Gerard and Culpeper wrote of the vegetable 'increasing seed and stirring up lust'. Madame de Pompadour, with her eagerness for aphrodisiac foods, lived off asparagus tips and egg yolks with an occasional dish of truffles, celery leaves and vanilla. She succeeded in giving her name to a recipe – asperges à la Pompadour – which uses egg yolks, but unfortunately it has cornmeal to thicken the sauce, an ingredient she was unlikely to have had at her disposal.

The most striking characteristic noticed by people who have consumed asparagus is the strong pong that emanates from the urine. It was noted by Dr Louis Lemery in his *Treatise Of All Sorts Of Foods* in 1702, 'asparagus causes a filthy and disagreeable smell in the urine as everybody knows'. The smell is caused by the excretion of methyl mercaptan, triggered off by the sulphur-containing amino acid methionine in the asparagus. All people who have eaten asparagus excrete the same. I stress this as there are some that I have met who claim they have never noticed their urine pong in such a way. The explanation is that our ability to detect this odour differs from person to person.

Food writers and connoisseurs of this delicious vegetable direct you to peel the spears from below the tip before cooking. I have never found this necessary, as the whole spear can be eaten down to the woody base. An asparagus kettle, where the tied bundle stands upright, so that the tips are steamed while the base stands in simmering water, is without doubt the best method of cooking the spears. Simmer for five minutes, no longer, though the time does depend on the thickness of the spears. Better by far, though, to have the asparagus a little on the raw side than soggy. If you haven't got a kettle, stand the bundle upright in a large saucepan and wedge it with new potatoes which you boil in water, and cover the top with a dome of foil. No need to eat the potatoes at the same time, though their flavour is superb; they will make an excellent salad.

I notice that my cooking of five minutes is a great deal less than that given by the late Jane Grigson – her writings we accepted like the Tablets from Moses. She says: 'time will vary from 15 minutes to 45; it depends on the variety and quality of the asparagus'. My asparagus either comes straight from the garden or from a nearby farm and perhaps the freshness of the vegetable demands such a modest cooking time. Test by piercing the lower end of the asparagus with a sharp knife.

Quite another method of cooking which has lately found favour, ensuring an al dente spear with quite a bit of crunch, is grilling. Melt some butter in the grill pan and lay the washed spears in it, turning them so that they are covered, then grill for up to five minutes turning the spears so that they are briefly seared on all sides.

What to dip these spears into should not tax the connoisseur too hard for, like Julius Caesar, I have little doubt that melted butter is the most delicious, though I would add the juice of half a lemon to sharpen it. Both hollandaise and an aioli mayonnaise are excellent, but the simplicity of the dish is now blurred and the calories are mounting up. A vinaigrette made from sherry or balsamic vinegar is particularly good and is perhaps the simplest to contrive.

If you have a generous supply of asparagus in that short season, as I do, you can go to town and use the spears in other recipes. They are, for example, after being boiled, uncommonly good chopped in scrambled egg, a simple yet magnificent supper dish. They easily make a delicious soup: the spears are boiled, the tips saved for decorating the soup, then the cooked spears are blended with stock with the addition of a little cream. Be sure to sieve the mixture after blending as nothing is more unappetising than coarse threads.

When asparagus is used in a recipe, one pound will happily feed six. Cut off the fibrous ends before steaming or poaching.

ASPARAGUS TIMBALES (SERVES SIX)

1 LB/450 G ASPARAGUS, TRIMMED
2 EGGS, BEATEN
½ PINT/285 ML MILK
SEA SALT AND FRESHLY GROUND BLACK PEPPER

METHOD

Cut off 6 of the asparagus tips and reserve. Simmer the remaining asparagus in a little boiling salted water, until tender.

Drain the asparagus well and blend to a purée in a blender or food processor. Add the eggs and milk and blend again. Season to taste with salt and pepper.

Butter 6 ramekins and place an asparagus tip in the bottom of each one. Pour in the asparagus mixture and bake at 400F/200C/gas mark 6 in a bain-marie for 20 minutes or until set.

Remove from the oven and leave to stand for a few minutes before unmoulding.

Asparagus Soufflé

- I LB/450 G COOKED FRESH ASPARAGUS
- 4 EGGS, SEPARATED
- 5 FL OZ/150 ML SINGLE CREAM
- I OZ/25 G Gruyère cheese, grated
- SEA SALT AND FRESHLY GROUND BLACK PEPPER

Method

Cut off the tips of the asparagus stems and reserve. Place the rest of the stems in the blender and reduce to a purée. If it still looks fibrous, put the whole lot through a sieve. In a mixing bowl beat the egg yolks, cheese, cream and asparagus purée. Add seasoning and stir in the asparagus tips. Butter a 2½ pint 1.5 litre soufflé dish. Beat the egg whites until stiff and fold them into the mixture. Pile the soufflé mixture into the dish and bake in a preheated oven at 425F/220C/gas mark 7 for 20 minutes, or until risen and golden brown.

A V O C A D O S   I N   I S R A E L

Until recently, my liking for avocados was matched by my ignorance of how they grow. So a sixty-foot tree laden with the green fruit, its branches curved to the ground, was a spectacular sight, like something out of an illuminated medieval manuscript. One almost expected a serpent coiled around the trunk and a Cranach-shaped Eve poised to offer the pear. The more so because I must have been standing not all that far from the original Garden of Eden, after passing along the road to Armageddon through orchards for which the Persian word was paradise. I was in Israel to look at the fruit and vegetable industry.

The avocado is a fruit of Central American origin, named from the Aztec word ahuacatl, which the Spanish called *aguacate*. It was ignored as tasteless for centuries though we did plant a tree in the Botanical Gardens, Bangalore, in 1819. At the end of the last century, American breeders got to work improving the fruit.

Today's avocado stems from three distinct races: the Mexican, which has a thin skin, small fruits, anise-scented leaves and a high oil content, and is the hardiest; the Guatemalan, which has medium to large fruits with a thickish skin and a lower oil content; and the West Indian, which will grow well only in the tropics but whose fruits will reach the size of a small melon. From these three races, there are nearly 500 varieties.

Commercially, we require a smaller avocado (only Embassy dinners demand the West Indian type) and the ones in the shops are Mexican and Guatemalan hybrids. Of these, there are four different types – Ettinger, Fuerte, Nabal and Hass. The last is the small knobbly black one which has the smallest seed and takes the longest time to ripen. It will then keep happily in the refrigerator for a week.

The avocado is the only fruit that contains protein. Its antibiotic properties also make it useful in cosmetics. Both the Ettinger and the Fuerte are pear-shaped and ripen early in the year. The Nabal is rounder and can be picked from the middle of January to June. (The avocado can hang on the tree fully grown but ripening for nine or ten months.) The Hass can stay on the tree from October until the following June.

The first seeds were planted in Palestine in 1895 but it was not until

1956 that Israeli commercial farming began. Growing avocados requires a large investment as there is no fruit for the first six or seven years but then trees can go on bearing for up to eighty years. In Mexico, it is not uncommon to have a 150-year-old tree.

In 1957, Israel exported seventeen tons of avocados to Europe. In that first year, we ate nine tons of them, the only year when we ate more avocados than France. This year, Israel expects to export 70,000 tons, 8,000 tons to Britain. France eats more avocados than any other European country. Though we now see this fruit everywhere, our national consumption remains one avocado per person, per year. In France, it is four and in Israel fourteen. Mexicans get through one or two per person per day.

The tree produces its fruit once every two years. (It flowers every other year as the fruit stays on the tree for so long.) From a few feet away, the flowers look like rhododendrons after the petals have fallen. On close inspection, these rather skeletal stems and branches bear hundreds of tiny blossoms. One of these may be pollinated by an insect and bear fruit.

Insects play another role in avocado farming, for Israel is proud of its bio-control, claiming that it is the only country exporting avocados which does not use pesticides on the crop. Farmers control the pests by importing parasites from other countries which lay their egg in the pest. The eggs grow and consume their host.

A delicate balance has to be kept in the food chain between parasitic insect and fruit pest for, if the insects devour the pest completely, they have no host to lay their eggs in. These beneficial insects are minute and barely visible. At the Biological Institute in Rehovot, the Director talks of them with the compassion and concern that Moses must have given to the Lost Tribes.

He refers to the prudent parasite which will never completely eradicate its host and the stupid parasite which lays more than one egg in its host and thus wastes itself. And he sees the whole of life as a delicately balanced food chain, referring to God as 'the highest predator that feeds off all of us'. A novel concept for modern Judaism.

Farmers often do not believe that the beneficial insect exists, for when they are released by the Institute nothing is visible. To satisfy a farmer, quite often the biologists will bring a placebo and release a phial filled with common house flies. Customs officers are also bewildered by the import of near-invisible beneficial insects, and on their forms they are written down as 'non-edible pets'.

The avocado begins to ripen twenty-four hours after it is picked. It will then take four to ten days at a temperature about 42F/5C. Once the fruit has ripened, it will keep in the refrigerator for a few days more. The Hass avocado has the highest oil content, 12 per cent when it is ripe, and is favoured by connoisseurs.

In Israel, they cook with avocado more than we do, but the flesh must never do more than heat in the oven beneath its sauce for, if it starts to cook, the flavour becomes bitter. The avocado flesh will blacken if exposed to air but painting it with lemon juice halts the process. The flesh is delicious if scooped out, seasoned with sea salt, black pepper and a little lemon juice, and then kept in a closed jar in the refrigerator for use as a spread. In Israel, the children have avocado-spread sandwiches as ours and the Americans eat peanut butter.

HOT STUFFED AVOCADO
(SERVES FOUR)

¼ LB/100 G MUSHROOMS SLICED
I LARGE ONION, DICED
I OZ/25 G BUTTER
2 TABLESPOONS SOUR CREAM
I OZ/25 G GRUYÈRE CHEESE, GRATED
I OZ/25 G PARMESAN CHEESE, FRESHLY GRATED
I TABLESPOON GREEN PEPPERCORNS
2 LARGE RIPE AVOCADOS
A LITTLE SALT TO TASTE
CHOPPED PARSLEY OR CHIVES

METHOD

Cook the mushrooms and the onion in the butter until they are soft, reduce any liquid from the mushrooms by raising the heat. Then add the sour cream, cheese and peppercorns, stir until the cheese has melted, taste and add a little salt. Preheat oven to 300F/150C/gas mark 2. Halve and stone the avocados, cut out some more of the flesh from the cavity and add that to the sauce, then fill the four halves with the sauce and place in an earthenware dish in the oven for about 5 minutes. Sprinkle with some chopped parsley or chives before serving.

Avocado and Butter Bean Salad

1 RED PEPPER
2 STICKS OF CELERY
½ CUCUMBER
1 MEDIUM CARROT
3 TABLESPOONS OLIVE OIL
1 TABLESPOON LEMON JUICE
SEA SALT AND FRESHLY GROUND BLACK PEPPER TO TASTE
1 LARGE AVOCADO (OR 2 SMALL)
4 OZ/115 G BUTTER BEANS, SOAKED AND COOKED, OR
    ONE 15 OZ/425 G TIN BUTTER BEANS
1 LARGE FIRM TOMATO
6 BLACK OLIVES

METHOD

Deseed and slice thinly the red pepper. Slice celery and cucumber. Grate the carrot coarsely. Mix together. Mix the oil, lemon juice and seasoning together. Peel and slice the avocado. Add to the vegetable mixture along with the beans. Pour the dressing over and mix thoroughly. Slice the tomato. Mince the olives. Sprinkle the minced olives on top of the salad. Arrange tomato slices in a border round the edge and serve.

Apple and Avocado Salad

4 EATING APPLES
1 LARGE AVOCADO
4 OZ/115 G SALTED CASHEWS
BUNCH OF WATERCRESS
VINAIGRETTE DRESSING

METHOD

Core apples but do not peel. Slice thinly. Peel avocado, halve and slice thinly. Chop cashews coarsely. Combine avocado, apple, cashews and watercress and toss in a vinaigrette sauce. Serve at once.

AVOCADO AND SPINACH SALAD
(SERVES FOUR)

Spinach leaves, if young, make an excellent salad. They go particularly well with avocado. If you have some young dandelions on the front lawn, pick the leaves and add them too.

6 OZ/170 G FRESH YOUNG SPINACH LEAVES
I RIPE AVOCADO, PEELED AND SLICED
I TABLESPOON PISTACHIO NUTS
I TABLESPOON SOUR CREAM
I TABLESPOON LEMON JUICE
I TABLESPOON HAZELNUT OR OLIVE OIL
SEA SALT AND FRESHLY GROUND BLACK PEPPER

METHOD

Wash and dry the spinach. Place in a bowl with the avocado slices and scatter the nuts. Mix the sour cream, lemon juice, oil and seasoning together and pour over the salad.

ICED GUACAMOLE SOUP
(SERVES SIX)

The traditional Mexican recipe for the purée guacamole, in its dip form, includes tomatoes, but this cool summer soup version omits them because the fresh green colour of the dish is essential to its visual charm.

3 RIPE AVOCADOS, STONED AND PEELED
2–3 GREEN CHILLIES, SEEDED AND SLICED
I LARGE CUCUMBER, CHOPPED
ZEST AND JUICE FROM ONE LEMON OR LIME
GENEROUS HANDFUL OF FRESH PARSLEY, CHOPPED
SEA SALT AND FRESHLY GROUND BLACK PEPPER
I CLOVE GARLIC, CRUSHED
2½ PINTS/1.5 LITRES WATER
2 TABLESPOONS FRESH CORIANDER, CHOPPED

Method

Chop the avocado flesh and place it in a liquidiser with the rest of the ingredients, except the coriander. Whizz until you have a smooth soup, flecked with the green of the parsley and cucumber. Check the seasoning, then refrigerate for a couple of hours. Finally, sprinkle the coriander over the soup before serving.

Spiced Sweetcorn and Avocado

The seasoning in this recipe is aromatic but not overpowering. The dish can be a starter, salad or side vegetable dish.

> 1 PACK (ABOUT 20) FRESH, WHOLE BABY SWEETCORN
> 1 TABLESPOON WALNUT OIL
> 1 TABLESPOON GINGER ROOT, FINELY GRATED
> ½ TEASPOON TAMARIND
> ¼ TEASPOON EACH OF NUTMEG, FRESHLY GROUND, CLOVES, FRESHLY
>   CRUSHED
> 1 FIRM BUT RIPE AVOCADO
> ZEST AND JUICE FROM 2 LIMES
> SEA SALT AND FRESHLY GROUND BLACK PEPPER

Method

Throw the sweetcorn into boiling salted water for 1 minute. Drain well. Heat the oil in a wok or pan and add the spices, squashing and breaking up the tamarind, then stir-fry the corn for about 2 minutes.

Peel and slice the avocado flesh into strips, add to the pan with the zest and lime juice, stir-fry for about 30 seconds. Season and serve.

Avocado Flan

> 1 COOKED PASTRY CASE
> 2 EGG YOLKS
> ½ PINT/275 ML SUNFLOWER OIL
> 2 CLOVES GARLIC, CRUSHED

3 AVOCADOS, STONED AND PEELED
3 OZ/75 G CURD CHEESE
3 OZ/75 G COTTAGE CHEESE
12 BLACK OLIVES, STONED

METHOD

Make a mayonnaise with the egg yolks, sunflower oil and crushed garlic. Purée one half of one avocado and beat this purée into the mayonnaise. Combine the curd and cottage cheese and add about one third of the mayonnaise. Spoon this mixture over the cooked pastry case. Slice the rest of the avocados and arrange them in the purée. There should be enough to fill the case. Spoon the rest of the avocado mayonnaise over the top, decorate with halves of the stoned olives and a little watercress. Let the flan rest for an hour or more before serving.

TWO PEAR SALAD
(ENOUGH FOR SIX)

HEART OF A CRISP LETTUCE
2 LARGE RIPE AVOCADO PEARS
2 LARGE RIPE EATING PEARS (COMICE OR CONFERENCE)
1 TABLESPOON TARRAGON VINEGAR
2 TEASPOONS TARRAGON MUSTARD
1 SMALL CARTON SOUR CREAM
SEA SALT AND PEPPER TO TASTE
1 HANDFUL CHOPPED TARRAGON (OPTIONAL)

METHOD

Arrange lettuce leaves on six individual plates. Peel, stone and core all four pears, slice them across in thin slices and arrange on the plates interleaving the avocado with the conference or comice. Mix the tarragon vinegar with the tarragon mustard and stir it into the sour cream, season with salt and pepper and spoon over the pears on each plate. If you have some fresh chopped tarragon sprinkle that over the top.

HOT AVOCADO WITH CHESHIRE CHEESE (SERVES FOUR)

3 FL OZ/75 ML FRESH DOUBLE CREAM
3 OZ/75 G CHESHIRE CHEESE, FINELY GRATED
¼ TEASPOON PAPRIKA
SEA SALT AND FRESHLY GROUND BLACK PEPPER
4 SLICES WHOLEMEAL BREAD
2 RIPE AVOCADOS

METHOD

Lightly whip the cream, fold in the grated Cheshire cheese with paprika, pepper and a little salt. Toast the wholemeal bread. Peel and slice the avocado pears and place on toast. Spoon the cream and cheese mixture on top and glaze under the grill. Serve hot.

B ALLS
Green Pasta Balls • Spiced Potato Balls • Walnut Balls

B ASIL
Pesto

B EANS
Chilli Beans • Creamed Butter Beans • Broad Bean Tartlets • Broad
Bean and Courgette Salad • Broad Bean Soup • Spiced Butter Beans •
Spiced Black Beans

B EETROOT
Harvard Beetroots

B UBBLE AND S QUEAK
Bubble and Squeak

BALLS

I have always been attracted to balls. They come in all sizes, shapes and flavours. They are sometimes canapés or appetisers, for a selection of balls makes an enticing first course, or they can be fashioned into larger ones for a main course. Yet because of the *double entendre* I have hitherto avoided naming them. Instead I choose to shape a mixture into something else, a flattened disc, a cake or a croquette. But a ball is a ball is a ball, and popping them into one's mouth is a pleasure not to be denied. Besides, part of the shaping requires modest but satisfying manual dexterity, the kind used for mud pies, not the potter's wheel.

If we ignore all those Middle Eastern balls made out of minced beef, fish, herbs and spices, we are left with balls made from nuts and vegetables. The classic ball is made to a formula. First, a purée, which is thickened by either breadcrumbs, pasta, nuts, cheese, flour or potato. This mixture must be well flavoured, if not strongly flavoured. A bland ball gives little pleasure. The mixture is then refrigerated for an hour or more (lowering the temperature glues the mixture together). It is then cut into portions, rolled in the hand and on a board, then floured, dipped in beaten egg and breadcrumbs, and refrigerated again before being deep or shallow fried. Balls are delicate objects and moulding them must be done lightly with the fingertips and palm of the hand.

When making the mixture for your ball, a decision has to be made on whether you want its interior to be soft or firm, whether the ball when cut oozes out in a slight goo or stays in place. I confess to enjoying, when biting into my ball, the sensation of a crisp exterior and a rather juicy inside. Besides, a light ball is a delicacy while a rather heavy one is a sadness. If the ball rolls rather slowly across the table then it spells doom to the stomach.

If you are dining out and meet with such a ball, the household pet will often deal with it for you. Even a senile dog will chase wearily after a heavy ball. Beware, though, how you drop it below the table; the sound of a heavy thud is a dead give-away.

Balls can be poached rather than fried. Gnocchi and quenelles are prime examples and a stunning first course can be three poached balls in a sauce in small puff pastry turnovers. Balls can be eaten cold, warm or hot, and some do not even have to be cooked, like the walnut balls below.

There is an infinite range. Here are but three recipes to entice you into a *ballon d'essai*.

Green Pasta Balls

4 OZ/115 G DRIED GREEN TAGLIATELLE

1 LB/450 G SPINACH LEAVES

4 OZ/115 G RICOTTA CHEESE

2 OZ/55 G GRUYÈRE CHEESE, GRATED

2 OZ/55 G PARMESAN CHEESE, GRATED

2 TABLESPOONS DOUBLE CREAM

PINCH OF NUTMEG

2 EGGS

SEA SALT AND FRESHLY GROUND BLACK PEPPER

WHOLEMEAL BREADCRUMBS FOR COATING

Method

Cook the green tagliatelle in plenty of boiling salted water until soft. Drain well. Cook the spinach leaves in a saucepan over a low heat until they have become a third of their bulk. Drain well. Combine pasta and spinach and place in a blender jar, reduce to a rough purée. Add all the rest of the ingredients except for one of the eggs and the breadcrumbs. Mix well. Place the mixture in a bowl and refrigerate. Beat the remaining egg. Fashion the mixture into balls. Dip into the egg and coat with the breadcrumbs. Refrigerate again. Then shallow or deep fry.

Spiced Potato Balls

1 TABLESPOON SUNFLOWER OIL

1 TEASPOON EACH OF THE FOLLOWING: CRUSHED CORIANDER,
   CUMIN, MUSTARD SEED AND CARAWAY

2 LB/900 G POTATOES, BOILED AND MASHED

1 TEASPOON ASAFOETIDA

1 TABLESPOON GARAM MASALA

2 TABLESPOONS CHOPPED GREEN CORIANDER

2 TABLESPOONS CHOPPED PARSLEY

I EGG, BEATEN

SEA SALT AND FRESHLY GROUND BLACK PEPPER

A LITTLE GRAM (CHICK PEA) FLOUR FOR COATING

METHOD

Heat the sunflower oil in a frying pan and sauté the spices (coriander, cumin, mustard and caraway) for a moment to release their oils; when the mustard seeds begin to pop they are done. Add the mixture to the mashed potatoes with the asafoetida and garam masala. Mix well, then add the chopped herbs, beaten egg and seasoning. Mix thoroughly, fashion into balls, then cool for 1 hour, before coating with the gram flour and frying.

WALNUT BALLS
(MAKES SIXTEEN)

2 OZ/55 G GROUND WALNUTS

I OZ/25 G WHOLEMEAL BREADCRUMBS

½ TEASPOON SEA SALT

A PINCH EACH OF GROUND CORIANDER, GROUND CUMIN AND CAYENNE
   PEPPER

TAHINI

ROASTED SESAME SEEDS FOR COATING

METHOD

Mix the first four ingredients together in a bowl. Add enough tahini to make a dry paste – about two teaspoons for this amount. Refrigerate. Then roll into small walnut-size balls. Roll in the roasted sesame seeds and refrigerate again before serving.

B A S I L

Yesterday I dropped my pagoda basil (marked 'rare' in the Suffolk Seeds catalogue). It somersaulted and landed upside down in a seed tray amongst some globe artichoke seedlings. This disaster made me ponder on the new strains of basil that are around this year. Basil, more than any other herb, draws us together in a chorus of fervent praise for its singular aroma and flavour. Food writers often go into simulated orgasm at the mention of a dish or ingredient but you can bet that basil, above all, draws from them the most intoxicated cry. The newcomers will certainly prompt new dishes and the reappearance of old ones.

The basil we all know, use, eat and make pesto out of is known as sweet basil or common basil or Genovese basil. This has the strongest aroma and flavour. It is an annual, like all the basils, and must be grown in our temperate climate under glass unless we have a very hot summer. It will also absorb a lot of water. Once the plant is around five inches high, pinch out the centre and let it bush. Also pick off the flowers as they appear, which will ensure that you have the longest time to enjoy the leaves.

Another basil that we see in the Mediterranean is the Greek basil which makes small clumps of tiny-leafed bushes. In those countries it is often kept on the window-sill, some will tell you as a plant to keep flies away; others, that it is a token that the household still has a marriageable daughter. They are slightly shocked if you pluck a few leaves and eat them, casting you in their mind's eye as barbarian. You may, after all, have just swallowed a portion of the dowry.

In the last few years, more varieties of basil seeds have been appearing in the herb catalogue. Dark opal has leaves the size of the sweet basil and looks pretty enough, being the vibrant shade of pickled red cabbage. But a sauce made from it for a pasta dish was disappointing in flavour. Its colour does not lift a tomato salad. Rather the opposite, red on purple reminding one of the church at its most ritualistic.

The new ones I am growing for culinary use this year appear far more exciting than dark opal. There is the lettuce basil with large floppy leaves that taste strongly, with more than a hint of anise. An arrangement of these leaves beneath a tomato salad would look striking and taste good.

Ruffle basil has large, crinkly leaves and it has a purple cousin. Again these are going to look wonderful in a salad. They taste (my plants are still fairly small) almost as strong as the sweet basil we have always used, though the purple ruffle has a slightly bitter flavour.

Then there is a lemon basil, which has fairly small leaves. The smell is strong, a fusion of verbena, a touch of clove and basil. I inhale deeply every time I pass the plant.

Lastly, the pagoda basil which was planted by Hindus to guard against evil spirits. Mine has a bent stalk after its fall but it smells strongly of cloves as well as basil and is used in India as a seasoning. A light curry dish or warm salad with a few of these crushed leaves would be both exciting and satisfying.

We all have different ways of storing basil through the winter. The Italians pack the dry leaves with sea salt in a jar. I do a pesto half-house; that is, I blend the leaves with lemon juice and enough oil to make a green purée and keep this in the refrigerator in a closed jar. Then I add crushed garlic and pine nuts to the mixture for pesto. Or I use it, as it is, for a sauce with salads. You can of course buy pesto in jars (from Wales as well as from Italy) and these are perfectly good. But it doesn't take much room to grow a few plants on a sunny window-sill. They will thrive with the smallest amount of care.

Pesto is, of course, a famous sauce and there are hundreds of recipes for it. The blender has made it a doddle.

PESTO

FRESH BASIL
JUICE OF 1 LEMON
SEA SALT AND FRESHLY GROUND BLACK PEPPER
2 CLOVES GARLIC, CRUSHED
2 FL OZ/50 ML OLIVE OIL
1½ TABLESPOONS PINE NUTS
1 TEASPOON PARMESAN CHEESE, FINELY GRATED

METHOD

You will need a couple of handfuls of the leaves. It doesn't matter if you have a bit of stalk. Throw these into a blender, add the lemon juice, a tiny pinch of sea salt, a heavy grind of black pepper, the crushed garlic cloves and the olive oil. Turn on the blender until you get a dark green sludge, then add enough pine nuts, probably 1½ tablespoons, to stiffen the sauce slightly. Blend again to crush the nuts. Finally, add the finely grated Parmesan and blend for the last time. Taste and adjust the flavourings. The predominant flavour should still be the basil, heightened by the garlic and lemon, softened by the pine nuts, given a little salty bite by the Parmesan.

BEANS

Finding the dried bean in a Twelfth Night cake made you king for the day. Otherwise dried beans have normally had a bad press. Pythagoras banned them altogether.* Then Varro recorded the belief that beans carried the souls of dead men and for that reason priests should never consume them.

I have always ascribed the ancient superstition against beans to the side view of the broad bean, which is a charming echo of the female pudenda. So eating one was, of course, taboo. Anything which resembled the generative organs was considered to have miraculous properties and therefore was treated with a mixture of awe, respect and fear.

I do not believe that the theory of Pythagoras had anything to do with the tendency of beans to produce flatulence. For in ancient Greek there are five different words for the sound of various farts, from one which is like a maiden's sigh to another word which can also mean to bugger a horse. It must be left to each of our individual imaginations as to what the latter sound could possibly be.

Beans have actually carried far too much responsibility for the wind that is always with us. For fifteen per cent of all the carbohydrate that we eat cannot be absorbed by the small intestine and in attacking the indigestible matter the bacteria in our gut turn it into gas. Beans, and all vegetables high in dietary fibre, contain various sugars (in beans it is stachyose and raffinose) which cannot be assimilated into our system.

Purées of dried beans, however, can make a delicious spread. After they have been soaked and have trebled in bulk, boil them fiercely for ten minutes, then throw away the water. This destroys a toxin only identified a few years ago. Then heat a little olive oil, throw in some herbs or spices, grated ginger root, chilli or garlic, add the beans then simmer in stock until they are tender. Then any liquid is drained away and they are puréed with either a good olive oil, as hummus is made from chick peas, or mixed with fromage frais, quark, sour cream or yoghurt. Season at this stage and add finely chopped fresh herbs. This purée can be eaten with toast or biscuits, or you can use it to stuff courgettes or tomatoes. It can also be firmed up in the refrigerator, then cut into shapes, breadcrumbed and fried in oil.

In Latin America there are forty different kinds of beans. We don't have so many on the market here, but there are many more than there used to be. We now can choose from the Japanese aduki, the Chinese mung, the Mexican black as well as all the varieties of kidney beans.

But the haricot bean is my own favourite. This is of course the French bean, which is eaten in three stages: the young green pod, the young green dried beans, which are then called flageolets, and the last stage where the bean has fattened out and lost its green colour. One of the most delicious dishes is a mixture of the green pods and the cooked flageolets, served in a béchamel sauce seasoned with nutmeg and enriched with cream. Beans should never be dull; their full earthy flavour makes a most satisfactory complement to both hot spices and a rich cream sauce. Here are two recipes which reflect that idea. 12 oz/340 g of dried beans makes plenty for four to six people.

CHILLI BEANS

12 OZ/340 G DRIED RED KIDNEY BEANS
¼ PINT/145 ML OLIVE OIL
I TABLESPOON PAPRIKA
I TABLESPOON CRUSHED CORIANDER
6 CLOVES PEELED GARLIC
3 DRIED RED CHILLIES
SEA SALT AND FRESHLY GROUND BLACK PEPPER
I LARGE ONION
I RED PEPPER

METHOD

Soak the beans overnight, or at least for 2 to 3 hours. Boil them fiercely for 10 minutes and throw away the water.

Pour the oil into a pan, add the paprika, coriander, garlic and chillies, stir for a moment, then add the beans. Keep them on the move in the oil and spices for a couple of minutes, then add enough water to cover them by about an inch and a half. Simmer for 1½ hours or until they are tender.

Taste and season. Slice the onion and red pepper thinly and stir them into the beans. Put the lid on the pan and let them stand for about 10 minutes, so that the onion and pepper just soften but are still raw.

There should be no liquid, but drain off any there is. Either serve warm as a side vegetable or cooled as a winter salad.

CREAMED BUTTER BEANS

12 OZ/340 G BUTTER BEANS
2 OZ/55 G BUTTER
2 FL OZ/55 ML OLIVE OIL
1 TEASPOON DRIED OREGANO
SEA SALT AND FRESHLY GROUND BLACK PEPPER
¼ PINT/145 ML DOUBLE CREAM
3 TABLESPOONS FINELY CHOPPED PARSLEY

METHOD

Treat the beans as above for the initial stage. Melt the butter and the oil in a pan, add the oregano, then the beans and cook for a few minutes, keeping the beans on the stir. Then add enough water to cover them and simmer for 1 hour, or until they are tender. Watch that they do not dry out.

Taste and season, then stir in the cream and chopped parsley. Reheat gently.

BROAD BEAN TARTLETS
(SERVES TWO)

1 PKT (SMALL)/250 G SHORTCRUST PASTRY
1 LB/450 G BROAD BEANS
1 OZ/25 G BUTTER
1 OZ/25 G FLOUR
½ PINT/285 ML MILK
GENEROUS HANDFUL OF PARSLEY, FINELY CHOPPED
SEA SALT AND FRESHLY GROUND BLACK PEPPER

METHOD

Roll out the pastry and cut out four shapes to fit tartlet tins. Bake blind at 400F/200C/gas mark 6 for 10 minutes. Meanwhile, pod the beans and simmer them until tender, about 5 minutes.

Make a roux with the butter and flour, add the milk and parsley to make a smooth sauce. Drain the beans, add them to the pastry cases and pour the sauce over each one. Season with sea salt and ground black pepper.

Replace in a warm oven for 5 minutes before serving. Eat with new potatoes or a salad.

BROAD BEAN AND COURGETTE SALAD (SERVES FOUR TO SIX)

Young, fresh vegetables taste so good that often the best way of serving them is a salad to begin the meal.

2 LB/900 G YOUNG BROAD BEANS
I LB/450 G BABY COURGETTES
2 TABLESPOONS SESAME OIL
2 TABLESPOONS OLIVE OIL
I LARGE SPANISH ONION
4 OZ/120 G FETA CHEESE, CHOPPED
I TABLESPOON RED WINE VINEGAR
I TABLESPOON RED WINE
I TABLESPOON CAPERS
I TEASPOON SEA SALT
5 GRINDS OF BLACK PEPPER

METHOD

Pod beans, slice courgettes thickly; simmer both in salted water for 3 minutes. Drain; heat the sesame and olive oil in shallow pan and fry cooked vegetables for 30 seconds. Add thinly sliced onion. Stir-fry for 1 minute. Add feta cheese and the rest of the ingredients. Toss well.

BROAD BEAN SOUP

Young broad beans can be eaten whole; the pods are boiled lightly with the beans inside. They are surprisingly filling. If the pods have begun to get stringy make this soup.

4 OZ/125 G CHOPPED ONION
2 CLOVES GARLIC
2 OZ/60 G BUTTER
I LB/500 G SHELLED YOUNG BROAD BEANS
12 BEAN PODS, TRIMMED
ONE TABLESPOON CHOPPED SAGE
SEA SALT, PEPPER, SUGAR
4 TABLESPOONS DOUBLE CREAM
I TEASPOON LEMON JUICE
2 OR 3 CHOPPED SPRING ONIONS

METHOD

Soften the onion and garlic in the butter. Add about 3 pints of water, the beans and the bean pods. Bring to the boil and simmer for 10 to 15 minutes, or until the beans are tender. If young they will not need peeling. Take out a few of the beans for garnishing.

Blend the soup and sieve it. Reheat, adding the young beans, the sage, seasoning and cream. Taste after a few minutes and add the lemon juice and lastly the chopped spring onion.

SPICED BUTTER BEANS
(SERVES FOUR TO SIX)

When winter is upon us we need hot, filling food.

> 3 TABLESPOONS OLIVE OIL
> I LARGE ONION, CHOPPED
> 5 CLOVES GARLIC, CHOPPED
> 2 GREEN CHILLIES, SLICED
> 2 DRIED RED CHILLIES, BROKEN UP
> 8 OZ/225 G BUTTER BEANS (SOAKED FOR I HOUR OR OVERNIGHT)
> I TABLESPOON GARAM MASALA
> 2 PINTS/I.I LITRES VEGETABLE STOCK
> GENEROUS HANDFUL OF PARSLEY, CHOPPED
> SEA SALT AND FRESH GROUND BLACK PEPPER

METHOD

Heat the olive oil in a large pan, throw in the onion, garlic, and chillies. Sauté for a moment or two before adding the drained butter beans. Stir for 2 minutes then add the garam masala and the vegetable stock. Bring to the boil, then simmer for 45 minutes. Watch to make sure it doesn't absorb all the stock; if it does, add more water. When the beans are tender, add the parsley and seasoning; stir well, then serve.

SPICED BLACK BEANS

You can be generous with Worcester sauce in cooking. I just hope the black cook pinched some of the master's sauce for this dish. Black beans were considered slave food for a long time.

8 OZ/225 G BLACK BEANS, SOAKED OVERNIGHT
4 TABLESPOONS OLIVE OIL
I LARGE ONION, SLICED
3 CLOVES GARLIC, CRUSHED
ZEST AND JUICE FROM 2 LEMONS
2 TABLESPOONS WORCESTER SAUCE
2 TABLESPOONS TOMATO PURÉE
SEA SALT

METHOD

Drain the water from the beans, heat half of the oil in a large pan, add the onion and garlic, sauté them for a minute, then add the beans, stir thoroughly for another minute before adding enough water to cover by one inch. Pour in the lemon juice and half the Worcester sauce. Simmer for 45 minutes or until the beans are just tender. Pour off the liquid. Add the rest of the oil, the tomato purée and the sauce with the lemon zest. Season with a little salt. Stir thoroughly and simmer for 3 minutes.

B E E T R O O T

 Beetroots are marvellous raw, simply grated in a lemon and honey vinaigrette. Their main problem is that their dense colour runs into anything else on the plate; indeed, they leave a purplish trail wherever they go, even through the body. My mother used to cook beetroot with a plain white (béchamel) sauce; but the sauce, by the time the dish reached the table, had gone pink in uneven splodges, somewhat ruining its appeal. This is another way of cooking beetroots and is one of the most delicious. It is an American recipe which originated in middle Europe. It can be eaten either hot or cold and is particularly good with new baby beetroots.

H A R V A R D B E E T R O O T S
(S E R V E S S I X)

2 LB/900 G BABY BEETROOTS, BOILED AND SKINNED
5 FL OZ/150 ML CIDER VINEGAR
3 FL OZ/75 ML RASPBERRY VINEGAR
ZEST AND JUICE FROM 1 LEMON
1 OZ/25 G GINGER ROOT, PEELED AND GRATED
1 RED DRIED CHILLI, BROKEN UP
2½ TABLESPOONS SOFT BROWN SUGAR

M E T H O D

If having this hot, keep the beetroots warm while you cook the sauce. Heat the two vinegars with the zest and lemon juice, adding the ginger and chilli. Simmer for 3 minutes and then add the sugar to make a syrup. Simmer for another 2 minutes until it is of a sticky consistency and pour over the beetroots. Toss them in the sauce so that they are well covered, and serve.

BUBBLE AND SQUEAK

Bubble and squeak are traditional leftovers, originally cold boiled meat and greens brought back to life by frying. The source of the name is that the greens bubbled as they boiled, then squeaked in the pan as they fried. Now it means just cooked potatoes and leftover green leaves, spring greens, cabbage or even sprouts and it has long been a Monday dinner accompaniment to the cold joint from the Sunday roast. But those days are over and the dish is worth resurrecting in the winter as a vegetarian supper dish. Spring greens give the strongest most peppery flavour, the true flavour of the brassica, but some people find this too harsh and prefer cabbage. I think this dish is worth making specially from scratch. It is a little like the Irish colcannon. It can accompany almost anything, even cheese and pickles.

BUBBLE AND SQUEAK

I LB/500 G POTATOES, UNPEELED
I LB/500 G SPRING GREENS, CHOPPED
I TEASPOON SUNFLOWER OIL

METHOD

Boil the potatoes and steam the chopped spring greens above. Drain the potatoes then mash them, slicing the skins into small pieces, if necessary. After draining, mix in the spring greens thoroughly.

Heat a heavy iron pan or non-stick frying pan and paint the teaspoon of oil over the surface with a brush. Tip in the potato and greens, smooth them down over the pan, place the pan over a moderate to high heat and leave for 5 minutes so that the underside is brown and crisp. Turn over and do the uncooked side in the same way.

CABBAGE

Cabbage with Bitter Marmalade • Cabbage with Coriander • Pickled Cabbage
Red Cabbage Spiced Red Cabbage • Sweet and Sour Red Cabbage • Red Cabbage with Chestnuts • Viennese Red Cabbage • Caramelised Red Cabbage

CALABRESE

Warm Calabrese Salad • Cauliflower in Tahini Sauce

CELERIAC

Celeriac and Egg Salad

CHICORY

Braised Chicory • Chicory in Mustard and Soy Sauce • Lancashire
Stuffed Chicory • Chicory, Orange and Pistachio Salad

CHRISTMAS

The Alternative Christmas Menu Walnut Pears • Stuffed Avocado Pancakes
with Tomato and Malt Whisky Sauce • Layered Vegetable
Mould • Pumpkin, Ginger and Potato Gratin • Lime and Almond Ice Cream
Christmas in France Tarte à Tante Tatin

COOK ISLANDS

COURGETTES

Courgette and Parsley Soup • Vegetable Casserole

CABBAGE

 Boiled greens are disgusting, so let us revalue the cabbage. For even a closely packed Dutch white, if it is not boiled and never over-cooked, can taste wonderful: it is rich in vitamin C and it has the fresh sparkle of a good crisp salad.

The vegetable stems from a wild species, *Brassica gleracea*, which still grows around the coast of Europe. It is a fecund parent for it has produced the cauliflower, kale, Brussels sprouts, broccoli and kohlrabi. The savoy cabbage, which is probably the nicest, was developed in Savoy in the Middle Ages and introduced to Britain in the seventeenth century.

As different varieties of cabbage heart at different times of year, we can produce fresh cabbage all the year round. The Dutch white shreds well and is now used for making sauerkraut, which we tend to think of as being just part of the dull Teutonic diet, but sauerkraut in the past had great value. It was the only source of vitamin C in the icy winters of central and northern Europe when nothing fresh could be grown. Captain Cook credited the good health of his crew to sauerkraut.

It is a method of salting sliced cabbage so that it is preserved by the lactic acid in the fermentation. Nowadays the cabbage is flavoured with caraway, juniper and sometimes fennel. I do not advise making your own sauerkraut, unless you have a large cool cellar and a handy wooden tub, with the time to skim off the yeasts and fungi that rise to the surface in the three weeks' fermentation.

But sauerkraut can be bought in glass jars or sometimes from a tub in a delicatessen. It can be enjoyed as a salad or cooked briefly in its own liquor for four to five minutes. If eaten hot it is best to flavour the sauerkraut by adding garlic or chopped onion in a little oil before heating the vegetable. I intensify the flavour it already has by adding more caraway, juniper or coriander.

Whatever the type of fresh cabbage, my own method of cooking the vegetable remains the same. Slice the cabbage thinly and steam it in olive oil or butter. Avoid adding unnecessary water to food which is already high in water content itself.

Treat your cabbage with respect by throwing away the exterior leaves and keeping the interior well away from any water. Inspect for insects and wipe the leaf if any bug is resting there. Then slice the leaves paper thin, cut out the stalk and slice that thinly as well.

Choose a thick-bottomed saucepan with a close-fitting lid, heat the butter or oil and any spices, then throw in the sliced cabbage, shove it around with a wooden spoon so that the pieces are sealed by the fat, then put the lid on the saucepan, lower the heat and leave it to steam in its own moisture for about four minutes. Never salt the vegetables at the beginning of cooking. Salt will make the vegetable sweat and lose its liquid and you will finish up with boiled cabbage and not steamed. Salt and pepper the cabbage just before serving.

The cabbage and marmalade recipe given here sounds bizarre but is delicious. Instead of marmalade you could use a good Dijon or Meaux mustard, you could add a teaspoon of green peppercorns or a sprinkling of hard cheese, Parmesan or Gruyère.

Not long ago I experimented with cooking the cabbage in a tiny amount of apple juice, and after the cabbage was cooked, stirred in a spoonful of quince jelly. There is another recipe which cooks red cabbage in blackcurrant juice: this is not to my taste as the dish is too sweet, for cabbage has a particular sweetness of its own, which should be complemented by the bitter fruit purées. So choose a high-class marmalade for the recipe below.

CABBAGE WITH BITTER MARMALADE

I LARGE WHITE OR SAVOY CABBAGE
I OZ/25 G UNSALTED BUTTER
I CLOVE GARLIC, CRUSHED
I TABLESPOON GOOD-QUALITY BITTER MARMALADE
SEA SALT AND FRESHLY GROUND BLACK PEPPER

METHOD

Slice the cabbage thinly. Melt the butter in a thick-bottomed saucepan and fry the crushed garlic for a few seconds. Chuck in all the sliced cabbage, turn it about in the butter with a wooden spoon, put the lid on, lower the heat and leave for 4 minutes. The cabbage should have shrunk by a third. Now add the marmalade, salt and pepper, stir and serve.

Cabbage with Coriander

I LARGE WHITE OR SAVOY CABBAGE
2 TEASPOONS CORIANDER SEEDS
2 TABLESPOONS OLIVE OIL
2 TEASPOONS CHOPPED CORIANDER LEAVES (OPTIONAL)
SEA SALT AND FRESHLY GROUND BLACK PEPPER

Method

Slice the cabbage thinly. Crush the coriander seeds with a pestle in a mortar so that they become a powder. A slightly strenuous task this, but you do not want those tiny crisp shells lurking amongst the cabbage. Pick these out and throw them away. Heat the oil in a saucepan and fry the coriander powder for a minute so that it thoroughly flavours the oil. Throw in the sliced cabbage, turn it around with a wooden spoon so that it is sealed by the hot oil. Place the lid on, turn the heat down, leave for 4 minutes. Add salt, pepper, and the coriander leaves if you have them.

Pickled Cabbage

This is simplicity itself if you prepare it over two days. It is for lovers of hot dishes which clear the sinuses in one swallow.

I MEDIUM–SIZE WHITE CABBAGE
2 TEASPOONS SEA SALT
2 TEASPOONS CASTOR SUGAR
2 TABLESPOONS SESAME OIL
2 OZ/50 G GINGER ROOT, PEELED AND GRATED
2 GREEN CHILLIES, THINLY SLICED
I TABLESPOON SESAME SEEDS
2 TABLESPOONS RICE WINE VINEGAR

Method

Slice the cabbage thinly, throw into a bowl, sprinkle with sea salt, mix well and leave for a day. Then squeeze out all the moisture with your hands; be vigorous as if wringing clothes. Sprinkle with the sugar. Heat the sesame oil and throw in the ginger root, chillies and sesame seeds. Fry for a moment until the ginger is crisp and the seeds are popping, then pour on to the cabbage. Stir and toss the cabbage thoroughly. Finally add the rice wine vinegar. Allow the cabbage to stand for another day.

RED CABBAGE

Red cabbage is a curious vegetable, full of nutty flavour when raw and magnificent when cooked very slowly in a casserole with spices, nuts and fruit, but treat it like the white cabbage, steamed or boiled very lightly, and it is a huge let-down.

It grates well and makes a fine autumn salad, tossed in walnut or sesame oil with a little crushed garlic and a few chopped walnuts and lemon juice. Or it can be sliced paper-thin if you want to have more crunch in the salad, but it still merits a good flavoured oil or vinegar.

The long slow cooking method derives from middle and eastern Europe where the red cabbage was cooked with smoked sausage, bacon or pork and was left in a great iron pot all day over the fire. In autumn and winter it was and still is eaten with venison and game.

At the beginning of the nineteenth century in France, Carême was still using massive chunks of lard and hunks of smoked bacon but had also added apples, nutmeg and brandy. Whilst in Vienna, the lard was much reduced and instead the cabbage was cooked in a beef stock and wine vinegar with yoghurt or sour cream stirred in at the last moment; the latter mixed with a little flour to stop the cream from curdling.

Impervious as ever to cooking traditions upon the Continent, we in the British Isles merely pickled the red cabbage in malt vinegar and there is still plenty of that around. Apart from the undeniable fact that its colour and sliced form has a pleasant aesthetic effect, the taste of pickled cabbage is not something to titillate the gourmet's palate.

All these recipes for stewing the red cabbage slowly are especially good if eaten the day after. They will also freeze well.

To prepare the cabbage, discard any damaged outer leaves, chop it roughly but cut out the central stem for finer slicing. It will take longer to cook if the stem is left in chunks. Start cooking with it immediately. Once cut it will stain surfaces blue, so it needs sealing in fat or oil.

S P I C E D R E D C A B B A G E

I LARGE RED CABBAGE
3 LARGE COOKING APPLES, PEELED AND CORED
3 CLOVES GARLIC
2 TABLESPOONS OLIVE OIL
I TEASPOON CINNAMON
I TEASPOON ALLSPICE
4 TABLESPOONS WINE VINEGAR
SEA SALT AND FRESHLY GROUND BLACK PEPPER

M E T H O D

Choose a large earthenware or enamelled cast-iron casserole dish which has a close-fitting lid and which will go on top of the stove as well as in the oven.

Slice the cabbage, cut apples into chunks, peel garlic and chop coarsely. Heat the oil, stir the garlic, cinnamon and allspice into the oil, cook for a few seconds before adding the sliced cabbage, turn the cabbage over so that it is sealed in the oil. Add the apples as a layer on top, pour on the wine vinegar, raise the heat so that it steams, then place the lid on the dish and put it into a preheated oven at 350F/180C/gas mark 3–4 for 2½ to 3 hours. Add salt and pepper before serving. If you add salt while cooking the cabbage will lose too much moisture and flavour.

S W E E T A N D S O U R R E D C A B B A G E

I LARGE RED CABBAGE
I LARGE ONION
IO CLOVES GARLIC
2 TABLESPOONS OLIVE OIL
2 TABLESPOONS SULTANAS
I TABLESPOON MALT VINEGAR
I TABLESPOON SOY SAUCE
2 TABLESPOONS HONEY
I TABLESPOON MUSCOVADO SUGAR
I TABLESPOON GRATED BITTER CHOCOLATE
SEA SALT AND FRESHLY GROUND BLACK PEPPER

METHOD

Chop cabbage and onion, peel and chop garlic, heat olive oil in a heavy casserole and throw in the vegetables. Stir and turn the cabbage, then add the sultanas, the malt vinegar, soy sauce, honey and sugar. Cook in the oven at 350F/180C/gas mark 3–4 for 2½ to 3 hours. Add the bitter chocolate when it has finished cooking, with a little salt and pepper.

RED CABBAGE WITH CHESTNUTS

½ LB/225 G DRIED OR FRESH CHESTNUTS

I LB/450 G COOKING APPLES

2 TABLESPOONS OLIVE OIL

10 CLOVES GARLIC

3 BAY LEAVES

I LARGE RED CABBAGE

I LARGE ONION STUCK WITH CLOVES

2 GLASSES RED WINE

METHOD

If dried, pour boiling water over the chestnuts and leave them to treble their bulk. It will take them about an hour. If using fresh chestnuts, slit the tops, then pop them into a saucepan of water, bring to the boil, let them cool and skin them.

Peel and dice the cooking apples. Heat the oil in a heavy casserole, add the peeled chopped garlic, bay leaves and then the chopped cabbage; turn in the oil so that it is sealed, add the onion stuck with cloves, apples, chestnuts and the red wine. Cook it as for the spiced red cabbage and then add salt and pepper.

VIENNESE RED CABBBAGE

I LARGE RED CABBAGE
I ONION
I LARGE COOKING APPLE
2 TABLESPOONS OLIVE OIL
4 TABLESPOONS CIDER VINEGAR
2 TABLESPOONS MUSCOVADO SUGAR
I TABLESPOON PLAIN FLOUR
5 FL OZ/150 ML SOUR CREAM OR YOGHURT

METHOD

Chop the cabbage, onion and apple, heat the olive oil and seal the cabbage, then add the vinegar and sugar, stir vigorously, then cook in the oven as in the above recipes. When it has cooked mix the flour and sour cream into a paste, season the red cabbage with the salt and pepper, place the dish on a low flame on top of the stove and stir in the cream and flour paste bit by bit, until the sauce begins to thicken and the flour is cooked through.

CARAMELISED RED CABBAGE

This recipe, from Brian Turner's restaurant, seems to me the best I have ever come across for red cabbage. It is effortlessly simple but a bit expensive on the booze.

I RED CABBAGE, FINELY SLICED
5 FL OZ/150 ML PORT, MADEIRA OR MARSALA
2 TABLESPOONS DARK BROWN SUGAR
SEA SALT AND FRESHLY GROUND BLACK PEPPER

METHOD

Throw the sliced cabbage into a thick-bottomed saucepan. Add the rest of the ingredients. Bring to simmering point, then lower the flame so that it is just cooking and leave it for 2 hours. If all the liquid has not gone by that time, raise the heat and just slightly caramelise the cabbage. Excellent hot or as a cold salad.

However, delicious as the above is, all that red cabbage really needs in order to become a huge treat is long, slow cooking and a basic sweet/sour/hot addition. Thus, adding red wine vinegar, dark brown sugar and a dried red chilli, or any variation of that mixture plus perhaps a little ginger and garlic, and cooking over a very low heat for 4 to 5 hours will do the trick.

CALABRESE

Calabrese is part of the cauliflower family; it is a type of winter-growing broccoli. The curd-like flowers are particularly rich in vitamins and folic acid, especially important in pregnancy. These vegetables also have a calcium content, so they are useful for those suffering from lactose intolerance.

WARM CALABRESE SALAD

Warm salads, where the vegetables are briefly cooked, not only retain all the flavour, colour and vitamins but they add to winter comfort.

I LARGE CALABRESE HEAD, CUT INTO FLORETS
4 TABLESPOONS OLIVE OIL
3 CLOVES GARLIC, SLICED THINLY
I TABLESPOON MUSTARD SEEDS
I TABLESPOON GARAM MASALA
ZEST AND JUICE FROM I LEMON
SEA SALT AND FRESHLY GROUND BLACK PEPPER

METHOD

Peel the calabrese stalks, then slice and place in the salad bowl. Put the florets, stalk side down, into a little boiling salted water and cook for 2 minutes. Drain.

Meanwhile, heat the oil in a pan, throw in the garlic and mustard seeds and fry until the seeds begin to pop. (Put the lid on the pan to stop the seeds peppering the walls of the kitchen.) Now add the garam masala, zest and lemon juice and seasoning, stir and simmer for a minute. Tip the calabrese into a salad bowl, pour over the dressing and toss thoroughly.

CAULIFLOWER IN TAHINI SAUCE

3 TABLESPOONS TAHINI OR SESAME PASTE
JUICE OF 1 LEMON
3 TABLESPOONS WATER OR MORE
SEA SALT AND FRESHLY GROUND BLACK PEPPER TO TASTE
1 LARGE CAULIFLOWER

METHOD

Mix the tahini or sesame paste with the lemon juice and water, add a little salt and black pepper. The tahini at first thickens when the water is added, then begins to turn into a creamy paste. You need the consistency of a runny sauce. Taste and correct the seasoning. Boil the cauliflower in a tiny amount of water for about 3 to 4 minutes after cutting it into medium-sized chunks. Drain well. Lay the cauliflower in a fireproof dish and ladle the sauce over the top. Pop into a warm oven for 10 minutes before serving.

C E L E R I A C

 How good it is to see that celeriac is now more available in both markets and self-service stores than it was a few years ago. In the winter, it is a most valuable addition to a limited range of fresh vegetables. I once tried to grow it but my sandy soil was not conducive to the root swelling (like celery, it needs a dark, rich clay soil) and the seedlings grew instead into thick leaf. This was cut and used as a fresh green celery herb and served an excellent purpose but I missed out on the vegetable itself.

Celeriac is a turnip-rooted variety of the cultivated celery. The paler it is, with a slight greenish colouring on the top, the fresher it will be. Celeriac grows dingy with keeping but it has a thick outer skin with many roots which has to be deeply peeled and however old it looks on the outside, the interior, once cut, will smell pungently and pleasantly of celery.

For years recipes have come up with only two basic methods of treating and eating celeriac – celeriac remoulade, where it is grated, blanched, dressed and eaten raw; and celeriac purée, where it is boiled or steamed, then mashed and treated rather like a superior swede. I think the vegetable deserves better than this for the root is similar to the much-prized nutty core of celery, which is generally eaten by the cook while preparing the celery stalks.

If using it raw, try mixing the grated root with finely chopped celery stalks and the dark green leaves of the celery herb, even adding celery salt instead of sea salt to the vinaigrette.

I make a variety of salads from celeriac, where the root is partially cooked, or use it in pies and tarts, or puréed as a sauce. Fortunately, it has the ability to soak up flavours while not being swamped. This is the basis of the remoulade, where the blanched celeriac is marinated for a few hours, but I don't believe this treatment really brings out the flavour. Celeriac raw is not as tasty as part-cooked. This applies to most root vegetables, except beetroot which tastes good, but different, raw or cooked.

Therefore, to make salads, peel then slice the celeriac into large chip or finger sizes and steam for ten minutes. While still warm, toss in a flavoured vinaigrette or mayonnaise. Add chopped fresh herbs and serve. Particularly good if eaten while still warm. Celeriac done this way tastes marvellous with a mayonnaise flavoured with tomato, or a rouille type, spiced with chillies, or back to the traditional remoulade with a generous amount of whole seed mustard in it.

Or try cooking celeriac peeled and cut into the same lengths, as a hot vegetable, as part of the vegetarian main meal or as a side dish with game or fish. Melt 1 oz/25 g of butter in a pan. Add three crushed cloves of garlic, then ¼ pint/150 ml each of dry white wine and water to 1 lb/ 450 g of prepared celeriac. Poach in the liquid for fifteen minutes, when it should have absorbed most of the stock. Take the lid off the pan, raise the heat and let it reduce to almost nothing. Cooked this way and mixed with mushrooms or Italian dried fungi, then placed in a herb butter sauce, it makes a marvellous filling for pies or individual tartlets.

The whole root can be stuffed and baked, though a certain amount of trimming is necessary. Peel and trim one root, cut it in half and slice the base so that it will sit comfortably. Cut out a central hole to take the stuffing made from garlic, onion, parsley, tomato and cheese. Fill the hollowed centre with the stuffing and bake in a hot oven for twenty minutes.

CELERIAC AND EGG SALAD

2 MEDIUM TO SMALLISH CELERIACS, PEELED
JUICE AND ZEST FROM 1 LEMON
3 EGGS, HARD-BOILED AND SLICED
1 ONION, FINELY CHOPPED
2 TABLESPOONS CAPERS
3 TABLESPOONS HOME-MADE MAYONNAISE
3 TABLESPOONS PARSLEY, FINELY CHOPPED

METHOD

Cut the celeriacs into chiplike pieces and poach them in boiling salted water with the zest and lemon juice for about 5 minutes. They should be al dente. While still warm, tip into a bowl and add the eggs, onion and capers. Give a good stir, then after a few minutes add the mayonnaise and parsley. Taste and adjust seasoning if necessary.

CHICORY

Chicory was discovered by accident in the middle of the nineteenth century by a horticulturist at the Brussels Botanical Gardens, a M. Brezier. It is said that in growing chicory roots for coffee he found that some had sprouted white leaves. On discovering that these were delicious, the sensible man grew them every year but kept them for himself and his family. When he died his widow told his successor at the gardens the secret so that she could enjoy a life interest in the chicory.

Eventually in 1872, the first chicory (in Flemish *witloof*, meaning white shoots) travelled to Paris and began to be eaten widely. It is an economical crop to grow, for many roots will thrive in a small space. All it needs is warmth, water and complete darkness. When you see it in the shops interleaved with blue paper, the purpose is to keep out the light and to ensure the vegetable's freshness as long as possible.

But on the other side of the Channel asking for chicory can be confusing. The closed white bud or chicon is called by the French *endive* and the French *chicorée* is what we recognise as the curly leaved endive or batavia. All were developed from *Cichorium endivia*, but this sheds small light upon the matter.

Nowadays gourmets, salad lovers and gardeners may be even more confused, for the *witloof* has spawned other relations. There is the Italian *cicorie* with its stunning shades of cardinal and purple reds, and there are many varieties, which can be grown happily through an English winter if sheltered by a cloche. Sadly the red-coloured ones go brown in cooking. All of these endives have varying depths of bitterness, but this in my opinion only adds zest to the dish.

It is a great pity that the white Belgian chicory is not cooked more often. The shoots make a simple dish which is easy to prepare. They can be steamed or poached in water or stock, they can be baked in the oven with a little butter, or served with a cream or cheese sauce.

Buy the chicory with care. It should be firm and tightly closed, a creamy white with yellowish tips tinged faintly with green. Avoid chicory that has soft loose leaves tinged with brown. There is little nutritional value in it. The low calorie content makes it excellent for dieters, but as always it is what one puts on the vegetable or what one cooks with it that makes it fattening. Here are several ways of treating chicory during the winter. It might seem expensive, but all of it can be eaten, though some cooks like to cut out the bitter central core. Dutch growers have been asked whether they could breed a chicory without this bitterness. But as they wisely say, what would be the point of that?

BRAISED CHICORY

1½ LB/625 G CHICORY HEADS
I GLASS DRY SHERRY
JUICE AND ZEST FROM I LEMON
¼ PT/145 ML CELERY STOCK
SEA SALT AND FRESHLY GROUND BLACK PEPPER
2 OZ/55 G BUTTER

METHOD

Butter a shallow earthenware dish. Trim the chicory and slice them in half. Cut out the core if you wish. Lay the chicory in the dish, fitting them neatly together. Add the sherry, lemon juice and zest to the stock, sprinkle the chicory with a little salt and pepper and pour the stock over. Dot with pieces of the butter and place in a preheated oven at 400F/200C/gas mark 6 for 20 minutes, or until the chicory is tender. Pour off all the juices and reduce to 3 or 4 tablespoons, pour that back over the chicory and serve.

CHICORY IN MUSTARD AND SOY SAUCE

1½ LB/675 G CHICORY
I OZ/25 G BUTTER
I TABLESPOON PLAIN FLOUR
4 FL OZ/115 ML WATER
2 TABLESPOONS MOUTARDE DE MEAUX OR STRONG
    WHOLE-GRAIN MUSTARD
4 FL OZ/115 ML SOY SAUCE (SHOYU)

M E T H O D

Trim and slice the chicory as above, then steam it for 20 minutes. Meanwhile make the sauce. Melt the butter in a pan, add the flour and make a roux, slowly add the water and then the mustard and soy sauce. When the chicory is cooked, lay it in a shallow dish and pour the sauce over it. Let it rest in a warm oven for about 5 minutes.

L A N C A S H I R E   S T U F F E D   C H I C O R Y

6 GOOD HEADS OF CHICORY
I TO 2 OZ/25 TO 50 G ONION, FINELY CHOPPED
I½ OZ/40 G BUTTER
3 OZ/75 G MUSHROOMS, CHOPPED
SEA SALT AND FRESHLY GROUND BLACK PEPPER
I TABLESPOON MIXED CHOPPED HERBS
2 TABLESPOONS FRESH BREADCRUMBS
4 OZ/100 G LANCASHIRE CHEESE, FINELY CRUMBLED

M E T H O D

Preheat oven to 375F/190C/gas mark 5. Trim the heads of chicory. Blanch for 3 to 4 minutes. Split each head lengthways through and lay in a buttered fireproof dish.

Soften the onion in 1 oz/25 g of the butter. Add the mushrooms and cook another 1 or 2 minutes then turn into a bowl. Add seasoning, the herbs, breadcrumbs and the crumbled Lancashire cheese. Fill the heads of chicory with this mixture . Spoon over ½ oz/15 g melted butter. Cover with foil and put into the oven for 20 to 30 minutes.

Chicory, Orange and Pistachio Salad

- 2 OR 3 HEADS OF CHICORY
- 2 ORANGES
- 2 OZ/50 G PISTACHIO NUTS
- 2 TABLESPOONS OLIVE OIL
- 1 TEASPOON WINE VINEGAR
- SEA SALT AND FRESHLY GROUND BLACK PEPPER

Method

Tear the leaves from the chicory and slice the middle section. Arrange the leaves on a large platter so that they radiate outwards. Peel the oranges over the jar of a liquidiser so that the juice goes into it, and slice the oranges across and then in half. Make sure each chicory leaf has a piece of orange in it.

Blend the nuts, oil vinegar and seasoning together into a purée. If too thick, add more oil and the juice of an extra orange. Spoon a little of this sauce into each chicory leaf.

CHRISTMAS

THE ALTERNATIVE CHRISTMAS MENU

Walnut Pears

Stuffed Avocado Pancakes with Tomato and Malt Whisky Sauce
Layered Vegetable Mould
Pumpkin, Ginger and Potato Gratin

Mixed Green Salad with real Stilton

Lime and Almond Ice Cream

Here is an alternative Christmas dinner which includes no meat, fowl or
fish. It is also trouble-free for Christmas Day. Everything except the
potato gratin can be made beforehand and combined in the morning. The
layered vegetable mould can be covered in foil and reheated in the oven.
The pancakes can be filled with the avocado stuffing, laid in a shallow oven
dish with a little of the tomato and malt whisky sauce dribbled over each
one, and heated in an oven at 400F/200C/gas mark 6 for 10 minutes.

WALNUT PEARS

4 OR 6 LARGE RIPE PEARS
4 OZ/110 G BROKEN WALNUTS (FRESH IF POSSIBLE)
4 OZ/10 G FETA CHEESE
5 OZ/150 G CURD CHEESE
FRESHLY GROUND BLACK PEPPER

For the sauce

5 FL OZ/150 ML SOUR CREAM
1 TABLESPOON WALNUT OIL
1 TABLESPOON DRY SHERRY
SEA SALT AND FRESHLY GROUND BLACK PEPPER

Method

Ensure that the pears have their stalks on and peel them carefully. Cut the bottom of each one so that they stand up nicely. Carefully core the pears from beneath. Bring some water to the boil and cook the pears in it for a brief two minutes. Drain them well.

Grind the broken walnuts so that about a third of them are a powder. Break up the feta cheese and mash walnuts, feta and curd cheese together. Season with black pepper. Stuff the pears with this mixture.

They can now be kept covered in a refrigerator for a day. Before serving, make the sauce by beating the ingredients together. Stand the pears on individual plates and dribble a tiny spoonful of sauce over the top of each one.

Stuffed Avocado Pancakes with Tomato and Malt Whisky Sauce

For the batter
(Makes 8)

4 OZ/110 G PLAIN FLOUR
4 OZ/110 G WHOLEMEAL FLOUR
½ TEASPOON SALT
2 EGGS, BEATEN
½ PINT/275 ML MILK
½ PINT/275 ML WATER

For the filling

4 OR 5 SHALLOTS
1 OZ/25 G BUTTER
2 LARGE RIPE AVOCADOS
GOOD HANDFUL OF FINELY CHOPPED PARSLEY
5 FL OZ/150 ML SINGLE CREAM
SEA SALT AND FRESHLY GROUND BLACK PEPPER

For the sauce

2 LB/900 G TOMATOES
3 FL OZ/75 ML MALT WHISKY
3 CLOVES GARLIC, CRUSHED
SEA SALT AND FRESHLY GROUND BLACK PEPPER

METHOD

Sieve and mix the two flours together with the salt. Make a well in the flour and add the beaten eggs. Mix to form a paste, then slowly add the milk and water, beating all the time to get air into the mixture. Cover the bowl and let it stand for 1 hour, then just before cooking thoroughly beat the mixture again. Heat a griddle or frying pan, smeared with a minuscule amount of oil and measure the pancake mixture out with a ladle so that they are roughly 6½ inch/16 cm in diameter. Cook until air bubbles appear on the surface and the underside is dry, then flip the pancake over and very briefly cook the other side. Interleave with greaseproof paper and store in the refrigerator. To make the filling, chop the shallots and cook them in the butter until they are soft. Take the flesh from the avocados and chop that, adding it to the cooked shallots. Mix in the parsley, cream and seasoning. Put in a bowl and cover with clingfilm until you need it the following day.

To make the sauce, cut the tomatoes in half and place in a saucepan with the rest of the ingredients over a low heat. Put the lid on the pan and simmer for 10 minutes. Allow to cook, then put through a sieve. Refrigerate until the following day when the sauce can be reheated gently.

LAYERED VEGETABLE MOULD

5–7 LARGE SPINACH LEAVES
1½ LB/700 G SPINACH, WASHED AND CHOPPED
2 OZ/50 G BUTTER
2 LARGE FREE-RANGE EGGS
2 OZ/50 G GRUYÈRE CHEESE, GRATED
1 OZ/25 G TOASTED WHOLEMEAL BREADCRUMBS
SEA SALT AND FRESHLY GROUND BLACK PEPPER
1½ LB/700 G BRUSSELS SPROUTS, TRIMMED AND SLICED

METHOD

Blanch the 5–7 large spinach leaves in boiling water and leave for 1 minute. Drain. Cook the chopped spinach in half the amount of butter until soft – about five minutes. Blend to a purée. Empty into a bowl and add one egg, 1 oz/25 g grated Gruyère and half the breadcrumbs. Season. Do the same with the sliced Brussels sprouts. Cook them in the butter until soft, blend and add the rest of the ingredients.

Butter a 6½ inch/16 cm, 2½ pint/1.5 litre soufflé dish and arrange the spinach leaves so that they cover the bottom and go up the sides with about a quarter hanging over the outside edge. Fill with ½ inch/1 cm of the Brussels sprout purée, smoothing it down flat, then cover with ½ inch/1 cm of the spinach purée. Continue in alternating layers until the dish is full. Then fold over the overhanging parts of the spinach leaves so that the top is completely covered.

Place the dish in a baking tin with room for about 2 inches/5 cm depth of boiling water round it. Cover the top of the mould with buttered paper. Place in a preheated oven at 400F/200C/gas mark 6 for 45 minutes.

Take the mould from the oven and let it rest for 8 minutes, then unmould by covering it with a plate and upturning it. Refrigerate if need be for a day, then reheat by covering with buttered foil and placing in a preheated oven at the above temperature for 15 minutes. Slice like a cake.

PUMPKIN, GINGER AND POTATO GRATIN

I OZ/25 G BUTTER
3 FL OZ/75 ML OLIVE OIL
I OZ/25 G GINGER ROOT, GRATED
I TEASPOON CUMIN
½ TEASPOON CARDOMOM SEEDS
I½ LB/700 G PUMPKIN FLESH, CUBED
I½ LB/700 G POTATOES, BOILED FOR I5 MINUTES, THEN SLICED
SEA SALT AND FRESHLY GROUND BLACK PEPPER
I OZ/25 G TOASTED WHOLEMEAL BREADCRUMBS

METHOD

In a large frying pan melt the butter in the olive oil. Sprinkle in the ginger root, cumin and cardomom, then toss in the pumpkin and potato. Fry for 8 to 10 minutes, until the pumpkin is soft on the inside and crisp on the out and the potato has browned slightly. Season well with sea salt and black pepper. Pour contents into a gratin dish and sprinkle the top with breadcrumbs. Place under a hot grill until the top is crisp and the interior bubbling.

LIME AND ALMOND ICE CREAM

3 OZ/75 G FLAKED ALMONDS
6 EGG YOLKS
10 OZ/275 G CASTOR SUGAR
1½ PINTS/850 ML SINGLE CREAM
JUICE AND ZEST OF 4 LIMES

METHOD

Toast the almonds in a hot oven until they are golden brown and reserve. In a bowl, whisk the egg yolks and 3 oz/75 g of the sugar until smooth and thick. Bring half of the single cream to the boil. Take from the heat and add to the egg and sugar mixture. Stir well, and put back on the heat in a double boiler to make a custard. Let it cool, then add the rest of the ingredients and mix well. Place in the freezer and whisk it just before freezing and again 1 hour later.

CHRISTMAS IN FRANCE

To cook for oneself in France is like hearing Bach in a cathedral. The context is perfect and the material is of impeccable quality. All the more unexpected, then, to experience the French making a hash of a favourite dish in their own home. Looking back on it I cannot help but feel a twinge of *schadenfreude*.

One Christmas in Brittany three of us were invited to dine with a young doctor and his wife. We explained that we did not eat meat – always a surprise to the French, though they told us that this phenomenon was becoming more common among their British visitors.

We ate in the kitchen and we knew immediately we walked in that here were people who loved good food; the rows of pickled vegetables and fruits in eau-de-vie, the combination of smells, oil, butter, Calvados and garlic reassured us as we sat down at a large plastic table which was swept clear of children's toys and the bric-à-brac of their meal – more plastic plates, spoons and cups.

It was the young doctor himself who did most of the cooking. His wife taught at the local school, and they both gardened and grew all their produce. Any vegetables and fruits that were not consumed fresh were bottled and pickled; nothing, interestingly enough, was frozen. 'Freezing erases the flavour,' the doctor said and continued to explain that pickling intensifies it. On the principle that reducing a vegetable to a mass of ice crystals is one way of drowning it, while pickling is submersion in a flavoured bath, he may have a point.

The high point of the meal was the dessert. Tarte à Tante Tatin, or upside-down tart, or as Ann Willan calls it tarte des demoiselles Tatin. Is it the aunt's or the spinsters' pie? Ann Willan says it comes from the Loire. Madame Leclerc claimed it was a Breton dish and the secret of the rich pastry was the crème fraîche as well as the butter that it was made with.

Madame Leclerc began by sitting at the plastic table in front of apples so wizened and shrunk I would have thrown them on to the manure pile. (I certainly would have been ashamed of the guests seeing them.) She peeled, cored and sliced the apples into small chunks. Then into an aluminium shallow dish she sprinkled castor sugar and a little water and a few cubes of butter. She placed the dish on a high flame with the apple in it, cooking the apple and caramelising the sugar. She put the dish aside and took a mound of golden pastry which she rolled out. She explained that every week they had this tart so as to use up the crème fraîche.

Ann Willan in her recipe in *French Regional Cooking* (Hutchinson) does not mention the crème fraîche added to the pastry, so perhaps this is a tarte Tatin Breton version. Madame Leclerc heaped the cooked apples into a small mound and covered it with the pastry. She baked the tart.

Now, here is the first error that this good French cook made. She forgot that the tart was in the oven. It might well have been the sparkle of our conversation, or my own excitement at discovering Muscat (a sweet wine in which you taste the grape pip) or the fact that the ten-month-old baby was sitting on my lap throwing the plastic cutlery at the sheepdog. Whatever the reason, Madame forgot the tart and the tart was black. The tart was promptly put upon the window sill outside to cool down. For nothing much upsets French cooks. Anything, they feel, can be saved with a little adjustment.

But here was the next mistake. Madame forgot the tart again and it was snowing outside, not exactly on the tart, but near enough to half freeze it. Madame, recalling the tart, brought it back into the kitchen.

She then set to and scraped the black from the dome. She then tried to turn it the right way up, but it had stuck. And so, the last calamity, the tart was never turned upside down with its caramelised apples inside the pastry saucer.

But undaunted, Madame cut chunks of tarte Tatin and we all began to eat it, with a little more crème fraîche. It was amazing after the rigours of its creation that it was still a revelation of deliciousness, though both the baby and the sheepdog managed to make large inroads into my portion.

The following evening in our primitive cottage we started to make the tarte Tatin. We checked on Ann Willan to see how long the baking time should be. We added enough crème fraîche to make a stiff paste. We froze the pastry for an hour. We caramelised the apple and a sliced quince, we placed its pastry helmet on and baked it. If cooked for the right time, the tart will invert beautifully without the caramelised fruit sticking to the base.

Our tart was a dream. It looked like haute pâtisserie and melted on the palate like instantaneous paradise. We wolfed it down with some of the Muscat wine and, unlike Madame who made it once a week, we continued to make one almost every night. If you cannot find Muscat, and have not come across any here, drink a glass of Calvados with the tart. Use double or sour cream instead of the crème fraîche. Our strong white bread flour is the nearest to the French flour for baking, but you can enrich it more by adding a little soya flour.

TARTE À TANTE TATIN

1 OZ/25 G UNSALTED BUTTER

2 OZ/50 G CASTOR SUGAR

2 TABLESPOONS WATER

3 LARGE COOKING APPLES

For the pastry

4 OZ/100 G UNSALTED BUTTER, ICE–COLD

6 OZ/175 G STRONG WHITE BREAD FLOUR

2 OZ/50 G SOYA FLOUR

1 OR 2 TABLESPOONS DOUBLE OR SOUR CREAM

METHOD

Use a shallow baking dish that you can put on top of the flame as well as in the oven. Melt the 1 oz/25 g of butter with the sugar and water in it, dice the apple and let it brown, raise the flame so that the juices will evaporate. Let it caramelise.

Grate the ice-cold butter into the flours and quickly make a paste. Add enough cream to make a stiff dough. Refrigerate for 1 hour. Roll out the dough to about ½ inch/6mm thick. Heap the apple in the centre of the dish and cover with the dough, cut around it and return the unused pastry to the refrigerator. (Optional: you could decorate the top, as we did, with a sculptured representation of part of tante Tatin's anatomy.) Bake in a preheated oven at 400F/200C/gas mark 6 for 10 or 15 minutes or until the top is golden brown. Overturn tart with a palette knife and scoop all the apple into the centre. If the apples are bland in flavour, add a little cinnamon or grated ginger after they have caramelised.

COOK ISLANDS

The first Pacific island I dropped in on had been visited a week before by Cyclone Sally. This was Raratonga, the main island in the Cook Island group.

Because of Sally, one cliché was omitted: there were no frangipani leis to greet visitors. Twenty-two days after her devastating visit, there was just enough frangipani blossom for the visitors to have one flower thrust behind their ear. (It is said that if you wear the blossom behind the right ear, you are married; behind the left ear, free: and in the middle of the hair, just desperate).

I somehow missed the frangipani when I arrived but was given a lei two days later and it smelt fragrant and heady. The weather was humid and, on the second day, it pelted with rain, recalling Maugham's short stories where frustrated planters' wives shot their lovers.

How the European colonists fared with local food is rarely mentioned by fiction writers, and frenzied madness might come about, I thought some days later, if one had to survive on a diet of taro root, sago and yam. Cyclone Sally had ensured that we were back with staple foods; these were high in carbohydrate but a record low in flavour.

Sally had tossed coconuts, avocados and mangos from their lofty perches and washed them out to sea. She had knocked down breadfruit, guava, pawpaw, lemon, orange, lime and mandarin trees. Worse still, Sally had sunk the small banana boats which chug between the islands bringing fresh fish and produce to Raratonga.

All of the South Pacific islands are related, having been colonised from Taiwan between 5000 and 3000 BC. The people who were to go on to colonise New Zealand ate taro, yam, banana, breadfruit, coconut and rice, all staples of mainland south-east Asia by 3000 BC.

Their methods have not changed and even today food is either cooked in a pit or boiled in salt water. Once the rain came, pelting straight down in unceasing sheets of solid water, the thought of umu (the name of the oven) or the umukai (the name of the feast) was not likely to bring much of a sparkle to my eye.

The umu is prepared by digging a two-foot pit. This is filled with twigs and logs and a fire is lit which is then covered with riverstones.

'Why riverstones?' I asked.

'Because they are there,' Mr Koteka, my Cook Island guide replied. Philosophically, I felt this was sound enough and would have been satisfied but, after a pause, Mr Koteka enlarged upon the logic. 'Because you do not have to dig them up.'

The food is then prepared, wrapped in banana leaves, placed upon the hot stones and covered with more banana leaves and palm fronds. The meat is placed in the centre, the fowl are arranged around it, then vegetables and fish. It is left to cook for twelve hours or more.

The umukai is not just a tourist attraction but the usual method of cooking for everyone. The pit is always there in the backyard with the remains of yesterday's fire, and so are the riverstones.

The results of the umu were, I have to say in all honesty, dull and dreary. Food is overcooked and tends to be presented undressed, looking wan and shredded. But there were notable exceptions. I was excited by a new flavour in vegetables. This was rukau, the taro top leaves, which are cooked to a purée, then mixed with a little minced onion and coconut milk. They said it was like spinach, but rukau has less oxalic acid, so less assault on the palate. It was more like the flavour of chard stalk. Taro root, the ancient staple food, is something else – a doughy compound, cloying and insipid upon the tongue.

The other great delight was ika mata, a speciality of the islands. This is sliced fish marinated in lime juice with coconut sauce and chilli. The dish is known all over the South Pacific, in various guises and titles. Raw fish, in fact, is as commonly eaten here as it is in Japan. Yet the Cook Islanders are far less adventurous about what they eat from their lagoons and beaches than either the Japanese or Chinese. Brandis in the Raratonga Hotel is the only restaurant completely run by Cook Islanders which also has a menu in Maori. I couldn't understand why the bread and pasta were so leaden until I asked my old friend Mr Koteka. The flour has to come by sea and it gets damp on the voyage. A pity, for an ika arautea, which was a shrimp and mushroom ravioli in a dill sauce, tasted sensational, apart from the fact that the ravioli were little pouches of bleached leather.

To conclude there was a superb fruit salad. The islanders had snatched from the jaws of Sally a pawpaw, a mango, a green kiwi and a peach, which they had artfully sliced and then arranged so that they spilt cornucopia-like from an inedible pastry basket.

It took the Raratonga Hotel four days to recover from the cyclone, but it will take me a lifetime to forget the taste of taro.

Courgettes

 Courgettes always grow in great abundance, so one must remember to cut them when small, as their flavour is distinctly more intense than when they are allowed to get larger.

Courgettes can be cut from the plant when they are as small as 3 inches/17.5 cm. Their flavour then is at its best. They can be steamed whole for three minutes – no longer for they should never be as soft as a sponge. Alternatively those small whole courgettes can be stir-fried in olive oil in a wok and will be cooked in the same time.

Most of us eat courgettes when they are around 6 inches/15 cm long. This is the size you find them in the shops and markets. See that the colour is a dark burnished green. If the green has yellowed and looks dull and the outside skin has hardened, they have been around for more than a couple of weeks. This size of courgettes can be halved, sliced into four and stir-fried. They can be boiled whole and served with fresh chopped herbs or a light parsley sauce. They can also be sliced across and salted for an hour, so that they lose some of their water content, rinsed, then dried in a clean cloth and fried in olive oil and a little crushed garlic. In Italy these pieces of zucchini are dropped either in seasoned flour or a light batter before deep frying. Always cook them unpeeled.

Small courgettes are also good raw. Grate them, then place in a colander with a little salt, leave for an hour, squeeze the liquor out of them and toss in oil and vinegar with a few finely chopped herbs, mint, marjoram, basil or parsley. Alternatively, they can be cut and sliced into julienne strips – pieces the size of a matchstick – salted, drained, and then tossed in sauce vinaigrette.

Then there are courgette salads, which involve parboiling or steaming of the vegetable. The courgettes are sliced across into ½ inch/1 cm chunks, or down their length into 3 inch/7.5 cm slices, cooked for a moment or two, so that the interior flesh is still resistant to a fork, then drained well and tossed in a sauce – yoghurt and fresh herbs or oil and lemon.

Larger courgettes can be stuffed with various fillings. Soups can be made from them. They are one of the main ingredients in ratatouille. They can be made into a soufflé, an omelette, a tart or quiche, their flavour enhanced by different herbs and cheeses – I have used marjoram, basil, tarragon and rosemary. They are excellent in a vegetable casserole.

The courgettes that have turned into marrows are best either stuffed, or cubed and fried in olive oil with grated root ginger and garlic. They need to soak up flavour.

COURGETTE AND PARSLEY SOUP

I GENEROUS BUNCH OF PARSLEY
2 BAY LEAVES
2 LB 3 OZ/I KG COURGETTES
I TABLESPOON OLIVE OR WALNUT OIL
I CLOVE CRUSHED GARLIC
IO FL OZ/275 ML YOGHURT

METHOD

Make a stock by bringing 2 pints of water to the boil with the parsley stalks and bay leaves, simmer for 20 minutes, then throw away the parsley and bay. Meanwhile slice the courgettes and toss them in the oil with the garlic in a pan over a modest heat. Add the stock, bring to the boil, and let them simmer until soft. Add the chopped parsley and liquidise the lot. Return to the saucepan and reheat, adding the yoghurt. If the soup seems too thick, add either more yoghurt, skimmed milk, or stock.

VEGETABLE CASSEROLE

14 OZ/IOO G DRIED CHICK PEAS
I SPRIG ROSEMARY OR I TEASPOON GROUND ROSEMARY
2 LB 3 OZ/I KG TOMATOES
I GLASS RED WINE
4 SMALL GREEN PEPPERS
2 LARGE ONIONS
4 MEDIUM COURGETTES
2 TABLESPOONS OLIVE OIL
I TEASPOON PAPRIKA

METHOD

Soak the chick peas overnight, or pour boiling water over them and leave for an hour until they have tripled in bulk. Cook them in their water with the rosemary either in a pressure cooker for 20 minutes, or by simmering in a saucepan for 1½ hours. The chick peas are done if they break apart when stuck with the point of a knife. Liquidise half of the chick peas in their stock and reserve the other half whole.

Cook the tomatoes with skins and green calyx in the wine in a pan with a close-fitting lid over a low heat. They will be cooked within 10 minutes. Put them through a sieve and discard the skins and pips. Slice the peppers, cut away the seeds and pith, slice onion and courgettes, and cook in a pan in the oil and paprika for 10 minutes.

Pour into a large casserole dish the chick peas, tomato sauce and the vegetables. Mix well. Bake in a preheated oven at 400F/200C/gas mark 6 for 30 minutes, so that the flavours amalgamate and the sauce thickens a little.

DEMONSTRATIONS
Harrods Glamorgan Sausages
Jenners of Edinburgh Tyropitta (Cheese Pie)

DINNER PARTY
Avocado, Grapefruit and Purslane Salad • Spring Vegetable Soup •
Spinach Pancakes • Cauliflower Almonds

D E M O N S T R A T I O N S
H A R R O D S

On the second floor at Harrods in their kitchenware department they do cookery demonstrations. In 1985, I did one to publicise my book *Cordon Vert*. I had never before cooked in public, and as my cooking at home is consistently hampered by the unexpected – the kitchen roll falling into the soup or one of the cats sitting upon the pastry – I went into the experience believing that anything could happen.

I cooked six dishes in two hours and was expected to give a running commentary on what I was doing through that time. An audience of fifty women sat on chairs in neat rows before me. There was one middle-aged man among them who took notes. He was American: the CIA again? A few other people ambled around on the edges. I had a mike and an able assistant, Marilyn Aslani, who arranges these events and who wrote *The Harrods Cookery Book*.

It was an unexpected place to find myself, as shopping at Harrods is rarely on my programme. Mind you, one step into the food hall and I am seduced by the display. But here I was selling an upmarket book of fifty-two vegetarian dinner-party menus, aiming at a cuisine of style and lightness.

For the six dishes I had chosen old favourites: pipérade, oeufs durs soubise, Chinese potato pancakes, Glamorgan sausages (I'm fond of the Welsh touch), a spinach mould and an apricot cream cheese. Marilyn had done all the initial preparation and there were little piles of chopped vegetables, measured oil, milk, eggs, wine and tiny heaps of chopped herbs.

Such a precise regimen laid out before me in a kind of boxed dais, surrounded by gas rings and a tiny sink big enough to bath a hamster, made me realise how artificial a form the recipe is. Every oven is different, every ring and every saucepan reacts in different ways to the application of heat. Cooking, then, is always something of a gamble if taken straight from the recipe printed. But surely most of us modify a recipe as we go? As I looked about me, having quite forgotten the dishes I was supposed to cook, or what went into them, it seemed as if I would have to do exactly that.

There was the CIA taking notes, and I was still in the introduction, which covered, I hoped, any possible mishaps by informing them that there was nothing professional about my cooking. But I could see as they stared up at me they did not believe one word. The dishes were arranged in an order and I was to begin with the spinach mould as it needed forty-five minutes' baking. The recipe required four or five large spinach leaves to blanch, so as to cover the inside of the mould and to reach over the top. Harrods spinach leaves had obviously been grown for tiny tots' tea-time and I tell you, you can't stretch a spinach leaf. A whisper to Marilyn set her sorting through a mound of spinach leaves in search of a few longer than three inches. I continued to talk and moved two pudding basins around to look busy. After a few minutes we came up with a dozen small leaves and I made a patchwork quilt out of them.

To cook the six dishes I would have to start one, continue with another and sometimes talk about a third.

I remembered what actors always say about a sticky audience: look around for one with a sympathetic face and address your remarks to that person. Luckily for me, there was a woman dead centre who sat there beaming at me right from the beginning. I prayed she wouldn't leave to buy a pound of sprouts downstairs. But this audience seemed gripped (perhaps it was the way things boiled over – I am not sure) and the man from the CIA continued to take frenetic notes. I pointed out that he could save himself a lot of trouble by just buying the book. It was around then that a dreadful revelation visited me. I realised that some of my recipes were just not adequate.

In the mould recipe it said half a pint of milk and I found myself using less than a gill. Reason: Harrods spinach had more liquid in it than the leaves picked from the garden. I had stipulated wholemeal bread-crumbs when at home I use toasted wholemeal breadcrumbs. For the recipe for Glamorgan sausages, the amount of herbs assembled looked pathetically tiny. Back at home I would have trebled them, but this, I told myself, was my recipe. The scales at Harrods cannot weigh light, surely? And then, of course, the wholemeal breadcrumbs were all fluffy so that the sausage mixture was doughy rather than gooey and in the pan they burnt. Not only did they go black on one side but they tended to flatten out as if exhausted by the whole business. No wonder. My patter was beginning to flag. The third blow was that there were no fresh apricots at Harrods. Yes, can you believe, it in the top people's food emporium there were no apricots. Just think – for a whole day or maybe more, the duchess had to go without apricots. So did I. I did the recipe with peaches. I don't think it made much difference.

The food, as it was cooked, was cut up in tiny portions and passed around the audience. I stared at part of a blackened sausage and thought, rather you than me. I give below the recipe for Glamorgan sausages because it has become a favourite – when it is not burnt. As to the mould, when that was upturned the audience clapped – perhaps with relief. But for the first time in my life I felt like a top chef.

GLAMORGAN SAUSAGES

6 OZ/170 G LANCASHIRE CHEESE, GRATED
4 OZ/115 G TOASTED WHOLEMEAL BREADCRUMBS
1 LARGE BUNCH OF SPRING ONIONS, CHOPPED
3 EGG YOLKS
1 GENEROUS HANDFUL OF PARSLEY, CHOPPED
1 TABLESPOON EACH OF FINELY CHOPPED TARRAGON, BASIL,
    CHIVES AND CHERVIL
1 TEASPOON MUSTARD POWDER
SEA SALT AND FRESHLY GROUND BLACK PEPPER
1 EGG WHITE
MORE TOASTED WHOLEMEAL BREADCRUMBS (FOR COATING)
SUNFLOWER OIL FOR FRYING

METHOD

Mix all the ingredients up to and including the pepper in a bowl or in a food processor. The mixture should just stick together nicely with 2 egg yolks, but if it is too dry, add the third. Shape the mixture into 12–16 small sausages, dip each one into the egg white and roll in breadcrumbs to cover. Heat the oil in a frying pan and fry the sausages until golden brown.

They can be eaten with a home-made tomato sauce or with Dijon mustard, or moutarde de Meaux. They make a good appetiser or first course.

JENNERS OF EDINBURGH

The year following the Harrods demonstration I did one at Jenners of Edinburgh, an impressive and stylish store. (Perhaps some call it the Harrods of the Athens of the North.) But Jenners, unlike Harrods, is not equipped for cookery demonstrations, yet still believes they can be given.

I was led to a small kitchen table – with plastic tablecoth – near a cash register and a telephone in the kitchenware basement. On the table was a pile of vegetables, potatoes in their Safeway bag, peppers, onions, garlic and broad beans. No sink and no stove but a Baby Belling whose oven went off if you turned both rings on. The nearest water was in the ladies' loo, so I could not even wash my hands between crushing the garlic and peeling the orange. I asked for a damp cloth, a bucket of water and a range of implements, which we began to unhook from the wall.

'Delia Smith brings her *batterie de cuisine* with her,' I was told. 'Bully for her,' I replied and inquired where I could empty the bucket of potato-scrubbing water. I went on to pod the broad beans as Edinburgh house-wives squeezed past me to scan the microwaves.

'Do you stock Teflon ware?' one asked me. 'Try the second basement down.' (A polite way of saying go to hell.)

'And I want three mixing bowls of various sizes.' By this time, I had three assistants running around stealing baking trays, sieves, timers, oven gloves and zesters from the displays. My *batterie de cuisine* was beginning to look more impressive than the shop's – never mind what Delia Smith had.

'There's no sour cream.' In the whole of Edinburgh, not a carton of sour cream? By now the assistants were in a splendid flap, so I calmed them down by telling them that cooking was all a matter of improvisation. In this context, nothing mattered very much and very little mattered at all. We used a little fresh cream instead to purée the broad beans to go into the centre of the globe artichokes.

There were now about fifteen citizens standing around including some frail and elderly ones, but there were no chairs for them and certainly no mirror slanted above my table so that they could easily view any sleight-of-hand with the garlic cloves.

In the midst of a general explanation about the characteristics of Mediterranean cookery, the telephone rang. It squawked somewhere near my left shoulder. An assistant answered it *sotto voce*. Someone wanted to know where the Teflon ware was.

Two minutes later, while I was talking of the spices used in North Africa, the cash register rang repeatedly on a large order and my voice vied with it, projecting 'cardomom, cumin and coriander' as clearly as the rains in Spain.

I soldiered on to find that a description of the lack of dairy herds in southern Europe was becoming entangled with a persistent woman squeezing behind me in search of the best-quality kitchen scissors. 'Have the scissors changed or is the bacon rind more durable?' I heard her complain.

We came to the *pièce de résistance* – the Greek filo cheese pie, tyropitta. I picked up the filo sheets, holding one up to the light. A small girl insisted it was a Kleenex tissue. The audience thought it most unlikely that filo pastry could be bought in Edinburgh. But it can and it was. I give the recipe below, for it is a winner. The original Greek recipe I have adapted to make it less rich in saturated fats, using a polyunsaturated oil instead of butter between the pastry leaves.

The audience ate up all the pie and the five other dishes, even each artichoke leaf with its smidgeon of broad bean purée. All the recipes came from my *Mediterranean Vegetarian Cooking* (Thorsons).

They were a lovely audience. And they stood for two hours. But, please, Madam Jenner, next time give them chairs to sit on and a viewing mirror to look at and a quiet place where they can hear without the demonstrator having to compete with Ethel Merman. And please give your cooks a sink with running water, four gas rings and an oven with an adequate preparation area. The bucket of water can be used to dunk the cash register and the telephone.

TYROPITTA (CHEESE PIE)

PINCH OF NUTMEG

1 TEASPOON FRESHLY GROUND BLACK PEPPER

4 EGGS

12 OZ/340 G FETA CHEESE

8 OZ/225 G COTTAGE OR CURD CHEESE

4 OZ/100 G PARMESAN CHEESE, GRATED

3 CLOVES GARLIC, CRUSHED

2 TABLESPOONS FINELY CHOPPED PARSLEY

CORN OIL

1 LB/450 G FILO PASTRY

SESAME SEEDS

METHOD

Add the nutmeg and pepper to the eggs and beat them with a fork. Crumble in the feta cheese and stir in the other cheeses together with the garlic and parsley. Continue beating until you have a smooth sauce.

Oil a baking tray. Cut the sheets of filo pastry in half. Layer them on the baking tray, brushing each sheet with oil. Continue until half the pastry sheets have been used. Now place the cheese mixture over and then cover with the remaining pastry, oiling each sheet. Sprinkle with the sesame seeds and bake in a preheated oven at 400F/200C/gas mark 6 for 30 minutes.

Dinner Party

Here is a meal, which could be a dinner party for six to eight people, as some readers are still mystified as to how to structure a menu if you omit both meat and fish.

I would start either with the salad or the soup and conclude the meal with cheeses and fresh fruit, or, if feeling more than usually wanton, I might make a fresh fruit salad soaked in a little eau-de-vie.

Purslane can now be bought in London markets in the spring and summer. It is imported from Cyprus, though it is the Far Eastern population here that eat it. If you have a garden, it will grow easily throughout the summer.

Purslane itself grows wild in India where it has been eaten for thousands of years. It is cultivated in the Middle East and southern Europe. It has fleshy leaves and tastes slightly spicy; it is rich in minerals, vitamins and protein. It was popular in the days of Elizabeth I, and is eaten now as a salad in France.

Avocado, Grapefruit and Purslane Salad

3 LARGE PINK GRAPEFRUIT
I TABLESPOON CIDER VINEGAR
4 TABLESPOONS OLIVE OIL
½ TEASPOON DIJON MUSTARD
SEA SALT AND FRESHLY GROUND BLACK PEPPER
3 LARGE RIPE AVOCADOS
I BUNCH OF PURSLANE

Method

Peel the grapefruit, ensure that all the pith is taken off the fruit, break into segments and leave in a colander to drain. Make a vinaigrette sauce with the cider vinegar, olive oil, Dijon mustard, sea salt and black pepper. Peel the avocados, stone them and slice across.

Cut the tops from the purslane, then take the leaves from the rest of the stalks. Discard the stalks. Arrange on individual plates some purslane leaves, then interleave avocado and grapefruit segments, pour over some vinaigrette, and decorate with the tops of the purslane.

If you cannot find or grow purslane, then use lettuce for the base and deep-fried parsley for the decoration.

Spring Vegetable Soup

For the stock
2 HEADS OF CELERY
2 LARGE ONIONS
2 CLOVES OF GARLIC
PARSLEY AND WATERCRESS STALKS

For the soup
1 TABLESPOON WALNUT OIL
4 OZ/125 G NEW POTATOES
6 SMALL CARROTS
4 OZ/125 G FRENCH BEANS
4 YOUNG LEEKS
4 OZ/125 G RISONI
PARSLEY AND WATERCRESS LEAVES
SALT AND PEPPER

Method

Coarsely chop all the ingredients for the stock, boil 4 pints/2.3 litres of water, and add the stock vegetables, simmer for 1 hour, then liquidise and strain through a sieve. Throw away the used vegetables.

Heat the walnut oil in a saucepan, chop the potatoes and carrots in thumb-nail sizes and sauté in the oil. Add about half of the stock and simmer for 10 minutes. Add more stock and the French beans. Cook for 5 minutes more then add the leeks and risoni – a tiny pasta which will thicken the soup slightly. Cook for a further 5 minutes.

Put the parsley and watercress leaves into a blender and add the rest of the stock. Liquidise so that the herbs have flecked the stock green. Taste the soup for seasoning. Add salt and pepper and taste again. At the last moment add the flecked green stock and heat the whole soup. It is important that the watercress and parsley are not boiled, only heated.

SPINACH PANCAKES
(MAKES SIX TO EIGHT)

For the batter
4 OZ/125 G PLAIN FLOUR
4 OZ/125 G WHOLEMEAL FLOUR
½ TEASPOON SALT
3 EGGS, BEATEN
2 TABLESPOONS SUNFLOWER OIL
¾ PINT/400 ML MILK

For the filling
2 LB/900 G SPINACH LEAVES
4 OZ/125 G GRUYÈRE
4 OZ/125 G SOFT GOATS' CHEESE, RICOTTA OR CURD CHEESE
SALT AND FRESHLY GROUND BLACK PEPPER

METHOD

Sieve and mix the two flours together with the salt. Make a well in the flour and add the beaten eggs. Mix to form a paste, then slowly add the milk, beating all the time to get air into the mixture. Leave it to stand for a few hours. Add the oil just before cooking.

Tear the spinach leaves from the stalks, wash them well, then drain and pat the leaves dry. Place the leaves in a large saucepan without any water and cook over a low heat with the lid tightly on. The leaves should have reduced and be cooked through in 6 to 8 minutes. Take the pan from the heat and squeeze all the moisture from the leaves.

Grate the Gruyère and mix it into the soft goats' cheese, ricotta or curd cheese. Put the spinach into a bowl and let it cool, then beat the cheeses into the spinach and add a little salt and black pepper.

Make the pancakes, let them drain on absorbent paper, put about 2½ tablespoons of the filling into the centre of the pancake and fold the outsides in to form an enclosed envelope. Place in a large buttered earthenware dish, place a knob of butter on top of each pancake, and pop into an oven to reheat.

CAULIFLOWER ALMONDS

4 OZ/125 G FLAKED ALMONDS
I LARGE CAULIFLOWER

METHOD

Bake the almonds in the oven so that they become golden brown and crisp. Cut the cauliflower into small florets. Boil in salted water for no longer than 3 minutes, drain carefully. Melt a little butter in a pan, add the cauliflower and let it brown slightly. Serve with the baked almonds sprinkled over the top.

With this meal I would steam some new potatoes with mint.

EDUCATION
A Visit to St Christopher's School at Letchworth

EGGS
Oeufs Mollets Leek Purée • Caper Sauce • Potato Purée • Mustard and
Egg Sauce
A Reader's Plight and the Impossibility of Precise Cooking Instructions
A Simple Dish Eggs and Tomatoes

ÉLITIST FOOD

EDUCATION

A VISIT TO ST CHRISTOPHER'S
SCHOOL AT LETCHWORTH

 Recently I visited St Christopher's School, Letchworth. I planned to speak to the sixth form in the afternoon and to the local vegetarian society in the evening. What makes this school of particular interest is that ever since its foundation in 1915 it has been vegetarian in practice and principle, the only boarding school – though it also takes day pupils – which still is.

Letchworth itself was part of garden town idealism at the turn of the century. It was begun by Ebenezer Howard, a theosophist and fervent believer in the Utopia of newly planned rural settlements. (Only recently has Letchworth acquired any pubs. I was told that for decades the bar at the cricket pavilion did amazing business.) Before the First World War a vegetarian school must have seemed the natural and necessary outcome of Fabianism and those alternatives to the high consumerism of the urban bourgeoisie. This was the idealism that for years we associated in a derogatory fashion with home-spun tweeds, sandals and dandelion wine. Now that it has recently come out of the freak closet, it surely has a more appealing and potent force.

Today, confronted by the starvation of the Third World, and revolted at the beef and butter mountains which entrenched EEC policies have created, the clear principles of St Christopher's school and its brave statements about world hunger should compel us to look more closely at how it works.

The school was one of the pioneers with Summerhill, Bedales and Dartington Hall. It believed in no corporal punishment, in non-compulsory lessons, in sandals and shorts instead of uniforms, in self-government, in the use of Christian names for the staff, in parent involvement (St Christopher's began the first parent–teacher association in 1920) and, most shocking of all, in coeducational boarding houses. As with all such institutions, local myths abound that the children smoke in class and use their nut cutlets as cricket balls, that the lack of discipline leads easily to riots and that the mixed boarding houses can and do lead to you-know-what.

So the vegetarianism is part of a general liberal package which centres on respect for the pupil as an individual. The diet is based on fresh fruit, vegetables, grains, nuts and pulses, together with some use of milk, cheese, eggs and honey. It is in fact what we now know as the supreme healthy diet, low in saturated fats, high in dietary fibre with an emphasis on fresh produce and no canned or junk food.

For lunch I was offered a multiplicity of delicious salads, cooked and raw vegetables, nuts, beans and fruit with various dressings. For a school meal it was haute cuisine. I could not fault it and ate with gusto. However, later in the day I got the impression that though these salads were always there for lunch, with an alternative hot meal, people quickly got bored with them and there was an idea among the pupils that salads were not a proper meal. All I can say is that they do not know a good thing when they see one.

The pupils are encouraged to learn the principles of cultivation – there is a large vegetable garden – and how to keep goats, hens and bees. The nutritive and moral grounds for the school diet are carefully explained. The staff need not be vegetarian but are asked to eat as though they were while on the premises. There is a cooking school with room for twenty. I watched a class of fifteen girls and boys aged ten making individual cheese soufflés. It did my heart good to see the lads industriously stirring the sauces or enthusiastically whipping the egg whites. What a change from my youth, when if you attempted to make a roux you were immediately considered effeminate. These boys looked upon the cooking lesson as a necessary chore; they were no better and no worse than the girls, which makes me conclude the obvious, that the talent for cooking well does not belong exclusively to either gender.

The information dispensed at the school was on the exploitation of animals, on world food problems, and the stranglehold that multi-nationals have over the distribution of resources, on nutrition and diet. The school is keen to introduce pupils to a wide range of vegetarian diets, including vegan and macrobiotic, Chinese and Indian.

Yet how far do these high principles of behaviour influence the pupils? After my discussion with the sixth form I felt more cynical, for they seemed unaffected and unimpressed. Only about three of them came from vegetarian households; the rest happily returned home in the holidays and ate meat – in fact most of them looked forward to spearing a sausage on a fork.

Yet in the evening, when I discussed this with an enthusiastic crowd of vegetarians, the view from the floor was very much that the young people after leaving school would go on a meat binge and then return to a vegetarian diet later. Was this just wishful thinking? It might be, but how we are programmed in school and at home does have a lasting influence, even if only one of lasting revolt. Would these pupils when they left school wade into steaks, and then when they saw newsreel footage of famine in Ethiopia recall lessons in the distribution of grains (more now goes to feed animals than humans) and give up eating meat? I would dearly like to see St Christopher's do some research on the eating habits of old pupils.

Eggs
Oeufs Mollets

I have a particular fondness for oeufs mollets. We have no English word for the arrested cooking in a boiled egg. 'Mollet' describes an egg which stops cooking when the white is firm and the yolk is still raw or runny. Soft-boiled is the nearest equivalent, but is not as precise as mollet.

Oeufs mollets provides us with some of the most delicious ways of beginning a meal. Served in individual ramekin dishes, or cocottes, the soft-boiled egg, springy to a light-fingered touch, lies on a delicate vegetable purée and is glazed with a sauce. Delicious hot or cold, in either case they can be prepared for a dinner party some hours beforehand, leaving one free to tackle the main course.

But it is necessary to have a strict regimen and timing to achieve the right result. First choose a pan in which the eggs will fit, so that you can wedge them in without their moving. Wire egg holders do exist, in which you place the eggs before lowering them into the water. It sounds a perfect answer to the problem – I still have not acquired one.

For a large egg to be mollet it must be boiled for three and a half minutes and not a second more. Standard eggs need three minutes. Have your eggs at room temperature, wedge them into the saucepan and pour the boiling water down the side of the pan to cover them. If you pour the boiling water straight on to the eggs they will crack. Place the saucepan immediately over the heat so that the water quietly simmers and you can start timing. If an egg still cracks you will have to dispense with it and start again. When the time is up plunge the eggs into a basin of cold water, or let the cold tap run over them. They must stop cooking. If you just drain the water from them, there is enough heat in the egg to cook the yolk through.

Most recipes for oeufs mollets give a timing of four minutes for the cooking. But the minute they are immersed in boiling water they begin to cook a little and certainly there is a fraction of time to be allowed for after they are immersed in cold water. If half of the yolk is cooked through, there is, in my terms, no point in oeufs mollets. The whole enjoyment of the dish is the flavour of the raw yolk fusing with the purée and sauces.

Allow the eggs to cool. It is almost impossible to peel the shell from an egg still angry with heat, which is why oeufs mollets hot is more difficult to contrive. With the back of a teaspoon gently beat the egg so that hair cracks appear, and peel the shell with its inner membrane away. With luck the whole shell will fall away like a jacket.

If you want your oeufs mollets hot, have the ramekins warming up in the oven, and the vegetable purée hot in a saucepan. Spoon purée into each ramekin and place the egg on it. Have the ramekins standing in a baking dish, pour boiling water into the dish and pop it into the oven for about three minutes or until the eggs are just heated through. Any longer and the yolks will begin to cook. Meanwhile make your sauce, or reheat it, to cover the tops of the eggs. Pour a little of the sauce into each ramekin and serve immediately.

Here are some suggestions for purées and sauces.

L E E K P U R É E

I LB 5 OZ/600 G LEEKS
I OZ/25 G BUTTER
SEASONING

M E T H O D

Trim the leeks, split, wash and cut them across in ½ inch/1 cm slices, then pop them into a saucepan with the butter over a low heat. Place the lid on and leave them for a few minutes. They will steam in their own liquid and should be cooked within 3 minutes. Let them cool, then liquidise. Add seasoning, check by tasting. Place enough purée in each ramekin to cover the base by ½ inch/1 cm. Enough to serve 5. An onion purée is made the same way.

C A P E R S A U C E

I OZ/25 G BUTTER
2 TABLESPOONS CAPERS
5 FL OZ/150 ML WATER
GLASS DRY SHERRY
I TEASPOON CORNFLOUR

METHOD

Melt the butter and add the drained capers. Let them sweat in the butter, then add the water, bring to the boil and simmer for a moment. Add sherry, simmer for another moment, then thicken with cornflour. Pour over each egg in its ramekin.

POTATO PURÉE

    1 LB 5 OZ/600 G POTATOES
    2 OZ/50 G BUTTER
    2 TABLESPOONS DOUBLE CREAM
    SEA SALT AND FRESHLY GROUND BLACK PEPPER

METHOD

Peel and boil the potatoes. Drain, then put the pan back over the heat and stir for a moment, so that any excess water is driven off in steam. Shove all the potatoes through a sieve, add the butter, mix well, add salt, pepper, and cream, stir again. Enough here for about 8 ramekins.

MUSTARD AND EGG SAUCE

    2 COOKED EGG YOLKS
    3 TEASPOONS MOUTARDE DE MEAUX (OR MUSTARD POWDER)
    1 RAW EGG YOLK
    5 FL OZ/142 ML CARTON DOUBLE CREAM

METHOD

Make a paste of the cooked egg yolks and the mustard, add the raw yolk, a pinch of salt and stir in the cream.

All the above purées and sauces can be eaten hot or cold, except for the potato which is not very nice cold. You can make purées of mushroom, spinach, aubergine, avocado, even of the plebeian parsnip, though I would be tempted to use a few curry spices with it. You can also cover the egg with a simple sauce béchamel or mornay. Almost any sauce or purée will merge happily with oeufs mollets.

A Reader's Plight and the Impossibility of Precise Cooking Instructions

A *Guardian* reader tried making oeufs mollets and failed. He wrote in and said:

'Colin Spencer writes: "The English have no word for an arrested boiled egg." One can see why. Anglo-Saxon caution has stood us in good stead in the past.

'This morning I destroyed four eggs by peeling them and was led to let the vegetables boil dry. The preparation of a non-meal took two hours.

'Is Colin Spencer one of your humorous writers?'

This is an example of how impossible it is to rely on precise instructions in cooking, for there are so many uncertain factors: the age of the egg (the fresher an egg the faster it will cook), how hot the boiling water is when simmering, the type of saucepan used – copper will cook quicker than steel or aluminium or enamel. In order to master the art of oeufs mollets, I advise trial experiments. Also, if you are nervous of egg yolks being contaminated with salmonella, either make certain your supply of eggs is free of the contamination (a small free-range flock that you know is best) or avoid the dish altogether.

A Simple Dish

This dish gives a simple but satisfying fusion of flavours. Variations of this recipe appear in the cuisines of France, Spain, Italy, North Africa and Greece. As fresh tomatoes are often expensive and tasteless, use part of a small tin, well drained.

Eggs and Tomatoes

3 TINNED TOMATOES, CHOPPED
I TABLESPOON OLIVE OIL
I TABLESPOON TOMATO PURÉE
SEA SALT AND FRESHLY GROUND BLACK PEPPER
2 LARGE EGGS

Method

Drain the chopped tomatoes well. Pour the oil into a pan and heat it, add the tomatoes and stir in the tomato paste. Season, then break in the eggs and cook them on top of the tomatoes. When the whites are set, slip the eggs out on the top of the tomatoes and eat with plenty of fresh bread.

ÉLITIST FOOD

There was a letter in the *Guardian* listing pet hates which concluded with the dish vegetable terrine. How right he was, I thought, picturing this slab of striped and polka-dotted porridge that tastes of the pap that last dribbled down my chin at ten months. This is food pretending to be nutritious and tasty when it is neither; it is food which pretends to be gourmet and trendy, when in a few years time it will seem as ludicrously out of date as a kiwi garnish.

Such dishes make me feel I have been worked over by a con man. This is elitist food which has no connection with anything else, insulated by the company expense account

Not all elitist food is pretentious but it is veering that way. Food is becoming precious; it is being fiddled about with, tarted up in such a way that the frills do not show. Food has now become adroit, so that what appears natural is contrived and has really taken ten cooks five hours to prepare.

Yet corner a foodie and every time they will come up with a definition of good food which we all agree with. It would be something like the freshest of ingredients, prepared simply and cooked as briefly as is palatable. Yet though this food is praised, when it is discovered, even the most astute of critics is lulled into a mood of baroque celebration when the pompous food arrives. When will cooks stop composing pictures on a plate, when will they think of nutrition, taste and texture first, the visual aspect last?

But the worst crime of elitist food is that it dismisses the needs of society. It does not address itself to the single parent living in two rooms, it does not consider the unemployed, pensioners or anyone who cannot fork out £30 for a meal for one without wine. It does not, cannot, see food as survival, food as healthy body fuel, which at the same time can be appealing and original and not cost an arm and a leg.

FIBRE
Baked Beans • Fasoulia

FLYING
Why Not Take a Picnic?

FRUIT
Fruit Brûlée

FIBRE

A recent report on fibre in the British diet claims that though most of us know vaguely that eating it is beneficial, we are not quite certain what foods it appears in and few of us eat much of it anyway.

Dietary fibre (it used to be called roughage) has been widely recognised since the early seventies as an essential part of the diet, where it puts up a rearguard action against the avalanche of refined and processed foods. Yet though we have known this for the last ten years, we have hardly changed our eating habits.

Average consumption is about half of the recommended daily amount of 30 grams; only 7 per cent of the population consume that amount, and only one in five comes close, with 20 to 30 grams per day.

High-fibre foods are wholemeal bread, sweetcorn, kidney beans, and all the other pulses, bran and dried fruit. Forty-four per cent of us eat at least one of these foods in a day, wholemeal bread being the one most commonly cited. One must feel slightly dubious, however, as most people think that all brown bread must be wholemeal. The national food survey shows that only 6.2 per cent of bread bought is wholemeal, 11.6 per cent is brown and 70 per cent is white.

Medium-fibre foods are root and green vegetables, corn and wheat breakfast cereals and brown bread. Three-quarters of the population, as one would expect, eat some medium-fibre food every day. As they do low-fibre food, such as white bread, fresh fruit and salad.

High-fibre foods are eaten more in the south of England than in the north, which must make the Tory voter healthier than the opposition, while the highest intake of fibre is in London and East Anglia. I take this as a personal tribute as these are the places where I live.

Bran is synonymous with fibre for many people, but many do not like the taste or give it up because of the unpleasant side effects – another euphemistic phrase for gas in the lower bowel for which powdered bran is notorious, as is the F Plan Diet, which has helped to popularise the idea that a high-fibre diet is slimming as well as healthy.

No doubt about the latter – dietary fibre is beneficial because it helps the transit of food through the colon and protects against a variety of diseases associated with too refined a diet. But there is no evidence that fibre helps you to slim. If the F Plan Diet works it is because it is low–calorie, which all specialist diets must be if they are to work at all.

Of all high–fibre foods, I am most enthusiastic about beans, and damn the intestinal disturbances. I have recently been experimenting with making home-made baked beans, a perfect dish for anyone with a solid-fuel stove. Just put them into an earthenware crock, seal it with a lid or foil, and forget them for four or five hours.

You can also use an oven at a low temperature and leave them for the same time. Or you can cook them in a thick-bottomed saucepan on top of the stove over a low heat. In that case you will have to stir the contents every quarter of an hour to stop the beans sticking to the bottom.

Fasoulia is a kind of Greek baked bean dish that you eat cold as a first course and is, I think, the best way of eating beans ever devised. What makes it a rich and delicious experience is the amount of olive oil used, and the slowness of the cooking.

BAKED BEANS

I LB/450 G SMALL HARICOT BEANS OR NAVY BEANS, SOAKED
   OVERNIGHT, DRAINED
2 OZ/50 G BUTTER OR HARD VEGETABLE FAT
14 OZ/400 G TIN ITALIAN PLUM TOMATOES
3 TABLESPOONS TOMATO PURÉE
I TABLESPOON RAW CANE SUGAR
SEASONING

METHOD

Combine all the ingredients, except the seasoning, in an earthenware crock or marmite (or if cooking on top of the stove in a saucepan), bring to the boil and let it simmer. Add enough extra water to cover the beans by about 1 inch/2.5 cm. Cover with lid or foil. Place in a low oven at 275F/140C/gas mark 1 for 5 to 6 hours. Inspect after 4 hours and add a little salt and pepper.

Alternatively, if cooking in a saucepan, simmer over a very low flame for 2 hours. Inspect every 20 minutes or so to see there is enough liquid and the beans are not sticking.

FASOULIA

¼ PINT/150 ML OLIVE OIL
4 CLOVES GARLIC, CHOPPED
2 BAY LEAVES
1 TEASPOON OREGANO
SPRIG OF ROSEMARY
1 LB/450 G LARGE HARICOT BEANS, SOAKED OVERNIGHT, DRAINED
4 TABLESPOONS TOMATO PURÉE
JUICE FROM 1 LEMON
SEA SALT AND FRESHLY GROUND BLACK PEPPER
1 LARGE ONION THINLY SLICED

METHOD

Pour the olive oil in the earthenware crock, marmite or saucepan, add garlic, bay leaves, oregano, rosemary and the drained beans. Heat so that the beans are simmering in the oil and herbs for a few minutes. Pour in enough water to cover the beans by about 1 inch/2.5 cm, add the tomato purée and the lemon juice. Cook in a low oven as above. After 4 hours inspect the dish and if the beans are soft and gooey, season to taste and add the thinly sliced onion. Leave the dish covered off the heat for the onion to soften.

Alternatively, cook in a saucepan over a low flame for 2 hours, but inspect the dish for the same reasons as above.

Fasoulia is eaten cold and the sauce mopped up with good bread. I also like eating it on crisp lettuce, though the Greeks would consider that a very odd idea.

FLYING
WHY NOT TAKE A PICNIC?

 When the aeroplane is on its way, after the drinks have been served and when the small plastic trays have been set down in front of each passenger, I have a fantasy: with one accord we all fling the food into the gangway.

Yes, a bit hard on all those patient stewards and stewardesses, for the food is not their fault. The appalling quality of airline food is not even the fault of the caterers. It is our fault for the indifference we show in not complaining and sending it back. Hence, I wish to start a revolution. Take a flying picnic. If none of us ate the food and we all complained, standards might improve.

I am not hopeful though. There have been many times when I have asked for a vegetarian meal while booking my flight, but on the flight itself no one has heard of my request. I have complained in writing afterwards and still no one ever knows how such a request could have been neglected. It happens time and again. It has happened to other vegetarian friends. There have been only two exceptions. Singapore and Thai airlines both provided the most delicious vegetarian dishes on being told a few days before, but in the East the vegetarian tradition is an ancient one.

On short flights of under five hours it seems to me unnecessary to provide hot meals. They are rarely hot anyway, but lukewarm. Meals do not have to revolve around the boring old combination of meat and two veg, a pudding or cake, and a sliver of processed cheese. Too wide a variety of inferior food only stresses the poor quality of everything.

On longer flights, surely hot dishes could be served which are more appealing than meat or fowl in packet gravy with frozen peas and tinned new potatoes. Have the caterers considered pizzas, quiches, fish, game or vegetable pies, lasagne, risotto, stuffed peppers or aubergines?

Soups are obviously not served in the air because of the risk of spillage, but a jellied consommé could be, and very refreshing it would be. Though I bet (laying down the gauntlet) it would be beyond any caterer's range to provide a vegetarian jellied consommé.

Why on our national airlines do we not have national dishes? Why no steak and kidney pudding, no smoked haddock, no dumplings, no salad or raw marinated kippers? Why no pease pud, no bubble and squeak, no kedgeree, potted crab, pickled herrings? Why no Yorkshire pudding, no pancakes, no spotted dick or bloater paste?

Whenever I fly anywhere I now take a picnic. I warmly commend it. It passes the time beautifully: the aroma of one's own food fills the air around you so that passengers and staff stare with envy. It means one extra piece of hand luggage; indeed generally I manage to get it all into my own shoulder bag. A Thermos full of jellied consommé with a generous glass of vodka or sherry, first chilled and whisked into it, is no bad way to start the meal, especially if the airline is slow at serving the booze.

My picnics are built around a large container of mixed salad with a separate jar of aioli mayonnaise (home-made mayonnaise keeps beautifully in a sealed jar). The salad can be crudités: thin sticks of celery, courgette, carrot, pepper, chunks of fennel, cauliflower, broccoli, crisp lettuce. Or you can make a salad of grated vegetables already mixed in a saucy vinaigrette, but then you will either have to bring your own cutlery and plates or borrow the airline's.

I then either make a quiche or a pizza or cut sandwiches from a loaf, brown, white or wholemeal. The recipe below is probably the best way of taking a sandwich. It looks good and it is easy to eat.

The meal ends with fresh fruit and the best of British cheeses. The better and the more delicious your picnic, the longer you will linger over it. It is the only way I know of lessening the barbarian experience of being crushed like cattle, which flying now inflicts on one.

SANDWICH ROULADE

You will need one white sandwich tin loaf for this method. Brown or wholemeal will crumble and break when rolled. The roulade is usually made with smoked salmon. Two suggested vegetarian fillings are given below.

Slice the crust from the top and bottom of the loaf, leaving the crust on ends and sides. Slice the bread down its length as thinly as possible, so that you have a long strip. Spread the filling on each slice, making sure it is smooth and even. Then, starting at one end, roll the bread up, so that you have a shape like a small Swiss roll. A sandwich roulade for a party is then sliced across in quarter-inch portions but this is unnecessary for a picnic.

You may spread the bread first with butter or margarine, but with a strong enough filling it is unnecessary. Besides, there is always the risk of the fat soaking through the bread and looking unsightly.

T A P E N A D E

    4 OZ/100 G CAPERS
    2 OZ/50 G BLACK OLIVES
    JUICE FROM LEMON
    1 CLOVE GARLIC, CRUSHED

M E T H O D

Liquidise all the ingredients in the blender until you have a smooth purée.

S P I C E D   C U R D   C H E E S E

    4 OZ/100 G CURD OR SOFT CHEESE
    1 TEASPOON EACH CURRY POWDER AND GARAM MASALA
    1 TABLESPOON SOFTENED BUTTER OR MARGARINE

M E T H O D

Mash well to a good spreading consistency.

Since this article was written airlines have become much more sympathetic to providing good vegetarian food, if it is ordered in advance. Quite often the vegetarian food is of a higher quality than the rest of the food served. So fly vegetarian.

FRUIT

'Vegetables and fruits are a rich source of a number of nutrients. They are relatively low in energy but high in fibre, vitamins and minerals,' the WHO report mentioned in its introduction. It has also become obvious over the past decade that a diet which is good for the prevention of cancer is also good for the prevention of heart disease. This is partly because of the antioxidant vitamins, beta-carotene and vitamins C and E.

We ought to be eating fresh fruit and vegetables every day throughout the year, not only in the summer when soft fruits are in season. Mind you, the following pudding does use a whole carton of double cream which rather mars the healthy aspect of the dish. You could, however, substitute a low-fat yoghurt or fromage frais. I rather suspect that like sugar, saturated fats are addictive, so once you give them up for a length of time you actually end up not liking the taste.

FRUIT BRÛLÉE

This is a marvellous summer pudding, second only to Summer Pudding itself. It can be made in one shallow oven dish or six small ramekins.

> 1½ LB/675 G MIXED SUMMER FRUIT (STRAWBERRIES, RASPBERRIES, RED,
>   BLACK OR WHITE CURRANTS, GRAPES, PLUMS, PEACHES)
> 8 FL OZ/225 ML THICK DOUBLE CREAM OR FROMAGE FRAIS
> 4 OZ/120 G SOFT BROWN SUGAR

METHOD

Trim, stone and, if necessary, chop the fruit and place mixture in the dish or dishes. Refrigerate at this stage. Just before serving, light the grill, pour the cream or fromage frais over the surface of the fruit and sprinkle the top with a layer of brown sugar. When the grill is very hot, place the dish or dishes beneath it to caramelise the brown sugar. It should take just 30 seconds. Whip the dishes out immediately to the table.

GOOD FOOD
On Redefining the Word 'Good'

GOOD FOOD
ON REDEFINING THE WORD 'GOOD'

If you examine our idea of what good food is, it turns out to be at first glance nothing more than what is currently fashionable. Yet that too only applies to the minority, who feel they are part of the cultural elite. For them, now, nouvelle cuisine is good, while haute cuisine is bad. (The nineties fashion is for 'granny food', or simple peasant cooking, and this represents a return to real British food.) But the idea of good food to the wealthy philistine would still be a form of haute cuisine. The rich and the uninformed demand larger portions and richer sauces, which would seem both vulgar and crude to nouvelle cuisine. Yet good food to an agricultural worker or a coalminer means something else again.

Who is dictating the nature of good food for these various social groups? Economics obviously, which is why the majority are on a diet of junk food and are brainwashed into thinking it good and tasty. Food is a profitable industry. The Ministry of Agriculture and successive governments connive in the food policies to ensure the status quo of profits in the food industry and the myth that what we eat is good for us. But some of us know it is not. Some of us would ask why there is not a government subsidy for wholemeal bread so that it is cheap, hence we would all eat it and have our daily dietary fibre. There is no philanthropy in most governments, and a great deal less in the British governments of the 1980s and 90s.

Food is a political weapon, used here to ensure that the profits grow, but the idea of good food is used politically too. Food is a huge class divider, and in our country it is used as the material for the walls. There is more snobbery in food than in anything else. You could live in any district in any place in the British Isles and make it socially acceptable. But imagine ordering a sweet white wine with the grilled Dover sole or eating asparagus with a knife and fork. In twenty years' time both might be permissible, but now the kindest interpretation put upon such behaviour would be eccentric. To know, or to pretend to know, what good food is and what wine to drink with what dish is a form of superiority so potent that it emasculates the ignorant; such knowledge impresses far more than any exhibition of wealth and grandeur, for nothing can be more crushing or more formidable than the knowledge of how the cutlery is laid out and which year the Lafite-Rothschild failed.

Why should this be? Surely it is that food is our essential fuel, without it we die and if the food is of inadequate quality we become enfeebled and vulnerable to disease. Food is so essential and of such necessary significance to us that a mystique has formed around some elements of it to make it seem highly precious – the ritual of meals and restaurants – in a society where the quality of the food is usually commonplace.

The idea of good food bestows a moral worthiness upon some kinds of food which are out of reach of the majority of people. The gourmets and food gurus are like the priests of some ancient religion being allowed to feed off the best and most precious food, which will ensure their continuing possession of divine wisdom. Indeed, some food writers in their style do appear to be dispensing just that: for there is a tone of 'thou shalt not' and 'thou shall' about most food columns.

Time changes the concept of what is good, but place does as well. Good food is wholly different in Baghdad from what it is in Birmingham, yet not quite as different today as it would have been fifty years ago. As the world draws closer and different foods are shared by different peoples, one person's definition of good begins to merge with another – a trend worth fostering and encouraging. At least through food we may catch glimpses of other people's cultural riches and learn to adjust to them if not to enjoy them.

The world of good food is deliberately kept apart as a secret ritual. The precise details of why a food becomes good and is considered gourmet are kept a mystery, the use of French and other foreign names obscures the true identity of the food, the price of a meal can be a two-week package tour holiday for two. These three factors alone ensure that good food is kept for an elite minority in our society. Yet why a food seems good could be explained rationally, its identity need not be in a foreign language and it could be served at a reasonable cost.

'Good food', even in the *Good Food Guide* sense, means food that is unavailable to the majority, food which is the requisite of the unattainable lifestyle. It is food, then, which is not good in any real sense of the word at all, but food used as a form of oppression. Every obscure ingredient, every bit of the *batterie de cuisine*, is a weapon to keep them in their place, unemployed and on the streets. The world of good food is that world which the rulers of society inhabit, the restaurant ritual is their daily rite while the rest exist on a bag of chips. I would like to redefine good food. For a food to be good, it should do the consumer no harm, nor should it exploit the farmer or the land in which it grows, or brutalise the life of an animal. Food cannot be good if the source is factory farming, nor can it be good if it is over-processed and refined with additives and preservatives which destroy vitamin B1 and allow the re-emergence of diseases like scurvy. Food which tends to give us bad health cannot be called good.

Plants which provide the food must not impoverish the soil or the workers who till the soil. Cash crops in Third World countries generally do both under the patronage of multinationals. Good food has to be food which does not kill an animal unnecessarily and which does not endanger a living species.

Food to be good must be the best nutritionally for the greatest number of people and do as little harm as possible at its source.

Tall order. And it is political naivety to think such food is possible except for a Candide within the confines of his own garden.

HEALTH FARM
Shrubland Hall Carrot and Apricot Salad

HERBS
On Planting a Herb Garden
Unusual Herbs in Cooking

HEALTH FARM
SHRUBLAND HALL

I have always felt that health farms were the indulgent sport for the idle, overfed rich. Stories of people being starved and given a hard time by underwater jets rather pleased me. But I have now changed my tune, for on an impulse after a bad illness I decided that a few days at one of these places might be just the job. I opted for my local, Shrublands, feeling I could escape easily if I hated it.

Most preconceptions turned out to be false. Not much sign of the idle rich, for a start: a smattering of well-heeled bourgeoisie and plenty of suburban regulars who take ten days at the health farm rather than a holiday in Marbella. But my main surprise was that the food, raw and vegetarian, was exquisite.

Mind you, not many of the guests had the food. There was the fat lady who complained she was being starved for three days. 'Not a crumb passes my lips,' she announced. Then, the following morning, she complained of not sleeping. She suspected the cause was the broth, 'Very salty, that broth.' She made public statements to any of us in earshot about her bulk (fifteen stone), her age (forty-three), her diet (favourite food – pork sausages and trifle) and her decor (home-made rugs for wall coverings).

The remark about the broth got an immediate reaction. Another stoutish lady nodded fiercely and breathed the word 'Oxo'. This satisfied everybody but they were wrong. That evening, I was given some of the same broth: it was pure vegetable – I checked – flavoured with a little Vecon.

The kitchens of health farms must be the only ones which see no wastage returned upon the plates. If you are on a light diet, on the second day you are liable to get so hungry you can easily consume the apple complete with core and stalk. It is important that you drink plenty of fluids. For the night, you are given a Thermos of hot water, lemon and honey. I savoured each mouthful as if it was malt whisky.

Oddly, though the diet is austere, the garden that you stroll in could be the setting for a Roman orgy. It was designed by Sir Charles Barry in the style of the Villa d'Este. A flight of 100 steps, wound with clusters of vine and wisteria, leads to a formal display of hedge and lawn with classical arcades and statues of Diana the huntress.

When I was there, magnolia and rhododendron bloomed, the walks were scented with viburnum and syringa, and it still looked magnificent in the unceasing rain. The hall was built in 1740, a perfect setting for Congreve or Sheridan, and it gives you a sense of *folie de grandeur* reading a paperback in the library.

On the first morning I was confused with a Mrs Budd and given her treatment slip. I was briskly told my first appointment was at 8.30 a.m. We were awoken an hour before. At 8.30 a.m., there was the mysterious word 'vacusage'. This sounded like a form of torture invented by the French Revolution. I looked it up. 'Suction for breaking down hard and obstinate fatty tissue.' A kind of body Hoover.

Luckily, the mistake was adjusted and instead I was submerged in a warm tank for half an hour while a hose with a pressurised jet was moved over the joints. I decided, as I was there, I wanted everything and I left the treatment rooms dazed and glowing.

But it was the food that impressed me. A diet of raw vegetables sounds dull and repetitive but the salads were neither. The presentation of them upon plate or platter, however small the quantity, was always highly appealing. The supper of sliced pineapple, cherries and yoghurt looked as if it had been composed as a still life.

There were rings of fennel with grapefruit or grated fennel with lime juice and red kidney beans. Grated carrot and cheese rolled into balls. Grated celeriac with sliced raw mushrooms, lemon zest mixed with cress and diced olives. Diced celery, pineapple cubes and cress. Diced celery, black grapes, chopped fennel on dandelion leaves. Fresh peas, sweetcorn, tomato flavoured with tarragon and lemon balm. Raw shredded spinach with chopped onion, lemon juice and soy sauce.

These are but a few ways with familiar vegetables. Below is a salad I made after I returned.

CARROT AND APRICOT SALAD

6 DRIED APRICOTS, SOAKED OVERNIGHT

1 LB/450 G CARROTS, GRATED

1 TABLESPOON SUNFLOWER OR OLIVE OIL

1 TEASPOON MUSTARD SEEDS

2 RED CHILLIES, FINELY CHOPPED

1 TEASPOON CORIANDER

1 TEASPOON ASAFOETIDA

1 TABLESPOON CASTOR SUGAR

1 TABLESPOON WHITE WINE VINEGAR

1 TABLESPOON SMOOTH PEANUT BUTTER

SEA SALT AND FRESHLY GROUND PEPPER

METHOD

Chop the dried apricots and mix into the grated carrots. Heat the oil in a pan and add the spices, sauté for a moment so that the flavours are released, then mix in the sugar, vinegar and peanut butter. Pour over the salad and toss thoroughly, seasoning to taste.

Herbs
On Planting a Herb Garden

Early in 1983 I began planning a herb garden. It was dug and planted out in the spring; neatly geometric and painstakingly logical with the large plants like bronze and green fennel, elecampane, angelica and lovage all on the north side so that they would not shade the smaller plants from the sun. I became obsessed, planting every herb I could find, many I had never heard of before, and buying up every herbal book.

There are now just over eighty different herbs. I have managed to memorise their names but not yet all of their properties. Some have seeded themselves and romped away in directions far from the ones planned. A few dislike their neighbour (wormwood is a bad companion) and have sulked; most, though, have grown considerably, sprawling over the geometrical design, so that it looks like a very imaginatively planned bomb site. It bears no resemblance at all to the neat herb gardens and borders in the grounds of country mansions.

Yet it gives remarkable pleasures. To walk through the area in the evening is like being embalmed in a bowl of pot-pourri. The variegated foliage is as handsome as any in the herbaceous border, even if for most of the time it is out of control. The bees are clustered over every flower. I wish I knew whose honey I was flavouring.

Both animals and birds appear to get a high from certain herbs. The cats, indifferent to catnip, go crazy on the new growth of valerian. They roll over and over in it, then sit bolt upright and exocet across the lawn. A pair of jays peck at the camphor seeds. In the spring the wormwood has to be protected, for the birds will strip the plant of its new leaves. They are built into the nest, but why?

These are all the unexpected pleasures, for I planted most of the herbs to use in cooking and not to give wild and domestic life a dope paradise. Each season has its own requirements from the herb garden.

In very early spring, when it is still too cold for salad vegetables, three herbs sprout green leaves which can be picked, chopped and eaten as a salad, dressed with oil and lemon, either on their own or mixed with white cabbage. Angelica, usually grown for its stem, which is candied, is fragrant. Woad, which is the herb we used to paint ourselves blue with, has pinnate leaves with a slight mustard flavour. Lovage has been compared to celery, but it is stronger in flavour and quite distinct.

Even when the first lettuces are available, a green salad is transformed by adding all the fresh chopped herbs there are: fennel, tarragon, marjoram and chives. Or they can be stirred into soft cheeses, sprinkled over steamed vegetables and made into herb sauces.

In the summer too, herbs are used to flavour bean pâtés and terrines, rissoles and croquettes, and to decorate the base of jellied moulds or timbales. Salad burnet has featherlike fronds, which look charming when a dish is unmoulded, but with borage and marjoram flowers they can be used in a salad hors-d'oeuvre to decorate each individual plate. Nouvelle cuisine seems to have got stuck with a clump of lamb's lettuce, which seems a trifle unimaginative. The herb garden offers the artist cook a host of other more attractive possibilities.

The pickling begins in August. Gherkins or cucumbers are flavoured with dill weed. It is an annual and almost over by this time: possibly the reason why dill pickle exists. I confess, though, a need always to experiment, if not to break with tradition. So this year my gherkins grown in the greenhouse have been pickled with lovage seeds, fennel, and tarragon. Later in the autumn the chutneys are made from crops of apples, marrows, and green tomatoes. There are still plenty of mints for the apple and marrows, still plenty of thyme, sage and tarragon for the tomatoes.

Fish can be grilled or barbecued on a bed of stalks made up from fennel, rosemary, thyme or angelica. Smaller fish can be wrapped in angelica leaves and poached. Fish served with sorrel purée is one of those rare perfect complements.

At the first hint of frost, the pineapple sage and the lemon verbenas must be taken into the greenhouse: I might make a curry and use a few leaves of one bruised and ground into a paste, then stirred into a bowl of yoghurt.

All very well to be enthusiastic about the herb garden when most people count themselves lucky to have a backyard and a window box. But I would now urge even those with a tiny garden to grow more herbs.

Even without a garden at all, two window boxes will allow you to grow the most important culinary herbs: rosemary, sage, thyme, chives and parsley will all flourish if they have sun and are fed and watered adequately.

Herb lovers are in agreement that basil is their favourite. It is an annual and must be kept either indoors on a sunny windowsill or in a greenhouse. One packet of seeds will give you over a hundred plants. I harvest the leaves of mine every two weeks. They are stuffed straight into the blender with one crushed clove of garlic, juice from one lemon, and enough olive oil to make a stiff sauce. This sauce can be used on pasta, on sliced tomatoes or boiled vegetables. Or at this stage you can add crushed pine nuts and grated Parmesan to it and it becomes the classic sauce pesto. As pine nuts are expensive, you can use instead any mixed crushed nuts to make the sauce creamy. The sauce without these additions can be frozen and stored throughout the winter.

UNUSUAL HERBS IN COOKING

 Nothing in my garden has given me as much pleasure as the herb garden. Vegetable cooking, in my canon, needs strong and individual flavours, and many a herb has been used as an experiment to give punch to an otherwise monotonous dish.

May is the time to plant the herbs you are going to use. The traditional ones like mint, parsley, bay, thyme, rosemary and marjoram are easy enough to cultivate. Mint, if the roots are not contained in an old bucket or container, will take over; so will horseradish, burrowing beneath the soil and popping up in the lawn or formal bed. It is best, if you have the space, to let parsley seed itself in some part of the vegetable garden, while the three other herbs above thrive in a much tidier manner.

All are excellent for flavouring bean dishes. A sprig of bay, rosemary or thyme can be plunged into the boiling water and left to stew while the beans are cooking. Marjoram or oregano can be chopped and added after the beans are cooked.

But there are other herbs I have come to rely on as much for their beauty as well as the strength of their flavour. Angelica, a biannual, grows astonishingly tall: up to six feet in the spring. The herb's name distressed Culpeper who berated 'heathens and papists' for their blasphemy in calling angelica 'a herb of the Holy Ghost'. It was supposed to have flowered on the feast of St Michael the Archangel, 29 September, which is how it got its name, but I have a precocious plant: mine flowers in July.

Angelica is used commercially; not only are the stalks crystallised but the plant is used to flavour chartreuse and Strega. I use its leaves in salads, while the smaller stems are chopped up fine, adding much to a rice, grain or bean salad.

The tallest herb I know is lovage, which grows up to eight feet. A perennial once it has approved of where it is planted – it likes a fertile dark soil – lovage will grow into a clump of dark green stems covered in pinnate leaves. Both can be eaten raw or cooked, and when the plant has formed a huge clump its roots can also be boiled and eaten. It has a powerful, distinct flavour, its nearest relative in taste being celery, but it is in fact a member of the carrot family, and is a native of southern Europe.

It was used extensively by the Greeks and Romans. Culpeper says that the leaves will remove blotches and boils if 'fried with a little hog's lard'. I have made it into soup with cauliflower, or used it in a dark green sauce for pasta or fish. I have also used it as a layer in a vegetable terrine, but most of all I constantly pluck a leaf to chew as I pass.

Tarragon is another essential herb, but is not always easy to grow, demanding a rich well-drained soil; and it can easily be killed by hard frost. Many of the plants on sale are the inferior Russian tarragon, which has little flavour and will grow huge, spreading over the garden. This variety is eaten in Iran as a salad with grilled meat.

French tarragon is traditionally used with fish: a modest little fish cake made with cod is transformed by a couple of tablespoons of the chopped herb. It is also used to flavour vinegar: a stalk gathered before it flowers, placed in a bottle of white wine vinegar and left for two months, will do the trick. The French use tarragon extensively: the vinegar and the fresh herb is used in sauce Béarnaise; other famous dishes include poulet à l'estragon and oeufs en geleé à l'estragon.

A spice we completely ignore but which grows in many a suburban garden is sumac. The dried fruit, a dark red pyramid, stays on the bare tree throughout the winter. In Middle Eastern countries it is dried and crushed. It has an astringent, fruity sourness – due to malic acid as in sour apples – and is sometimes used instead of lemons. Sumac powder can be bought in some ethnic stores; it is widely used for sprinkling over meat dishes as they are cooking. Its sourness would cut across the fat but it is known to be a digestive. It is also used in fish soups and in salads. A simple but excellent dish to begin a meal with crudités and hummus is to mix a couple of tablespoons of sumac with half a pint/275 ml of strained yoghurt (labne), a recipe thought to come from Armenia.

There are some herbs one grows for their beauty which are only medicinal, or have limited uses. Wormwood (*Artemisia absinthium*) is among these: its silver feathery leaves are beguilingly handsome. It has a long medicinal history but is most notorious for its essential oil, absinthol. In large doses it is a cerebral stimulant and certainly heavy absinthe drinkers in the nineteenth century were poisoned by it.

Oberon used wormwood when he lifted the spell from Titania with the juice of 'Dian's Bud'. The herb is named after the goddess Artemis. A little of the herb, however, does no harm and can do a power of good. It is used commercially in vermouth. I have a sprig in a bottle of vodka, and it gives the spirit an extra bite.

ISRAEL

I S R A E L

The most telling impression which remains from Israel is the sheer energy of the country. Even if one naturally withdraws from the blatant aggression of Zionism, smiles at the orthodox Hebrew who – we were told – will not proselytise for his faith, for then, if everyone believed, they would stop being the Chosen People, and shudders at a view of women first formulated over 3,000 years ago, one cannot help but admire the grinding hard work and drudgery of building the kibbutz in sand and scrub, irrigating it, then planting and tending crops while fighting off the enemy.

All this is, of course, now old history, yet in this land one is vividly aware of the past having carved out the present and that many of the fruits and vegetables which the first settlers in the thirties began to plant, or replant, were those which echo through the pages of the Old Testament. They take a delight, for example, in saying that academics now believe it was the Sharon fruit which Eve used to tempt Adam. Certainly the translation 'apple' makes an unlikely choice in this subtropical climate.

As visitors to this land we were kept busy. The energy of the place pushed you on through the long day to see yet another kibbutz, more production plants, more farming assemblies, packing factories, export outlets, fish farming, research labs. In between this frenzied competitiveness with the rest of the world, the ancient sites teemed with devout and inquisitive tourists and the tension between Jew and Arab was tangible.

The boundless energy augments the familiar miracles. They don't just walk on the Sea of Galilee – they water-ski. And the fish familiar from the miracle of the loaves and fishes teem in hundreds of fish farms and are air-freighted to New York each day. It is named St Peter's fish from the Sea of Galilee, as it were a fresh-water version of John Dory. We ate it on the first day in Caesarea overlooking the Roman amphitheatre where the fish was so crisply grilled that the skin was like pork crackling.

We then went to see a fish farm and packing plant where they filleted the fish before sending it to America. It is no relation to the Dory and has no thumb print but appears to have the marks of four fingers, hence the myth that this was the fish which multiplied in the miracle.

The Israeli fruit industry is concerned about Portugal and Spain being in the EEC. The Iberian peninsula is their main competitor in the export of citrus fruits, with the advantage that their fruit comes in freight by road to us, whilst Israeli fruit has to go by sea to Marseilles for transhipment or else is air-freighted straight to London. Naturally, the latter takes less time than a lorry load from Madrid but is about thirty times more expensive.

The Israelis believe that they have a better product to sell. What they certainly do have is a wider range of fruit and vegetables with a determination to investigate new strains of fruit for farming and export.

The pomelo is about twice the size of a grapefruit and it has a thick yellow rind which can be easily cut away. The flesh will then divide into segments but it is further protected by a thick pith and skin which has to be peeled away before the fruit below is eaten. The fruit itself is tremendously juicy and tastes a little like a very sweet grapefruit but the flavour is not as strong. It needs no chemicals injected into the skin to prolong its shelf life, for the thick skin and inner pith are enough protection.

The red and rose grapefruit are both cousins of the grapefruit we know so well, as is another fruit, nauseously named sweetie. The latter is the size of a small grapefruit but is lime green in colour and verges on the sweet and insipid. The red grapefruit, on the other hand, has a superb colour – a glistening dark ruby – but its flavour too is not so bold as its colour. The rose grapefruit we know already.

Another fruit we tasted was the mineola. Its rather Walt Disney name is indeed Californian, it peels with insouciant ease and its flavour is mild. Kumquats, the interior flesh sweet and the peel sharp, were a delight consumed whole, a little like eating raw marmalade, when picked from tiny trees which grow no more than three feet. Limes in their turn have now spawned the limquat. These are very sharp indeed but are marvellous cut and squeezed into a drink.

Starfruit look unpromising but, sliced thinly, have a sharpness and intensity of taste as invigorating as a sea breeze. As to Eve's Sharon fruit, the dark amber pulp has something sensual about it and, matched with the red and rose grapefruits, they make a jewel of a fruit salad.

L EEKS
Leek and Green Peppercorn Tart

L EFTOVERS
On the Social Disapproval and the Secrecy of Their Consumption

LEEKS

Try always to buy the smallest, for they are sweeter. The best way of cleaning them is to slice them lengthways so that any mud between the leaves is clearly seen and can be washed away. They need brief cooking, merely softening in oil or butter for a few minutes. If steamed whole, they will take longer – perhaps ten minutes.

LEEK AND GREEN PEPPERCORN TART

1½ LB/675 G LEEKS
2 OZ/50 G BUTTER
2 TEASPOONS GREEN PEPPERCORNS
5 OZ/140 G RICOTTA OR CURD CHEESE
2 OZ/50 G GRUYÈRE CHEESE, GRATED
1 EGG BEATEN
SEA SALT AND FRESHLY GROUND BLACK PEPPER
1 WHOLEWHEAT PASTRY CASE, BAKED BLIND

METHOD

Preheat the oven to 400F/200C/gas mark 6. Slice the leeks lengthways to clean them, then cut them across thinly. Melt the butter in a pan and cook the leeks over a low heat until just soft: about 5 minutes. Pour into a mixing bowl and add the rest of the ingredients. Mix thoroughly, pour into the pastry case, and bake for 15 to 20 minutes. Let the tart rest for 10 minutes before slicing.

L E F T O V E R S
O N   T H E   S O C I A L   D I S A P P R O V A L   A N D   T H E
S E C R E C Y   O F   T H E I R   C O N S U M P T I O N

 Though we all have personal habits that we might be disinclined to discuss in public, I am somewhat puzzled as to why the subject of 'leftovers' is so often avoided. People actually feel guilty about confessing to sneaking them from the detritus of last night's dinner party, that is if the cat has not got to them first. I believe leftovers are something to be enjoyed and publicly celebrated.

Let's face it, so many dishes taste better the next day. So many scraps appear more succulent as a stolen nibble than as part of a three-course dinner. We all know stories of larder night-raiders. I have known people pretending to suffer from spasms of night starvation descending on the refrigerator and consuming mountains of cold curry. Highly spiced ethnic dishes often have a magnetic addictive quality; a chap I know used to breakfast happily on curry or Chinese dishes, such as crab, chilli and ginger, and wash it all down with strong black coffee.

But there is a perfectly good reason why some leftovers taste better the day after: any food which has a multiplicity of spices and flavourings added to it needs time after it has been cooked for the flavourings to become fused. This is something which the experienced cook plans for, knowing that there are many dishes which benefit from being cooked a day before you intend to eat them. A cassoulet, for example, gains immeasurably, the beans in that extra day soaking up even more of the herb-flavoured liquor.

However, the consumption of leftovers is still somehow considered far from *bon goût*; it is a little like nail biting, something to be indulged in in secret, alone. I suspect the notion of stealing food, even when it is from your own larder, makes the food much more enticing. Obviously this goes back to childhood when some of us were not allowed to raid the larder or refrigerator, or were imprisoned in a punitive boarding school where what scraps existed were both tediously bland and firmly padlocked.

But the greatest gustatory thrill surely is to steal food without the crime showing. Thus the solitary act, the cautious opening of the refrigerator door, the furtive selection of the appropriate morsel, popping it into the mouth and that moment as the food begins to dissolve, while the ivories are quietly champing, becomes pure ecstasy. Until, that is, someone calls out with an urgent question. What to do? Answer with your mouth full and give the game away? Try to swallow quickly? Pretend you never heard the question? Only the intrepid and experienced stealer of leftovers has the answer, has learnt to place only small portions of food in the mouth, so that in an emergency such as this an intelligent reply can be made while the fragment of food is quickly relocated at the side.

So let us bring the leftovers out of the closet. We could begin by answering with our mouths full. Or declaring within the family that the leftovers are the perks for the person or people who do the washing up. Or, alternatively, you could refuse to eat them plain as delicious messy finger food and choose instead to consider methods of rejuvenation – the Lazarus technique or How to Breathe Life into an Old Bean.

But first let us briefly deal with the problem of selection; no real problem for what you throw away is obvious. All leftover salad, especially if doused in vinaigrette, is fit only for the bin. (There are some people, I have heard, who try to make soup out of it. Ugh!) All food which tasted dull, or even unpleasant, first time around must be thrown out, for a second incarnation would be a crime. An attempt, for example, at reviving overcooked vegetables which only taste of tap water will be doomed to failure. Mush is mush and there is no way back.

But here follows the good news. Some types of food are better at being revived than others. Plain boiled rice can be perked up in an infinite variety of ways, from being used as stuffing to being fried with lots of tasty additions or made into rissoles or a kedgeree. All leftover grains, in fact, like millet, bulgar and buckwheat, will adapt in a similar way. One of the nicest leftover meals is a kind of do-it-yourself Chinese. All you need is a crisp fresh lettuce like a Webb's Wonder, a few chopped chillies, green coriander and spring onions, plus lots of flavouring sauces. Lea & Perrins now sell four different types of soy, flavoured with ginger, garlic, chilli or five-spice powder – these are perfect to accompany this simple feast. Your mound of leftovers, rice or grains, is flavoured individually to your own taste by some or all of the above, then spoonfuls are wrapped in a lettuce leaf and eaten.

The do-it-yourself stuffed lettuce technique can work with other leftovers too. Take vegetables, beans, courgettes, carrots, whatever, toss them in a sauce made from tahini, yoghurt and lemon juice, add some chopped onion or chilli if you wish. Part of the delight of these meals is the difference in texture between cooked and raw, the crunch of the lettuce which packages the goods. The most satisfying food entertains the palate. The charm of leftovers is that the successful dishes taste even better the following day because of the nostalgia factor. In fact, I would suggest the best leftovers are generally the vegetables re-invigorated with spicy sauces and freshly chopped zingy additions.

MAIZE FLOUR
Corn Sticks • Hush Puppies • Polenta

MALNUTRITION
Find Your Feet

MARROWS
Curried Marrow Soup • Chilled Marrow Soup • Gratin of Marrow and
Fennel • Fried Marrow • Green Pepper and Marrow Tarkari • Marrow
Tart • Gratin of Spiced Marrow • Marrow with Chilli and Coriander

MEDITERRANEAN
Malta

Mediterranean Cooking Artichoke Hearts in Tomato and Garlic Sauce •
Fried Artichokes in Batter • White Egg Fungi Soufflé • Stuffed
Tomatoes

MUSHROOMS
Spiced Mushrooms • Stuffed Mushrooms in Red Pepper Sauce

M a i z e   F l o u r

 A reader from Gloucestershire asked for information on 'cornmeal, polenta, maize flour, whatever it is called'. (Cornmeal does sometimes go under the name of maize meal and in Italian stores it might be known as polenta flour, for that is primarily what they use it as. It is a much-neglected ingredient over here but a staple food in America.

Cornmeal was one of the foods discovered by Columbus in 1492. Two Spaniards who had been sent to explore Cuba returned to report on a sort of grain they called maize, which was 'well toasted, bak'd, dry'd and made into flour'. The first settlers in Virginia found that maize was carefully cultivated and that the Indians would get three crops a year. In their widely varying languages and dialects the Indians gave corn different names, but they all meant the same thing – Our Life.

The Europeans were astonished at the efficiency of Indian farming. Fields were laid out on a grid pattern, every small square heaped with earth, the maize seeds were planted in each square in a circle, and later a few beans, squash, pumpkin and watermelon seeds were sown as well. The maize grew straight up, giving support to the beans, while the squashes grew down the mound and kept the weeds down.

The size of these maize plantations also amazed the first explorers. Diego Columbus, the brother of Christopher, declared he walked eighteen miles through a field of maize, beans and squashes. These three foods were always eaten together and in the Iroquois tribe's myth they appeared as three inseparable sisters.

The plant was brought back to Spain and grown in Andalusia. About 1530 it began to be distributed around the shores of the Mediterranean. Early on it became a success in the Middle East, and from there it was sent to northern Europe – which is why it appears in John Gerard's Herbal, in 1597, as Turkey Wheat. He was not impressed.

'Turkey wheat doth nourish far lesse than either wheat, rie, barly, or otes . . . Although the barbarous Indians, which know no better, are constrained to make a vertue of necessitie, and thinke it a good food: whereas we may easily judge, that it nourisheth but little, and is of hard and evill digestion, a more convenient food for swine than for man.'

For the next few hundred years the swine and the rest of the farmyard did eat it, and they still do. Corn, like the potato, was a despised food in Europe, but corn had another drawback which hampered its acceptance. Though the early American settlers grew to like it and for 200 years used the flour for all their baking, they ate it in a mixed and varied diet. Europe's poor, on the other hand, lived off the maize flour and nothing else. The result was pellagra. It was first noticed in the very poor of Andalusia by Philip V's doctor, Gaspar Casal. Then it appeared in northern Italy, Hungary, Romania, Turkey, Greece and Egypt.

A French doctor noticed that pellagra followed the spread of maize cultivation. Formerly, the European poor could survive on a diet of wheat or rye bread. But a sole diet of maize was a killer. Millions of Mexican poor lived off maize and little else, but they soaked the maize overnight in hot limewater before it was husked and ground. Once you added eggs, milk or a little fish to the diet, all signs of pellagra vanished.

Research in America early this century proved that the problem was caused by a vitamin deficiency, but it was not discovered until 1929 that the protein in maize is low in an amino acid, tryptophan, which the body transforms into the B vitamin niacin. Lack of niacin causes pellagra.

The Indians generously showed the settlers how to eat and cook the maize. Young corn must be picked and boiled immediately. Mark Twain was in complete agreement, suggesting that a cauldron of boiling water be placed over a fire in the middle of the cornfield. The flavour is astonishing when cooked immediately for, from the moment the cob is plucked, the sugar in the kernels starts to turn into starch. But though we enjoy sweetcorn we still do not much use its flour.

All of the maize recipes below are, in fact, Indian in origin. You must remember that, though nutritionally cornmeal is as good as other cereals, it contains no gluten, therefore when using it to make bread or pastry it must be mixed with wheat flour – one-third cornmeal to two-thirds wheat flour. Why bother to use it at all?, you may ask. Well, because the flavour, texture and colour of cornmeal much improves whatever it is added to. It turns a shortcrust pastry egg yellow and crumbly, it makes a pizza base taste almost as good as its topping, and pancakes are far tastier too. By the way, do not confuse cornmeal with what we call cornflour, which is starch and can be made out of rice.

These recipes come from *The American Heritage Cookbook*. I find their version of polenta, for example, far easier to cook than following an Italian recipe, which can ask you to stir the meal for up to half an hour.

Cornmeal is very obliging: all sorts of additions of your own can go into the recipes, and the flour still puffs up and bakes golden. My partner adds to the corn sticks, which are more like small crumbly rolls, a finely chopped chilli and three grated tablespoons of a hard goats' cheese. We often eat them with a thick vegetable soup for lunch.

CORN STICKS
(MAKES TEN TO TWELVE)

½ CUP SIFTED PLAIN FLOUR
2½ TEASPOONS BAKING POWDER
½ TEASPOON SALT
I TABLESPOON SUGAR (OPTIONAL)
1½ CUPS CORNMEAL
I EGG
3 TABLESPOONS MELTED BUTTER
¾ CUP MILK

METHOD

Sift together flour, baking powder, salt and sugar. Then stir in the cornmeal. In a separate bowl, beat the egg thoroughly, then stir in melted butter and milk. Combine with flour mixture, using as few strokes as possible (the batter will be lumpy). Spoon into a greased cake tin. Bake in a preheated 425F/220C/gas mark 7 oven for 20 to 25 minutes.

HUSH PUPPIES
(MAKES ABOUT FIFTEEN)

1½ CUPS CORNMEAL
½ CUP PLAIN FLOUR
2 TEASPOONS BAKING POWDER
½ TEASPOON SALT
I EGG, WELL BEATEN
¾ CUP MILK
I SMALL ONION, GRATED
OIL FOR SHALLOW FRYING

METHOD

Sift together cornmeal, flour, baking powder and salt. Mix egg, milk and onion in a bowl. Combine with dry ingredients and drop from a spoon into hot oil. When crisp and golden (about 1 minute), lift with slotted spoon and drain on paper towels. Serve hot with fried fish, Southern style. Made bite-sized, they are delicious served with drinks.

POLENTA
(SERVES SIX)

I CUP CORNMEAL
I TEASPOON SALT
½ CUP PARMESAN CHEESE, GRATED
3 TABLESPOONS BUTTER
PAPRIKA

METHOD

Bring 3 cups of water to a rolling boil. Combine cornmeal with 1 cup cold water and salt. Stir into boiling water and cook, stirring frequently, for about 10 minutes. Pour into a loaf pan and refrigerate until firm. Shortly before serving, cut the polenta into slices about ½ inch/1 cm thick and place in shallow baking dish. Sprinkle with Parmesan, dot with butter, and shake paprika over all. Grill until brown – about 4 to 5 minutes.

M A L N U T R I T I O N
F I N D   Y O U R   F E E T

 In the Second World War, the fear of a U-boat blockade of our food supplies prompted the discovery of a source of protein which was kept top secret. The raw materials grew in abundance all around us, indeed they flourish all over the world: green leaves. At Rothamsted in Hertfordshire, our oldest agriculture research centre, it was discovered that to extract the protein you only needed something like a large mincing machine, a saucepan to boil the juice, and a sieve to collect the curds.

'Eat up your greens, they're good for you,' is a familiar enough cry, as is the negative response from the child. What makes leaves so undesirable to a child is the large amount of fibre to be chewed before getting the benefit of the protein, vitamins and trace minerals. The wartime research discovered a technique of pulping the leaves, extracting the juice, then heating it to make a curd. One kilo of cabbage will give about twenty-five grams of leaf curd or concentrate. I've eaten some; it is a bit like green cottage cheese, rather soft and fluffy but quite delicious. It can be added to other foods, and like tofu can be sweet or savoury.

The advantages for Third World countries are astonishing. Find Your Feet, a registered charity, is promoting better nutrition for malnourished children through leaf concentrate. Any edible leaf can be used that is not so dry or glutinous as to make it difficult to handle. Local plants from the wild can be harvested, or plants that grow quickly can be cultivated. Nothing is wasted: after pulping, the fibre feeds cattle and after heating the brown whey can be used as fertiliser or be fermented and drunk as booze.

A tablespoon of leaf concentrate gives more protein than is listed in the recommended daily allowance the United States lays down for children aged between one and three years. It is also rich in vitamins A, B and E plus iron, calcium and magnesium. UNICEF estimates that forty per cent of the world's children under five are suffering from protein energy malnutrition. Small children are most vulnerable at the time of weaning and they need easily digested high-protein foods. One of the most devastating outcomes of a vitamin A deficiency is nutritional blindness (xerophthalmia), which is irreversible. Half a million children a year go blind from it, but a level teaspoon per day of leaf concentrate will give a five-year-old sufficient vitamin A for maximum health.

The staple diet in the developing world often provides poor-quality protein: leaf concentrate can improve this situation. In the last few years trials have been monitored in Sri Lanka, Ghana, Bolivia, Mexico and Pakistan. So successful have these been that sixty-six other countries have made enquiries about starting such programmes. In Sri Lanka (where the mincing machines are made from scrapped engines of old Morris Minors) there is a drink going back a good 2,000 years called Kola-Kenda, made from ground coconut, rice and leaf juice. It was simple to invite mothers to try substituting the leaf concentrate for the juice, and over a trial period of two years the children have thrived. Tell-tale signs of malnutrition, mouth sores and eczema, disappeared within a month of starting on the concentrate.

In Mexico, where 90,000 children die every year before they are three, a women's co-operative makes leaf concentrate out of alfalfa and adds it to pasta, churritos and fresh lemonade. So popular is their product that they have opened La Casa de la Salud, the house of health, to sell their foods. Over the border in California, a huge processing factory every hours turn sixty tons of alfalfa into concentrate pellets to feed cattle and chickens . . . such is life. And in Ghana, concentrate is supplied to schools and clinics, and the whey is fermented to produce yeast and medical alcohol.

Find Your Feet was hampered for many years in their promotion by the indifference of mostly male food scientists who had the attitude that a simple food process in the hands of village women must somehow be flawed or inadequate. Carol Martin, chairman of the charity (who has always been motivated by outrage that the Western world lives in abundance but can do so little to feed the hungry), says the idea that mere grass can be a valuable human food has been a difficult one for Western people to grasp, though not for the hungry. A mother working in a village co-operative once explained what she had got out of the experience. 'We like the responsibility.' The co-operatives think up new recipes all the time. Guacamole, for example, goes a stunning colour of chartreuse.

If there is a British food manufacturer who wishes his name to go down to posterity as a synonym for compassion, like Wilberforce, he could add leaf concentrate to anything from cocktail biscuits to sausages, market it and give a percentage of the profits to Find Your Feet to start 1,000 more village co-operatives.

Find your Feet, 13–15 Frognal, London NW3 6AP. 071-794 6435.

M A R R O W S

The British are fond of their marrows, though before the middle of the last century they were referred to as vegetable marrows to distinguish them from beef marrow.

They were considered to be food for country people, part of the cottage garden, the vegetable equivalent of hollyhocks. That snobbism still exists: food writers of distinction are not courteous to the marrow any more than the snob cuisines will favour it with even one recipe.

Pick or buy marrows when they are still young, no longer than 14 inches/35 cm and when the skin can still be broken with the finger nail. At this size they do not have to be peeled, and the skin has flavour. The marrow will obligingly soak up the flavours of herbs, oils and spices, which is why a simple dish of steamed marrow with mint is particularly good. The main problem is its high water content which boiling the vegetable only compounds, so tend to steam, bake or fry. Or salt the marrow and let it exude some of the moisture before cooking.

If eaten young the flavour is appealing, quite different from courgettes, and they make an excellent chilled soup. Courgettes allowed to grow too large should be treated like marrows. Both go well with home-grown tomatoes, onions, basil, garlic, parsley, and mint.

I have never found recipes for stuffing marrows very helpful, for if the marrow is cut in half the stuffing then leaks out from the middle. And if one end is sliced off, you cannot get all the seeds and pith out. I now favour the lid approach. Cut an oval shape out of the top quarter of the marrow, leaving the ends of the marrow intact. Prise this up with a grapefruit knife, sliding the knife around the whole shape, so that you then lift up a lid which is about ½ inch/1 cm in depth. The seeds and pith are easily scooped out with a spoon and the main bulk of the marrow resembles a dugout canoe. You can cram a lot of stuffing into this aperture and press the lid back down on it. It is then wrapped in foil and baked in a hot oven for an hour. It may need more time, for it depends upon the size of marrow. Some cooks favour blanching the whole marrow for fifteen minutes before it is stuffed. This cuts down on the oven time, but you will need a good-sized fish kettle or a very large saucepan to take the marrow.

While stuffing a marrow is no bad thing, depending on the piquancy of the stuffing, there are other ways of enjoying this vegetable, as in these recipes.

CURRIED MARROW SOUP

I SMALLISH MARROW
2 OZ/50 G BUTTER
I TEASPOON CRUSHED CORIANDER
I TEASPOON CURRY POWDER
I ¼ PINTS/900 ML VEGETABLE STOCK
I TEASPOON HONEY
SEA SALT AND FRESHLY GROUND BLACK PEPPER
2 TABLESPOONS YOGHURT OR SOUR CREAM

METHOD

Trim the ends of the marrow, deseed, and cut it into cubes. Melt the butter in a saucepan and add the coriander and curry powder, then the marrow. Place a tight-fitting lid on the pan and let the marrow steam in its own liquid for 5 minutes. Add the vegetable stock and honey. Bring to the boil and simmer for 15 minutes. Taste and season. Allow to cool then liquidise or put the soup through a mouli-legume. Reheat and add two tablespoons of yoghurt or sour cream before serving.

CHILLED MARROW SOUP

I MEDIUM-SIZE MARROW
I OZ/25 G BUTTER
3–5 CLOVES GARLIC
I ONION, SLICED
½ PINT/285 ML TOMATO SAUCE (SEE PAGE 270)
2 TABLESPOONS CHOPPED BASIL, MINT OR PARSLEY
¼ PINT/145 ML SINGLE CREAM
SEA SALT AND FRESHLY GROUND BLACK PEPPER

METHOD

Peel, core and deseed the marrow and cut the flesh into chunks. Cook in a pan with the butter and the garlic and onion for about 10 minutes. Place in the blender with its cooking juices, add the rest of the ingredients and mix to a purée. Taste and check for seasoning. Chill well.

GRATIN OF MARROW AND FENNEL

- 1 MEDIUM-SIZE MARROW
- 2 HEADS OF FENNEL
- 4 OZ/115 G BUTTER
- 2 BAY LEAVES
- SEA SALT AND FRESHLY GROUND BLACK PEPPER
- 1 OZ/25 G FLOUR
- ½ PINT/285 ML MILK
- ¼ PINT/145 ML SINGLE CREAM
- 3 OZ/85 G GRUYÈRE CHEESE, GRATED
- 2 OZ/55 G PARMESAN CHEESE, GRATED
- 2 OZ/55 G BREADCRUMBS

METHOD

Peel, core and deseed the marrow and cut the flesh into chunks. Trim and quarter the fennel. Cook in half of the butter in a pan with the bay leaves and a pinch of salt for about 10 minutes. Make a sauce by melting the rest of the butter, adding the flour and cooking it for a moment, before adding the milk, cream and the two cheeses. Season well with black pepper.

Pour the marrow and fennel into the sauce, discarding the bay leaves, so that it is well coated and then into a shallow earthenware dish (a tian or gratin dish). Sprinkle with breadcrumbs and bake in a preheated oven at 400F/200C/gas mark 6 for about 15 minutes.

FRIED MARROW

- 1 SMALLISH MARROW
- 2 OZ/60 G PLAIN FLOUR
- 1 TEASPOON GARAM MASALA
- SEA SALT AND FRESHLY GROUND BLACK PEPPER
- 2 OZ/60 G GINGER ROOT
- 3 TABLESPOONS OLIVE OIL

METHOD

Do not peel the marrow but trim the ends, then slice in half and extract and discard the pith and seeds. Cut the flesh into small cubes. Mix the flour, the garam masala and the seasoning together and toss the marrow in this. Peel and grate the ginger root and fry it in the olive oil for a second or two before adding the marrow cubes. Continue to fry for 4–5 minutes until the marrow is golden and crisp.

GREEN PEPPER AND MARROW TARKARI

I SMALLISH MARROW
4 SMALL GREEN PEPPERS
2 GREEN CHILLIES
I TEASPOON TURMERIC POWDER
I TEASPOON GARAM MASALA
I TEASPOON CRUSHED CORIANDER
JUICE OF I LEMON
2 TABLESPOONS CORN OIL
SEA SALT AND FRESHLY GROUND BLACK PEPPER

METHOD

Deseed and cube the flesh of the marrow. Slice the green peppers and chop the chillies, but discard their seeds. Heat the oil in a pan and fry the marrow, peppers and chillies until they are just soft. You will have to agitate the pan so that all sides are cooked and the pieces do not stick. Now add the spices and the lemon juice and immediately raise the heat, shaking the vegetables and spices together for about 2 minutes to drive off all the moisture. Serve sprinkled with a little sea salt and black pepper.

MARROW TART

8 OZ/200 G SHORTCRUST PASTRY
I SMALLISH MARROW
SEA SALT
I LARGE ONION
2 TABLESPOONS OLIVE OIL
I OZ/30 G BUTTER
2 OZ/60 G GRATED PARMESAN
2 OZ/60 G GRATED GRUYÈRE
4 EGGS, WELL BEATEN
HANDFUL OF CHOPPED PARSLEY
I TEASPOON DRIED OREGANO
2 TABLESPOONS SINGLE CREAM

METHOD

Bake the pastry case blind. Trim the ends of the marrow, slice in half and extract the pith and seeds. Cut the marrow into one-inch cubes. Sprinkle them with salt and leave for 1–2 hours to exude moisture, then rinse the salt off and pat the cubes dry. Slice the onion and fry it in the oil and butter with the marrow cubes over a high heat for about 3 minutes – you must seal the marrow so that the tart is not watery. Place in a bowl and leave to cool. Stir in the grated cheese, eggs, herbs and cream. Pour the mixture into the pastry shell and bake in a preheated oven at 400F/200C/gas mark 6 for 25 minutes or until the tart has risen a little and is brown.

GRATIN OF SPICED MARROW

3 TABLESPOONS OLIVE OIL
6 CLOVES GARLIC, SLICED
I OZ/25 G GINGER ROOT, SLICED
12 OZ/340 G MARROW FLESH, CUBED
SEA SALT AND FRESHLY GROUND BLACK PEPPER
2 TABLESPOONS HONEY
I TABLESPOON TOASTED SESAME SEEDS

METHOD

Heat the oil in a frying pan and add the garlic and ginger. Fry for a moment, then add the cubes of marrow. Fry quite fiercely, moving the pan vigorously. When the marrow is crisp on the outside, season, pour on the honey, and sprinkle on the sesame seeds. Place the pan under a hot grill until the honey bubbles and reduces.

MARROW WITH CHILLI AND CORIANDER (SERVES FOUR)

I SMALL MARROW
3 GREEN CHILLIES
I TABLESPOON CORIANDER SEEDS
OLIVE OIL FOR FRYING
SEA SALT AND FRESHLY GROUND BLACK PEPPER
2 TABLESPOONS CORIANDER LEAVES, FINELY CHOPPED
JUICE AND ZEST FROM I LEMON

METHOD

Peel and deseed the marrow and cut into small chunks. Slice the chillies with their seeds and grind the coriander to a powder. Heat a large pan with the olive oil in it and throw in the chillies and coriander, heat them in the oil for a moment then throw in the cubed marrow. Fry for 10 minutes, occasionally shaking the pan, and turning the marrow cubes so that they are crisp and brown. Add the seasoning and continue to cook for another 2 minutes. Finally, sprinkle the coriander leaves over with the juice and zest of the lemon.

MEDITERRANEAN
MALTA

From one perspective, Malta is an offshore island of Italy, like Sardinia. But after 150 years of British rule the heritage of the table bequeathed to the Maltese islands looks more like sausage, egg and chips, or fish and chips, or baked beans, pork pie and chips – all, of course, with tomato ketchup. Was there a national cuisine before such a travesty of food, and if so, could it have survived such an onslaught?

Malta has given its name to one sauce, which is a hollandaise made with blood oranges. There is no record of who created it. We can only guess. In 1770 Patrick Brydone visited Malta and went into ecstasies over the local oranges, calling them the finest in the world. He was told by the farmers that the blood oranges were produced from oranges grafted on to pomegranate stock. He noted that the crop was picked from November through to June. (It now ends earlier, in April.) So pleased was Brydone with his orange discovery that he took several chests of the oranges back with him to give to friends in Naples. He was also enthusiastic about the vegetables and the local fish. Sadly he does not note that with the fish he ate sauce maltaise.

It is thought that the Knights taught the Maltese how to cook. The Knights lived well. Vows of celibacy often make men indulge themselves in other ways and the accounts of the Knights' dinners show that they rival any royal banquet. They stocked the islands with game. (Now Maltese keep all the animals, including the game, penned in cages in their back-yards and allow the larger beasts an evening stroll.) Many of the present national dishes stem from the Grand Master's palaces and the kitchens of the Auberges.

As the Order was made up of eight Langues – Auvergne, Provence, France, Aragon, Castile, Italy, Germany and England – three of these being French, one would expect the dishes given to the islands to exemplify Gallic delicacy. But pasta – and heavy pasta at that – appears to be predominant. Sauce maltaise is lightness itself and my guess is that because of the orange tradition in Spain, the sauce may have emanated from the kitchens of the Auberges of either Aragon or Castile.

Timpana is perhaps the most famous Maltese dish; a baked macaroni with minced meat, chicken livers and hard-boiled eggs. When cold it can be sliced in chunks and it is then often eaten as a packed labourers' lunch. Kosksu, another form of pasta, is small pellets of dough, now made commercially, which can be added to soups, or mixed with peas or broad beans and eaten with a tomato and garlic sauce.

But it is in their pies that the Maltese come into their own. They make a splendid lampuki pie, torta tal-lampuki. Lampuki – dolphin fish – are caught in great numbers off the island's coast in the summer months. It is a fish full of flavour and bakes beautifully.

The Maltese make the pie by frying thick steaks of the fish and mixing these with vegetables. Alan Davidson gives a recipe in *Mediterranean Seafood* and rightly points out that the Maltese use a variety of vegetables: onions, peas, tomatoes, cauliflower and capers with the addition of mint and parsley. But I have also eaten this pie containing marrows, broad beans and black olives. The pie seems to work well whatever mixture it is.

Another notable pie is the one made from rabbit – torta tal-fenek. The rabbit is jointed, floured and fried then the bones are removed and the flesh is mixed with tomatoes, onions and peas. They often flavour the game pies with mixed spice. This tradition may stem from the Middle East and Africa, rather than from the Knights. Other specialities are stews made from rabbit, game or fish. There is frakassija tas-summien, a quail stew. The small birds are cooked in red wine, tomatoes and garlic, and flavoured with thyme and oregano which grows profusely over the cliffs and hills of the islands.

One of my favourite Greek dishes, fasoulia, made from haricot beans, olive oil, garlic, tomatoes and onions, appears in Maltese cooking as fazola and is exactly the same. Then there is ful bit-yewm, broad beans with their inner skin peeled away cooked in water, olive oil and a tablespoon of vinegar, with a third of their weight in garlic cloves: salt, pepper and chopped parsley are added when they are cooked through – in about five minutes.

Looking at these recipes I am not persuaded that the Maltese learnt much from the Knights. I believe that the most imaginative food stems from the lower classes, who by force of necessity have to make bland cereals interesting with hot spices and strong sauces. These ideas are pinched by the rich and quite often ruined by excess.

A visitor today to these islands would be wise to choose from the wide variety of fish on sale in the markets every day. Swordfish, plainly grilled with oil and lemon, is hard to beat. But there are other giant fish caught near, the most spectacular being the tuna, so dark red it looks unnervingly like a side of beef. Alan Davidson gives recipes for it from Algeria, Yugoslavia and Genoa among others. But he does not mention that if the fish is washed repeatedly in running water before cooking it loses a lot of its pigmentation and pungency. It is best in some form of casserole, cooked in oil with tomatoes, garlic and chillies.

Another great fish I have found on these islands is the merou, a sea bass, called cerna in Malta, which is similar to the Italian name cernia. The flesh is white and firm, full of flavour rather like a dense, fat haddock. It was here that the sauce maltaise came into its own. Merou with a sauce made out of blood oranges is sensational.

MEDITERRANEAN COOKING

 Maybe there are those who find self-catering holidays a chore. But I know that I seize the opportunity for another style of cooking based on different produce, often fresher and cheaper than we can find at home.

If you are renting a place on the Mediterranean, rely on your nose. Smell out the market and just enjoy wandering it. Observe the kind of produce the locals are buying. When they gather into an excited knot, see what mammoth of the deep is being carved up. An invaluable book for reference and recipes is *Mediterranean Seafood* by Alan Davidson (Penguin).

There are two types of shops, the one that caters for the tourists, so that the kids can still have fish fingers, and the shops that the local use. These are cavernous, dark, crammed with dusty sacks of rice, barley, beans and peas. From the beams hang salted dried fish, bundles of herbs, smoked hams; there are mounds of home-made pasta, jars of tomato paste, barrels of brine swimming with dark olives, bright green fresh capers, strings of crimson sausages larded with fat, jars of spices, tall cylinders of creamy cheese stuck with peppercorns; and beneath the counter, on show but in the cool, are unnameable slabs of local delicacies. A place that can alienate and bewilder the tourist or charm and delight.

The first shopping trip in a new place is always exciting and sometimes a revelation. Olive oil is at the top of the shopping list, but try to buy not only virgin oil (which is pressed without further refining) but extra virgin oil, which is the first pressing and has more flavour of the olive than any other. It is more expensive but you need less of it.

Never decide what you want to cook before exploring the markets and seeing what is at its best. I can recall finding small globe artichokes selling at the equivalent of 2p each. Because of their cheapness I could cook the two recipes given here, which in this country would have been an undreamt-of luxury.

Possibly you will find unexpected fruits, diminutive, but all the more intense in flavour: white peaches, apricots, quinces, plums and limes. You are sure to find, from the beginning of June, the magnificent purple fig, to be eaten with a mild soft cheese.

One winter in Orvieto I had a longing to buy truffles, but at £15 for 2 oz/55 g, it seemed a criminal absurdity. (I wish we could revive the truffle digging here. The last man who trained fox terriers to hunt truffles died early this century.) Instead, I made do with a jar of fungi in oil at around £2, which still seemed to me expensive enough, but thereby hangs a favourite dish.

The herbs that grow all over southern Europe and also near the sea are thyme, fennel, oregano, anise, and some sages and wild mints. On the first few days of your holiday, collect them all and use generously.

ARTICHOKE HEARTS IN TOMATO AND GARLIC SAUCE (SERVES SIX)

30 GLOBE ARTICHOKES
½ LB/200 G TOMATOES
6 GARLIC CLOVES, CRUSHED
2 TEASPOONS FRESH THYME
I TABLESPOON OLIVE OIL

METHOD

Cut the stalks and all the leaves from the artichokes. Boil in enough water to cover them for 20 minutes. Leave to cool. Wash the tomatoes, put them into a saucepan, skins and stalks as well, with the crushed garlic and simmer over a low flame. They will cook in their own juice and be ready within 5 minutes. Put them through a sieve. Sauté the fresh thyme in the olive oil, then add the sieved tomato and garlic purée. With the point of a knife take out the chokes from the artichoke hearts. Reheat the hearts with a little of the sauce poured over each one. Do not drown in the sauce.

FRIED ARTICHOKES IN BATTER

Choose small, tender artichokes. Allow 3 for each person. Cut off all the sharp, fibrous points from the leaves. Slice into quarters, dig out the embryo choke from each quarter with a pointed knife. Dip into batter and fry in olive oil until crisp.

White Egg Fungi Soufflé

ONE 12 OZ/350 G JAR OF FUNGI IN OIL OR I LB/500 G FRESH FUNGI OR
    FIELD MUSHROOMS PLUS 2 TABLESPOONS OF OLIVE OIL
4 OZ/100 G GRUYÈRE CHEESE, GRATED
4 EGG WHITES

Method

Empty the jar of fungi with its oil into a bowl, add the grated Gruyère, whip the egg whites until they are stiff, fold them into the mixture. Place in a well-oiled soufflé dish and bake in a preheated oven for 20 minutes at 400F/200C/gas mark 6, or until the soufflé has risen.

    If using fresh fungi or field mushrooms, slice them, then fry quickly over a fierce heat in the olive oil for about 2 minutes, or until they are just seared and shrunk a little. They must not begin to lose their juices, otherwise the soufflé will be too watery to rise.

Stuffed Tomatoes

4 VERY LARGE TOMATOES
4 CRUSHED CLOVES OF GARLIC
2 TEASPOONS EACH OF THYME AND OREGANO
2 TABLESPOONS TOASTED BREADCRUMBS
2 TABLESPOONS PARMESAN CHEESE, GRATED

Method

Split the tomatoes in half, scoop out the centre of each and place in a mixing bowl. Add all the other ingredients. Test for flavour and texture: it may need more breadcrumbs, black pepper, more garlic or cheese. Stuff the tomato halves with the mixture and place under a hot grill for 10 minutes or until the tops are brown and sizzling.

Mushrooms

At least now we have more variety of cultivated mushrooms to choose from than ten years ago. There are large flat ones, medium cups and small buttons; there are chestnut and oyster. There is no difference in flavour between the first four and all have an incredibly high water content so that they shrink alarmingly in cooking. Oyster mushrooms are by far the most tasty and have the smallest shrinkage so though more expensive they work out as a better buy. They are so delicious they only need a little sautéing in butter and oil with a touch of garlic.

If you can find them, wild field mushrooms are the most tasty of all the fungi, but it is well worth buying a comprehensive guide to mushrooms and fungi so that you can go out and pick your own.

Spiced Mushrooms

  2 TABLESPOONS OLIVE OIL
  I OZ/25 G GINGER ROOT, PEELED AND GRATED
  I DRIED RED CHILLI, BROKEN UP
  ½ LB/225 G MUSHROOMS, SLICED
  I TEASPOON ASAFOETIDA
  I TABLESPOON SOY SAUCE
  PINCH OF SEA SALT AND FRESHLY GROUND BLACK PEPPER

Method

Heat the olive oil in a pan and throw in the grated ginger root and chilli, cook for a second or two, then add the mushrooms. Leave to simmer, stirring occasionally for about 5 minutes, or until they are almost cooked, then sprinkle in the asafoetida and add the soy and seasoning. Cook for 1 minute more.

Stuffed Mushrooms in Red Pepper Sauce
(serves six)

You can now buy cultivated large mushrooms, excellent for stuffing. This makes a good first course. It can be eaten cold if you wish.

3 RED PEPPERS, CORED, DESEEDED AND CHOPPED
2 TABLESPOONS OLIVE OIL
SEA SALT AND FRESHLY GROUND BLACK PEPPER
2 OZ/50 G HAZELNUTS, ROASTED
GENEROUS HANDFUL OF CHOPPED HERBS: PARSLEY, BASIL, CHIVES, MINT
  OR CORIANDER
2 CLOVES GARLIC, CRUSHED
2 OZ/50 G BUTTER
6 LARGE MUSHROOMS
HERBS FOR GARNISHING

Method

Make sauce and stuffing first. Sauté the red peppers in the olive oil over a low heat in a saucepan with the lid on, until soft (about 10 minutes). When cool liquidise to a purée and season. Return to saucepan for gentle reheating.

Roast the hazelnuts in a closed pan, shaking the pan to stop burning, then rub between a teatowel to get the skins off. Liquidise the nuts in a blender with the herbs and garlic, mix with the butter and seasoning.

Place the mushrooms, inside down, under a hot grill for a minute. Let them cool, then spread the stuffing on the inside and place under the grill again to heat through.

Place in the centre of a plate and pour a little of the heated pepper sauce around each mushroom. Garnish each mushroom with a little fresh herbs.

OATS
Oatmeal Soup • Atholl Brose

OKRA
Okra and Mushrooms

OLIVE OIL
Farro Garfagnino

OATS

Oats are suddenly the new health food. A diet which includes one bowl of porridge and two slices of oat bread per day can, over a five-week period, lower the blood cholesterol by forty per cent. These statistics, Dr James Anderson of Kentucky University believes, are true even for a normal diet which includes animal fats – meat and dairy products.

Regular consumption of oats also smooths out the blood sugar level, which tends on the majority of diets to go up and down like a roller coaster. Oats, it is believed, somehow wrap up the more potent stimulants and in this way subdue their effect. We are, as a British doctor put it, Stone Age bodies now eating machine-made food and we should attempt to return to more suitable diets. That means oats.

Dr Anderson's claims may be true. But in Scotland, the home of oats and porridge, the incidence of coronary heart disease is higher than in the whole of the UK. Perhaps without porridge it would be higher still.

One factor which was ignored when the press was regaled with the news of this new miracle food was what you add to the oats. Do you make the porridge with water, skimmed milk or full-fat milk? The latter is high in saturated fats. It was mentioned in passing that most people add some salt or sugar to their porridge and it was considered by the two British doctors that these additions were so marginal they were insignificant on the general health picture. However, some salt or sugar might be putting it too modestly. When a small lad was asked what he had on his porridge, he replied, 'Butter, cream and brown sugar.' I cannot help concluding that the intake of saturated fats would be as high as that of soluble fibre and a dubious confrontation would take place – a view not altered by the recipes shown to us.

There seemed to be an almost frantic need not to allow the porridge to be eaten plain. The additions suggested were black treacle and cream, strawberry jam and cream, sultanas, raisins, currants and salted peanuts. There was porridge brûlée, mixed with rings of pineapple, covered in brown sugar and briefly sizzled under the grill; something called porridge paradise, which was sliced fruit and desiccated coconut (which looks innocent but is high in saturated fats); a spicy porridge, a herby porridge and a Scottish fruit fool.

Almost any food rolled in oats, or oats and herbs, or oats, salt and spices, is a huge improvement. The blandest rissole, croquette or fish cake is given a great boost by being covered in such a mixture before being fried. Fresh herring or trout rolled in oats and then fried or grilled is an old Scottish recipe.

Fine oatmeal can be added to wheat flour for bread, pastry and cakes. Use half oats to half wheat, as oats have a gluten that will not leaven bread. Oats make an excellent stuffing. Use them instead of breadcrumbs with plenty of chopped onion and herbs.

But perhaps where oats are of most use in cooking is for thickening sauces and soups.

Oatmeal Soup

2 LARGE CHOPPED ONIONS
2 OZ/50 G BUTTER OR MARGARINE
2 OZ/50 G ROLLED OATS
I PINT/570 ML VEGETABLE STOCK
SEA SALT AND FRESHLY GROUND BLACK PEPPER
½ PINT/275 ML MILK
HANDFUL OF CHOPPED PARSLEY

Method

Add the onions to the melted fat in a saucepan, cook for a few minutes until the onions are soft, add the oats, continue to cook but stir all the time so that the oats do not stick to the pan. (This gummy texture, by the way, is the very soluble fibre which is necessary to health.) Add the vegetable stock after a couple of minutes, bring to the boil and let the soup simmer on a very low heat for ½ hour. Finally, season to taste, add the milk and the chopped parsley, heat it and serve.

ATHOLL BROSE

- 2 TABLESPOONS ROLLED OATS
- 2 TABLESPOONS HONEY
- 2 TABLESPOONS WHISKY
- 1 PINT/570 ML DOUBLE CREAM

METHOD

Dry roast the oats in a pan so that they are browned, pour into a bowl and mix in the honey and whisky. Beat the cream so that it is stiff and mix with the other ingredients.

O K R A

 Sometimes referred to as ladies' fingers or gumbo, okra is part of the mallow family and a cousin of the cotton plant. People are often put off okra because its seeds are mucilaginous: to avoid this effect cook it quickly and enjoy its flavour all the more. Okra and oyster mushrooms are best in the winter.

O K R A   A N D   M U S H R O O M S

8 OZ/225 G OKRA
3 TABLESPOONS OLIVE OIL
8 OZ/225 G OYSTER MUSHROOMS
5 CLOVES GARLIC, SLICED

M E T H O D

Slice the okra down its length, heat the oil in a pan or wok and throw in the vegetables. Stir-fry over a high heat for a few minutes or at least until the okra is tinged with brown and is crisp, while the mushrooms have shrunk a little, but not lost their shape.

OLIVE OIL

There is good news for all lovers of olive oil. In the battle between the fats, saturated versus polyunsaturated, the mono-unsaturated olive oil had appeared to be neutral. But research published in the US in 1988 proved otherwise. In the *New England Journal of Medicine*, a paper by Scott M. Grundy studies the effect of mono-unsaturated fatty acids on lowering plasma cholesterol.

Up to now, the diet recommended for lowering cholesterol in the blood has been a low-fat diet. But in the Mediterranean countries, where large amounts of olive oil are consumed, the rate of coronary heart disease is low. Of all these countries, Crete has the highest consumption of olive oil and the lowest rate of heart attacks. This has always puzzled nutritionists. Now, Grundy has shown that a diet high in mono-unsaturated fats reduces total cholesterol to a greater extent than a low-fat diet.

Recently, on a trip to Lucca, I tasted a range of oils, including a new one by Bertolli – the first new olive oil for over 4,000 years, they proudly claim. The Bertolli factory uses extra virgin oil from ten different farms. Each farm oil is tested for acidity and impurities, then blended and filtered through cotton wool into huge vats. After the oil has gone through the cotton wool process, it is filtered a second time at pressure through 200 papers and aluminium plates. It leaves upon the plates a dark residue that you can draw on with a finger nail. The oil is now ready for bottling. The best one is extra virgin and it is expensive but this dark, well-flavoured oil is the lowest in acidity – less than one per cent.

Next in superiority is fine virgin which has an acidity of 1.5 per cent. Then there is ordinary virgin oil with a maximum acidity of 3.3 per cent. Pure olive oil is not pure at all; it is a blend, mostly oil which has been washed, decanted, centrifuged, filtered then flavoured and coloured with some extra virgin. There is not enough extra virgin oil to meet world demand.

The new oil which is called extra light is on sale now. It can be used for cooking, it has a high smoking point of 374–410F/190–210C. It will also make a light mayonnaise without the earthy flavour of the green Greek oils and the extra virgin oils of Tuscany.

The food of Lucca was a revelation of simple, earthy goodness. Olives are pickled with lemon salt, cinnamon and chilli peppers. Agnello con olive nere is a lamb and black olive stew. Or there is just olive oil with lots of coarse sea salt and black pepper in it used as a dip for crudités. A swirl of olive oil decorates many a dish like a wild hare and pasta leaf casserole, or this soup which we ate at the Buca di San Antonia in Lucca.

There are versions of this grain and bean soup – Gran Farro – around Tuscany. They use spelt, a hard wheat, available at health and wholemeal shops. Spelt needs a good hour's cooking but you could use buckwheat which only needs twelve minutes.

FARRO GARFAGNINO
(SERVES SIX TO EIGHT)

I LB/450 G SPELT OR BUCKWHEAT

I LB/450 G BORLOTTI BEANS, SOAKED

5 CLOVES GARLIC, CRUSHED

2 CARROTS

I SPRIG SAGE

I ONION, CHOPPED

3 CELERY STALKS, CHOPPED

½ LB/225 G TOMATOES, PEELED AND CHOPPED

I TEASPOON CINNAMON

SEA SALT AND FRESHLY GROUND BLACK PEPPER

5 FL OZ/150 ML OLIVE OIL

METHOD

If using spelt, cook it in water for 1 hour, then drain and reserve. If using buckwheat, do the same but only cook for about 10–12 minutes.

Meanwhile, cook the borlotti beans with the garlic, carrots and sage until tender, about 1 hour. Discard the sage. Reserve a quarter of the beans and blend the rest with their liquor in a food processor. Fry the onion and celery together with the tomatoes, cinnamon and seasoning in the oil. Add the bean purée and the wheat, bring to the boil and simmer for an hour. In the last 10 minutes, add the whole beans.

PARSNIPS
Parsnip Croquettes

PARTY
Summer Salad • Courgette Salad • Lasagne Verdi – 1

PASTA
Lasagne Verdi – 2
Gnocchi Gnocchi di Semolino • Gnocchi Verdi • Gnocchi di Patate

PASTRY

PEANUTS

PICKLING
Flavoured Vinegars
Home-Made Pickles Rhubarb Pickle • Quick Pickle • Spiced Quinces •
Lime Pickle
Nasturtiums

PILAF
Summer Pilaf • Millet Pilaf

PORTUGAL
The Market

POTATOES

Mint Salad Sauce • Potato Mint Croquettes • Potatoes Baked in Mint Stock • Gratin Jurassien • Salade Angevine • Moroccan Potato Casserole • Solyanka • Gourmet Potato Salad

PRESS TIPS
A Californian Experience

PROVENCE
Soupe au Pistou • Pistou Sauce
Pipérade Red Pipérade

PUMPKINS
Ginger Pumpkin Soup

PURÉES

PARSNIPS

 Parsnips tend to be underrated, merely thought of as winter fodder sprinkled around the roast joint. It was Jane Grigson who first made them into a curried soup and that dish has become a classic. But the natural sweetness of new parsnips can be used in other ways. This recipe teams them with an Indian spice too, cumin, but only a modest dash. Either eat them with just a green salad as a light lunch or supper or have them as part of a larger Indian meal.

PARSNIP CROQUETTES
(SERVES SIX)

2 LB/900 G PARSNIPS
2 OZ/50 G BUTTER
1 TEASPOON CUMIN
2 EGGS, SEPARATED
1 TABLESPOON GRAM (BESAN) FLOUR
SEA SALT AND FRESHLY GROUND BLACK PEPPER
2 OZ/50 G FRESH WHOLEMEAL BREADCRUMBS
BUTTER AND OLIVE OIL, FOR FRYING

METHOD

Peel and trim the parsnips. Cut them into chunks, put them in a saucepan and boil for 6 minutes, or until tender. Drain well. Melt the butter in a saucepan, add the cumin and sweat it for 1 to 2 minutes. In a bowl, mash the parsnips. Add the butter and cumin, and the egg yolks. Sieve the gram flour into the parsnip mixture and combine it well. Season with salt and pepper to taste. Mix thoroughly and chill for 1 hour.

Put the egg whites into a bowl and beat to combine; spread the breadcrumbs on a plate. Remove the mixture from the refrigerator, pick off pieces from the dough and roll into sausage shapes. Dip them into the egg white and then into the breadcrumbs. Continue until mixture is used up. Refrigerate croquettes until needed. Fry the croquettes briefly in a mixture of butter and olive oil, so that the outside is crisp and brown.

PARTY

 In 1983 on my birthday, I gave a luncheon party for about thirty friends which BBC TV filmed for a programme called *Vegetarian Kitchen*. Rightly, they thought that vegetarian food had been lumbered with the wrong earnest image for too long – food which, though good for you, is inherently unexciting and unimaginative. So the last programme of the series of six was devoted to food as celebration.

Cooking for thirty people is an undeniable challenge, but cooking in a torrid heat wave and taking it to the country homestead which is without electricity and sports only a small Calor gas refrigerator was something of a headache. The party was on a Sunday. On the Friday before, in London, I turned the thermostat of the refrigerator to its lowest and almost froze everything for twenty-four hours. On the Saturday morning I insulated every dish, packing them with layers of newspaper. I forgot to put clingwrap over some, so the lasagne verdi bore in mirror-image the whole of the *Guardian* leader column imprinted upon the cheese sauce. It was still there after we had cooked it.

I had planned to begin with an array of first courses. The cameras scrutinised them for longer than was good for them; I was convinced that in the heat the vegetable gelatine would melt and the terrine would sprout a fungus. I was filmed describing this cold collation, which I did with only about an eighth of my mind, as I was suddenly convinced that two of the guests, arriving at any minute, might decide to murder each other – an act not consistent with vegetarianism.

The meal was designed around four courses, the hors-d'oeuvre, then the lasagne verdi and salad, followed by some superb French cheeses, including a Brie and a Roquefort, obtained at a splendid local shop, Loaves and Fishes at Woodbridge, Suffolk. To finish there were soft fruits picked not an hour before from the garden, red, black and white currants, raspberries and strawberries. Later in the afternoon we also ate a chocolate cake made by a friend from one of Helge Rubinstein's recipes from her *Chocolate Book* (Penguin). We began with an excellent sparkling white Burgundy which seems like champagne, Crystal Dry. We then continued with a Côtes du Rhone, Château du Grand Moulas.

Among the first courses there were hummus, a tapenade made from capers, a fasoulia, a jajiki, two layered vegetable terrines, a platter of crudités, a ratatouille, tabbouleh, mushrooms à la grecque, tomatoes provençale, two onion tarts and various salads, raw grated beetroot, courgettes and mange-touts, coleslaw and the summer salad described below.

I have no idea what all this food was like, because I do not believe I ate anything. The cameras interviewed many of the guests, but will any of them have dared to criticise? There was one gourmet friend and brilliant French cook who bemoaned the fact that I had not placed a small nugget of meat especially for her – like a threepenny bit in the Christmas pud – within the lasagne. But she was a minority of one.

The weather influences what we want to eat and in that long, hot summer I devised more salads using lemon and yoghurt.

Summer Salad

½ CUCUMBER
JUICE FROM 1 LEMON
HANDFUL OF CHOPPED MINT
1 CLOVE GARLIC, CRUSHED
1 LB/450 G YOUNG BROAD BEANS
1 LB/450 G FRESH PEAS
5 SPRING ONIONS
5 FL OZ/150 ML LOW-FAT YOGHURT
SEASONING

Method

Slice the cucumber thinly, sprinkle salt over it and leave for 2 hours, then rinse beneath a cold tap and squeeze out all the moisture. Chop it finely and put it in a dish with the lemon juice, chopped mint and crushed clove of garlic. Steam the beans and peas. Chop the spring onions. Add everything to the cucumber and mix in the yoghurt. Season. Leave in the refrigerator for 1–2 hours before serving. Serve on a bed of crisp lettuce.

C O U R G E T T E   S A L A D

1 LB/450 G SMALL COURGETTES
HANDFUL OF CHOPPED MINT
JUICE FROM 1 LEMON
1 CLOVE GARLIC, CRUSHED
5 FL OZ/150 ML LOW-FAT YOGHURT
SEASONING

M E T H O D

Grate the courgettes into a colander. Sprinkle with a little salt. Let them drain for a while. Squeeze them dry and add the mint, lemon juice, garlic and yoghurt. Chill then serve.

L A S A G N E   V E R D I – 1
(S E R V E S   T E N   T O   T W E L V E)

2 LB/900 G SPINACH LEAVES
1 LB/450 G COURGETTES
2 LB/900 G FRESH PEAS
½ PINT/275 ML SINGLE CREAM
12 OR 14 STRIPS OF LASAGNE
2 TABLESPOONS OIL
½ LB/225 G PARMESAN CHEESE
½ LB/225 G GRUYÈRE CHEESE
BLACK PEPPER
½ LB/225 G MATURED CHEDDAR CHEESE
½ PINT/275 ML MILK
1 OZ/25 G BUTTER
2 OZ/50 G PLAIN FLOUR

M E T H O D

This is the lasagne devised for the party. The interior sauce is made from a purée of fresh peas and colours everything a delicate shade of green.

Chop and cook the spinach without water, on a low heat for about 5 minutes, then drain the moisture away and reserve for the cheese sauce. Slice the courgettes across and steam them with the peas. Add the courgettes to the spinach. Blend the peas with the single cream into a thin purée.

Cook the lasagne sheets in lots of salted boiling water and a tablespoon of oil. Depending on the thickness of the sheets they will be done any time between 5 and 20 minutes. Have a bowl of cold water and a little oil ready, take the lasagne sheets from the saucepan and put them into the cold water. Drain them on cloths and absorbent paper.

Butter a shallow dish and line the bottom and sides with the lasagne. Grate half of each of the Parmesan and Gruyère, add this to the spinach and courgettes, stir it in, then lay them over the lasagne. Now pour the purée of peas over the top, and season with black pepper. You will not need salt because of the Parmesan.

Place another layer of lasagne over the top. Make a thick cheese sauce with the rest of the grated cheeses, the milk and the spinach liquor, which is added to a roux of butter and flour. After it has thickened, let the sauce cool, then pour it over the top of the pasta. Cook in a preheated oven at 400F/200C/gas mark 6 for 45 minutes to 1 hour or until the top is brown.

P A S T A

Pasta served without meat sauce is lighter and more agreeable on the palate. Lasagne tends to be heavy, but when made with vegetable purées it can be almost as buoyant as a soufflé. Spaghetti, fettuccine, tagliatelli and vermicelli are all transformed once you have dumped the Bolognese.

I confess I have never made my own pasta. Nor have I been able to enjoy commercial brands of pasta which taste of flour mixed with chlorinated tap water. But now on the market, obtainable at wholefood shops, are some delicious types of pasta (some of the best are imported from Japan) of high quality, often made from buckwheat.

The recipe below uses wholewheat lasagne which has thankfully been with us for some time. A l lb/500 g packet costs about £1 and holds twenty-five sheets of pasta. As I estimate the recipe will feed eight people adequately and you need just ten sheets of pasta, the price is economical.

You will need a large pan filled with boiling and lightly salted water. The pasta needs to be boiled for twenty minutes. Do five sheets at a time. If all ten sheets go in at once, two can stick together and others may stick to the bottom of the pan. Keep a rolling boil going: stronger than a simmer, but not too fierce, or the pasta might tear. When they are done, lift them out with a perforated spoon and let them drain over the colander.

Make the lasagne in a large baking dish – one about 2½ to 3 inches (6 to 8 cm) deep and around 10 x 12 inches (25 x 30 cm) in size. Le Creuset makes a superb rectangular dish 10¼ x 15¾ (26 x 40 cm) of enamelled cast iron which does wonders for the biceps and the lasagne baked in it. But that size of dish would use double the amounts below.

Pyrex make dishes of about the right size, and an ordinary meat baking dish will do. But whatever the dish, do ensure the base and sides are well oiled or greased. You do not want to leave half of the pasta sticking to the dish when you come to serve it.

Prepare two or three different vegetables for the filling. Vary the texture of the strata by leaving one vegetable finely or coarsely chopped while another is puréed; vary the strata still more by what you add to them: eggs, cream, tofu or different cheeses, a herb sauce or chopped parsley.

The colours can contrast as well. This recipe uses green vegetables, but a proper lasagne verdi has spinach added to the pasta. And who cares if your lasagne has the strident vulgarity of a Neapolitan ice cream? We English are too often stifled by the concept of good taste.

It is up to you whether the layers of vegetables are separated from each other by pasta. I prefer not to do this, as the lasagne is too heavy, but if this is your inclination, you will need to boil more than ten sheets of pasta.

Most important of all, the vegetables should be only just cooked, without touching water. They are sautéed in a closed saucepan over a low heat in a tablespoon of olive oil, only for a few minutes, until they have just begun to get soft.

LASAGNE VERDI

1 LB/500 G LEEKS
OLIVE OIL FOR GREASING BAKING DISH AND COOKING VEGETABLES
2 LB/900 G SPINACH
1 LB/500 G COURGETTES
10 STRIPS WHOLEWHEAT COOKED LASAGNE
1 PACKET OF MORINAGA TOFU
SEA SALT AND FRESHLY GROUND BLACK PEPPER
2 OZ/50 G GRUYÈRE CHEESE
5 FL OZ/150 ML SINGLE CREAM
4 TABLESPOONS CHOPPED PARSLEY
2 EGGS, BEATEN
1 OZ/25 G BUTTER
1 OZ/25 G PLAIN FLOUR
4 TABLESPOONS SKIMMED MILK POWDER
10 FL OZ/275 ML SKIMMED MILK
4 OZ/100 G SAGE DERBY CHEESE
2 OZ/50 G PARMESAN CHEESE

METHOD

Split the leeks down the centre and clean the earth away. Then slice across in 1 inch/2.5 cm chunks. Use 1 tablespoon of olive oil at the bottom of the pan. Put the leeks in and the lid on the pan, and leave over a low heat for a few minutes, shaking the pan occasionally to ensure the leeks do not stick or burn. When they have begun to soften, give them a good stir and set aside.

Coarsely chop the spinach and cook in the same way. Slice the courgettes to about ⅛ inch/0.25 cm thickness, and cook in the same way – they will need a minute or two longer.

Oil the baking dish and lay the cooked sheets of lasagne on the base and sides, covering the dish completely so that there is no space between the sheets of pasta. Cover the pasta with the spinach. Drain the packet of tofu and spread over the spinach. Season with sea salt and freshly ground black pepper; grate the Gruyère and sprinkle over the tofu, pressing the layers down so that it is even. Next, spread the leeks out and season. Then pour the cream over, lay the courgettes over the leeks, season, sprinkle with chopped parsley and pour the beaten egg over the top.

Cover completely with another layer of pasta, then make a roux with the butter and the flour, adding the skimmed milk powder to the skimmed milk to enrich the sauce. Grate the sage Derby and the Parmesan into the roux and let the sauce thicken. When the sauce is cool, spoon it over the top of the pasta, making sure there are no bits sticking up out of the sauce. They will blacken and burn, so cut them away.

The dish is better if left at this stage for a day to settle. Then bake in a preheated oven, 400F/200C/gas mark 6, for 30 minutes, or until the top is brown and the interior bubbling a little.

GNOCCHI

I am fond of gnocchi – in Italy, I tend to go from one plate to another – and it is a dish by which a restaurant may be judged. I have had potato gnocchi that could have been used as rubber bullets when they should be light and fluffy like the interior of a soufflé.

So recently I enrolled myself on a day cookery course run by Catercall at a Cromwellian mansion in the depths of the Surrey Downs, bang in the middle of stockbroker country. Anna Del Conte was to give a cookery demonstration on gnocchi di semolino, gnocchi verdi and gnocchi di patate with a few other dishes thrown in for good measure. I could not help pondering on the irony of it all. Here was a bunch of the well-heeled watching how to make Italian peasant food. For gnocchi started off as the dumplings of the poor.

We all ate the results of Anna's demonstration and her potato gnocchi were as light as swansdown. The gnocchi verdi, she and I considered afterwards, may not have come out so well. I thought it was because frozen spinach does not give as good a result as fresh. Anna thought they had been kept warm in too hot an oven.

The gnocchi recipes do involve a lot of butter, but I made them at the weekend substituting Vitaquell margarine instead, and a French gourmet guest gobbled them up. I also used skimmed milk, and fried golfball-sized amounts of the semolina gnocchi in olive oil instead of baking them in the oven with more butter.

The potato gnocchi are the most difficult to make and if they break when being poached, it is always, Anna claims, the fault of the potato. You must make them with floury ones. She was dismissive (and rightly so) of electrical mixers and food processors for any of the purées. It must all be done by hand in a food mill for the right results.

GNOCCHI DI SEMOLINO

1¾ PINT/1 LITRE MILK
8 OZ/225 G SEMOLINA (PREFERABLY ITALIAN)
3 EGG YOLKS
PINCH OF NUTMEG
SEA SALT
4 OZ/100 G BUTTER
3 OZ/75 G PARMESAN CHEESE, FRESHLY GRATED

METHOD

Heat the milk in a heavy saucepan and when it has nearly reached boiling point, add the semolina in a thin stream, beating with a fork or whisk. Continue beating until the semolina has formed a thick mass and can be drawn away from the sides. Allow to cool, then add the yolks, nutmeg, salt, 1 oz/25 g of the butter and 4 tablespoons of the Parmesan. Mix properly until well blended.

Moisten a cold surface with a little cold water and spread over the semolina to a thickness of ½ inch/1 cm. Allow the semolina to cool completely, then with a 1½ inch/4½ cm biscuit cutter, cut into discs. Moisten the cutter every now and then in cold water.

Butter the bottom of an oven dish large enough to contain the discs in a single layer, slightly overlapping. Dot with butter and sprinkle with Parmesan as you lay the discs in the dish. Melt the remaining butter in a small saucepan and pour over the dish, sprinkling with the rest of the Parmesan. Bake for about 15 minutes in a preheated oven at 450F/230C/gas mark 8 or until a light golden crust has formed. Allow to stand for 5 minutes before serving. There will probably be enough here for a first course for six people.

GNOCCHI VERDI

I LB/450 G FROZEN LEAF SPINACH
2 EGGS
7 OZ/200 G RICOTTA CHEESE
7 OZ/200 G PLAIN FLOUR
PINCH OF NUTMEG
4 OZ/100 G PARMESAN CHEESE, FRESHLY GRATED
SEA SALT AND FRESHLY GROUND BLACK PEPPER
4 OZ/100 G BUTTER

METHOD

Cook the spinach for 5 minutes. Drain and as soon as possible squeeze all the water out with your hands. Chop it finely. Beat the eggs together, and mix in with the ricotta. Add the flour, spinach, nutmeg and half the Parmesan, salt and pepper. Taste and adjust seasoning. From this mixture, make some balls the size of a large marble. Put them on a floured surface. Bring a large pan full of salted water to the boil, add the gnocchi, about two dozen at a time, and cook for 3–4 minutes after the water has returned to the boil. Retrieve with a slotted spoon and let the gnocchi drain. Transfer to a heated bowl and sprinkle with Parmesan and melted butter.

GNOCCHI DI PATATE

2 LB/I KG FLOURY POTATOES, SUCH AS KING EDWARD
I EGG
I TEASPOON SALT
7 OZ/200 G PLAIN FLOUR
2 OZ/50 G FRESHLY GRATED PARMESAN

METHOD

Purée the cooked potatoes through a food mill, add the egg, salt and most of the flour. The mixture should be soft, smooth and slightly sticky. Knead for at least 5 minutes. Shape the mixture into sausage-like rolls about 1 inch/2.5 cm in diameter, and cut the rolls into ¾ inch/1.5 cm pieces. Shape gnocchi with a fork or butter pat, so that they are ridged.

Drop the gnocchi into a large pan of boiling water – use very little salt – and cook them for about 30 seconds after they have come to the surface. Drain well, transfer to a heated dish, sprinkle with Parmesan.

P A S T R Y

 For years now I have rather testily complained of the leaden quality of pastry made out of 100 per cent whole- meal flour. We all know those health food restaurants that give you an inch-thick pastry base which tastes and weighs like an engineering brick (the kind that resists a masonry nail), with a quarter of an inch of pallid custard and a few particles of leek adhering to it, and call it a quiche.

After one of these complaints Simon Hope, author and restaurant owner, wrote to me from Food for Friends in Brighton and said, let us prove to you that 100 per cent wholemeal pastry can be as light and fluffy as angel cake about to levitate. Huh, I said, some chance of that.

The head chef and pastry chef at Food for Friends is Philip Taylor. He and his pastry assistant, Bix Gatenby, enlightened me. They cooked a rum baba, a chocolate Swiss roll, a bande Napoleon and a Linzertorte. All were as light as swansdown, and tasty too. The bande Napoleon had been made with puff wholemeal pastry and its crispy wafers were dark and nutty; it was filled with cream with egg white whipped into it plus fresh strawberries and kiwi fruit. It would have graced any French patisserie window.

The rum baba was amazingly light, its exterior a glistening golden mahogany while the interior was flecked oatmeal, far prettier than that polystyrene look you get with most rum babas made with white flour.

The Linzertorte used wholemeal flour mixed with the same amount of freshly ground hazelnuts. Butter and an egg yolk added to this made a very sticky paste. This was refrigerated overnight with a view to rolling it out in the morning. If the pastry cannot be rolled, it has to be pressed into the flan base and then baked blind. On to this is poured a purée made from dried apricots. This pastry had the most delicious flavour as well as being crumbly and melting on the tongue.

At Food for Friends everything is real. Home-made mayonnaise for the potato salad, made with egg yolks and extra virgin olive oil, is used for its quality and its flavour. The coffee flavour in the cream for the Swiss roll came from a real bean and not out of a tin.

The restaurant opens at nine in the morning for breakfast – no eggs, no bacon, but muesli, waffles, muffins, wholemeal toast and plenty of home-made fresh apple and orange juice. It closes at ten at night. They feed 500–600 people every day at about 50 tables, and they are always packed at lunch time. The food is very reasonably priced, nutritious and full of ravishing flavours.

Simon Hope worked for a short time some years ago with Trust House Forte. That experience was crucial, for he saw how restaurant food had sunk to a travesty of what it could be. He then went to Food for Thought at Covent Garden where he had a Thai chef. There Simon went for freshness and simplicity, but dishes which had an Eastern flair and spice to them. Yet, as he admits, the pastry was still heavy and chewy, not something to jog along on. After he had opened the Brighton restaurant, Philip Taylor joined him and there the revelation struck Simon.

All Philip seems to have done is to bring to the making of wholemeal pastry the classical training and experience of a good pastry chef. When I asked him why we had to endure the horrors before, he thought it was the influence of brusque pastry directions in American recipe books. 'Mix everything together', that is, instead of going through the whole gamut of sifted flour, cold fat, mixing until you have a breadcrumb mixture, then adding just enough cold water to make a paste and no more. Another tip he gave me was to use a little lemon juice with the water. Lemon, Philip claims, acts on the gluten in the flour and makes it more elastic.

Filled with new zeal for wholemeal pastry I went back home and began. I had some vegetable curry over, so thought I would make some samosas for a quick Sunday lunch.

I took 12 oz/350 g of 100 per cent wholemeal plain flour and sifted it, then shook all the bran back in. I gave this a good pinch of salt and then grated into it 3 oz/75 g of ice-hard butter and 3 oz/75 g of ice-hard vegetable fat. I worked on this, crumbling the mixture in my fingers. It seemed a lot more like hard work than doing the same task with white flour and it took longer to get the tiny breadcrumb mixture falling freely through the hands.

I then squeezed the juice from a lemon and poured it into the bowl. Philip had said just give a squeeze of the lemon, but I have always been impetuous and a bit heavy-handed. I pummelled the stuff into a crumbly paste and found that no water was necessary. A delicious lemon aroma emanated from the bowl. I formed the paste into two balls, covered the bowl and left it in a cool place for an hour. Philip says just ten minutes will do, but this rest is essential.

When I tried to roll out the pastry it obliged to a thickness of about a quarter of an inch and then fractured into pieces. I stuck it together and tried again. It was hopeless. I cursed my liberality with the lemon, thinking that a little water might have done the trick and fused the wretched stuff together. Abandoning the idea of samosas. I plumped for a curry pie.

I smeared the pastry dough on the bottom and sides of a flan tin and baked it blind. The aroma in the last few minutes of cooking was heaven. It browned well and evenly. I filled it with the curried vegetables and then eyed the dough for the top of the pie. This would be a challenge.

Rolled out to a quarter of an inch thick, the pastry was still together, but at that thickness it would be an unpleasant wodge. Tenderly, I rolled it a little more, but no – it fractured into about five pieces. When I picked these up, they broke into more. So I fitted a few pieces on top of the pie and baked it. It looked like a pavement after the water main had broken. I baked it at 400F/200C/gas mark 6 for thirty minutes and then took it out and let it rest for another five minutes. The wrecked pavement effect had come together slightly. I had given a new meaning to papering over the cracks.

The flavour and texture of the pastry was sensational. It was crumbly and melted on the tongue. Never mind the disaster on the way, this was worth it. I shall experiment further.

PEANUTS

 Have you come across a stressed peanut lately? If the answer is no, it may be because you have not yet developed a peanut flavour consciousness, or been really exposed to a peanut experience. Once you have, there is little doubt that you would recognise that stressed peanut. It suffers from an off flavour like burnt plastic food, which comes from the peanut oil which has oxidised and gone rank.

My peanut consciousness was raised, widened, astonished and even somewhat alarmed at a Peanut Flavour Quality Seminar given by Gail Vance Civille, consultant in the field of sensory evaluation of foods, beverages, pharmaceuticals, paper, fabrics, personal care and – take a breath – other consumer products.

All this psychology of the inanimate derives from a panel of flavour and peanut specialists who have established a lexicon of flavours, backed by the US Department of Agriculture, no less. Basically, this concordance of unexpected adjectives to describe the characteristics of a nut is to boost the profits of the US Peanut Council, which is doing very nicely already.

But in England, the land of the class system, they are up against a view like that of Peter Fort of the *Financial Times*. 'The trouble is,' he confided to me, 'my mother taught me that peanuts were common. Can't even take that butter. Don't like it.'

The US Council forget to label some peanuts as upper-class and others as vulgar though I daresay Mrs Fort would have considered a stressed peanut pretty common. What she would have made of a painty, or a fishy, or a cardboard peanut, is anybody's guess. As for the fruity fermented peanut . . . well, a number of my closest friends could be described as fruity fermented.

But I am here to tell you about the normal peanut, a fresh-faced yuppy peanut, with spring in his step. The normal peanut has 'on' flavours, it smells roasted peanutty, raw beany, dark roast, sweet aromatic, and it tastes sweet, salty, sour and bitter; it has a woody hull and skin. This normal peanut is the US Control Peanut.

As in wine tasting, peanut samples are rolled over the palate, swilled around the mouth, and inhaled. Now how you can do that with a

gunge beats me; this is the way to lose a filling or displace a denture. As it is, the thick, viscous purée gets lodged into dental crevices like Polyfilla which, to my untutored palate, somewhat blurs the difference between green burnt nutty and sour sweet roasty.

Even what the average consumer calls yum and yuck could be confused when the teeth are coated with a clammy, tacky, gooey, colloidal emulsion that could taste leathery, putrid, mawkish, acerbic, coarse and corked.

All peanuts that do not meet the complex demands of US Control are inferior peanuts. They may even be off-flavour peanuts: chemical, phenolic, plastic flavours with a metallic-feeling factor. This peanut is our old friend, the stressed peanut.

Alas, unlike Ms Vance Civille who must have a distinguished palate and throat, I am not sure I feel aromatic volatiles at the back of the throat being transmitted to the olfactory nerve in the nasal cavity. These could be fruity, dairy, herbal, spicy, vegetative, animal, nutty, roasted, raw, burnt and chemical. And each of these categories can be split into many others.

'But how does a stressed peanut become stressed?' I asked, having an instinctive feeling for the underdog. With immense seriousness, Ms Vance Civille informed me that the plant physiology could be damaged by seasonal malevolence, by gross handling, by insensitive processing and inadequate storage.

Exactly. The environmental influences were not up to standard, so this is a deprived and maladjusted peanut we have here. Sadly, there was none to taste, but there were little jars of peanut butter. I noticed Peter Fort was unable to sample his.

PICKLING
FLAVOURED VINEGARS

 Flavoured vinegars are a boon to the pickle maker. Cucumbers or gherkins pickled in tarragon wine vinegar go down a treat, and even a mixture of vinegars can often work wonders with the blander type of vegetable. Red cabbage with a couple of tablespoons of raspberry vinegar mixed in with the cider is excellent. Alternatively you could use a garlic or shallot vinegar.

It is, of course, always cheaper to flavour these vinegars yourself. Branches of rosemary, marjoram, tarragon or mint can be placed inside the bottle and left to steep for three months. The garlic or shallots can be peeled and coarsely chopped and left for the same amount of time. Allow about six cloves of garlic or small shallots per pint of vinegar. The vinegar can then be strained and the vegetables discarded.

One of the most astringent vinegars, which if allowed to stand too long will become so strong it is likely to blow the top of your head off, is horseradish vinegar. It must be made from a fresh horseradish root. Peel and grate one root into a bowl with a couple of chopped shallots, heat the cider vinegar and pour it over the grated horseradish. When it is cool pour it into a jar, let it stand for two months and taste with caution. If you can endure it stronger, leave it for another month.

Another unusual vinegar is one made from elderflowers. Pick a large bunch when they are at the height of their flowering season in the summer, take the flowers from the stalks and half fill a pint bottle, pour the cider vinegar over them and leave for a month. Strain the vinegar through a sieve and rebottle. It is deliciously perfumed, but if left too long can smell like aftershave lotion.

In the Mediterranean I used to pickle my own capers. The bushes are low and hardy, grow out of minuscule cracks in the rock and their flowers are like birds of paradise. The capers are the closed flower buds and they can be picked when quite fat. They are pickled in salt and vinegar and can be used almost at once. These large fat capers are sold loose from a barrel and can be bought all over the southern parts of the Mediterranean to be eaten as a pickle with meat and fish.

It was the French who began making them into a sauce, perhaps most famously with black butter in the cooking of skate, when some of the vinegar is used in the sauce. The tender sweetness of the fish needs the complement of the hot, peppery caper, but a tablespoonful of the horse-radish vinegar added to the beurre noir is sensational.

Be adventurous in the use of flavoured vinegars. Don't just use them on the fish and chips, though the horseradish vinegar is excellent for cutting through the cloying flavour of fatty fish, and will certainly put plenty of zing into oven chips. Use them to add to sauces and soups. A tablespoon added at the end of a sauce being boiled can give an astonishing resonance, hard to track down but similar to the use of orange or lemon zest which is another ingredient lacking in so many recipes.

HOME-MADE PICKLES

Odd how the thought of pickles makes us certain that we are going to have our taste buds both stimulated and satisfied. Yet commercial pickles are pathetic scraps of tortured vegetable drowned in malt vinegar and dyed in E numbers. Home-made pickles are another matter, tasty, zesty and covering an infinite range of ingredients.

The *OED* defines pickle as 'to preserve', its origin unknown, the word dating from 1440. Tom Stobart notes the medieval spelling variations, Pykyl, Pikkyll or Pykulle. Preserving food in brine or vinegar goes back a great deal further: the first mention we find is Herodotus on the Egyptians, who pickled small birds in brine, while drying and salting fish for export.

The birds were eaten after a few days so they would have been cold-cooked as in the various ways we find today of preparing seviche. The Romans imported their pickles from Spain and if they had known the Chinese were superlative at it, they would have imported the large range of pickled vegetables, meats and fish which the Chinese are still adept at.

Pickling was for centuries part of the autumnal husbandry, preserving for the winter, using the harvest glut in bottling or layering in casks, so the vegetables most likely to be pickled would be the most abundant, the staple food of the area. In northern Europe that meant cabbage and onions, but anyone travelling abroad now will taste pickles which sometimes appear unexpected for that country, yet turn out to be traditional.

Pickled garlic is bottled from Korea to Cambridge, turnip from Lebanon to Sweden, while the small ridged cucumbers we call gherkins seem to be pickled in all countries I've ever visited.

There is no vegetable that cannot be pickled for three hours, or three years for that matter. The Japanese do a day pickle, not unlike the quick pickle below, though they add monosodium glutamate to the brine, and weigh the vegetables down.

Many vegetables can be layered in salt and they will make their own juice. The Indian lime pickle from Mysore does this and is amazingly delicious.

Golden rules to remember are: sterilise the jars and screw tops; and, because air is the enemy of preservation – it will cause discoloration and encourage moulds – fill the bottles to the brim, get rid of bubbles and if the pickles float to the top, weigh them down. Pickle in a 10 per cent brine, that is 100 g of salt in 1 litre of water, or 4 oz of salt to 1 quart of water, or in acetic acid or oil.

I refuse to use malt vinegar, as I find the flavour abrasive. I prefer cider or wine vinegar, but lately I have been pickling in a brine which includes sugar. This gives a solution which many of the Chinese and Far Eastern pickles are preserved in. Interestingly enough, the sweetness has given birth to various vinegar 'mothers' so I now have home-made wine vinegar on the go throughout the year.

Pickles can be flavoured with all manner of herbs and spices; they can also be cut and prepared in interesting shapes. There is a Lebanese pickle which slices small turnips like a book and we are familiar with commercial piccalilli and its shapes.

Vegetables can also be pickled in oil, but they should be blanched and dried for a day before being immersed. Mustard oil is used in Asian countries, while the more familiar olive oil is used to pickle sweet peppers or pimentos, for example, in the Mediterranean countries.

Keep pickles away from the light and in a cool place. The rhubarb pickle below is particularly spectacular, because it is cold-cooked by the acetic acid and it is ready in a month.

RHUBARB PICKLE

    1 PINT/560 ML CIDER VINEGAR
    2 TABLESPOONS SEA SALT
    2 TABLESPOONS CASTOR SUGAR
    1 OZ/25 G CLOVES
    1 OZ/25 G GINGER, THINLY SLICED
    1 DRIED CHILLI, BROKEN UP
    2½ LB/1100 G RHUBARB, TRIMMED

METHOD

Heat the vinegar with the salt and sugar until both are absorbed, then add the cloves, ginger and chilli. Boil for 1–2 minutes. Pack the sliced rhubarb into a jar, pour over the spiced cider and when cool screw on lid tight. The rhubarb will keep its shape and never get soggy.

QUICK PICKLE

    1 CUCUMBER
    1 HEAD OF CELERY
    8 OZ/225 G TINY ONIONS
    2–3 COOKING APPLES
    2 TABLESPOONS SEA SALT
    1 TEASPOON CHILLI POWDER
    4 TABLESPOONS SOY SAUCE
    2 TABLESPOONS DRY SHERRY
    SOME WINE VINEGAR

METHOD

Slice the vegetables and apple and mix them in a bowl with the salt and chilli powder. Pack them in a 2 lb/900 g jar, pour over the soy sauce and sherry, then top up with the vinegar. Leave for 24 hours.

In Far Eastern countries you can buy jars with weights; in some Eastern stores they have a plastic equivalent where the vegetables are pressed down with a screw. This helps the solution to penetrate the vegetable. The pickling solution can be re-used, but bring to the boil before adding new vegetables and add more sherry.

Spiced Quinces

3 LB/1.5 KG QUINCES
6 OZ/175 G BROWN SUGAR
1 PINT/560 ML CIDER VINEGAR
JUICE AND RIND OF 2 LEMONS
2 OZ/50 G ROOT GINGER
2 CINNAMON STICKS
2 VANILLA PODS
1 TEASPOON CLOVES
1 TEASPOON SEA SALT

Method

Slice the quinces in half and core them. Melt the sugar in the vinegar and add the rest of the ingredients. Add the quinces and simmer for 10 minutes. Cool and bottle. This pickle would work also with damsons or plums, but simmer them for only 3 minutes.

Lime Pickle

12 LIMES, SLICED
2 OR 3 DRIED RED CHILLIES, BROKEN UP
1 OZ/25 G GINGER ROOT, PEELED AND SLICED
SEA SALT

Method

Layer the limes in a jar and sprinkle each layer with the chilli, ginger and salt. Leave in the sun for a week. But as there is little sun here, I found after two months they made their own brine and tasted marvellous. Excellent with curries and spicy dishes.

NASTURTIUMS

 The nasturtium, an annual easily grown from seed in the garden or window box, is both attractive and edible. The whole plant can be eaten – its flowers and leaves in salads, and its seeds, when pickled, as a traditional alternative to capers.

It is a native of Mexico and South America and is not mentioned in the early herbals or in the later pseudo-scientific pharmacopoeia of Nicholas Culpeper (1649). But John Gerard, the Elizabethan physician who looked after Lord Burghley's gardens, refers to it in his earlier herbal (1597) as Indian Cress.

Gerard writes that the seeds came from the West Indies into Spain and thence to France and Flanders. Some people believe, he says, that the plant must be related to convolvulus or bindweed because of the tangled way it grows, yet Gerard is sure it must be a cress because of its smell and flavour.

It is because of this strongly individual aspect, its sharp peppery taste, that it now shares its name with the genus nasturtium, which comes from the fusion of two Latin words, *nasus* and *tortus*, meaning a sharp smell which wrinkles the nose up. However, it has nothing to do with watercress (*Nasturtium officinale*) or with horseradish (*Nasturtium armoracia*) but belongs instead with a subsection of the large geranium family.

The Elizabethans loved their exciting new plant. The gardeners enjoyed its lurid flowers and added them to the flowers they were already eating – violets, primroses, borage, cowslips, elder and broom. They also ate the nasturtium leaves, while the unopened buds and the young seeds were pickled.

Both Gerard and, a little later, John Evelyn carry on the more ancient concept of plant humours; thus Gerard talks of Indian Cress as tempering the coldness of lettuce and purslane. Fifty years later Evelyn calls it moderately hot and aromatic, saying that it will purge the brain and quicken the torpid spirit. Most of all he stresses that the flowers are an effective agent for expunging that cruel enemy, scurvy.

Nasturtium pickling is mentioned by Hannah Glasse and Eliza Acton. Both are rather perfunctory in their method, throwing the seeds into brine or vinegar with whatever spices you care to add. Neither mentions eating the leaves or flowers as a salad.

A cookery book of the 1890s redresses the balance slightly by giving a recipe for a sauce made from the flowers:

> Put the full-blown flowers into a quart bottle with a minced shallot or two and fill up the bottle with cold scalded vinegar. Let it stand for two months, then rub it all through a sieve, bottle off, seasoning with cayenne and salt to taste. (*Pickles and Preserves*, Queen Cookery Books)

It is possibly this recipe, or one like it, which inspired Ambrose Heath in *Good Jams, Preserves and Pickles* (1947). In his recipe nasturtium flowers are pressed down into a quart bottle. To a quart of vinegar he adds eight well-bruised shallots, six cloves, a teaspoon of salt and half a teaspoon of cayenne, which is all boiled for ten minutes then poured over the flowers and left for a month. Heath strains this liquid, then bottles it, adding only a little soy sauce.

More recent recipes than the eighteenth-century ones use rather more ingredients for pickling the seeds. This is Dorothy Hartley's method from *Food in England*:

> Gather and put them in cold water and salt for three days; then make a pickle of some white wine vinegar, shallot, horseradish, pepper, salt, cloves, mace and nutmeg quartered; put in your seeds and stop them close; they are cooked as capers.

Ambrose Heath also brines the seeds for three days, then packs them into jars with layers of tarragon leaves and grated horseradish. He then boils his white vinegar with shallots, salt, peppercorns, mace and nutmeg and strains it over the seeds.

A salad of lettuce or other leaves with a dozen or so variegated nasturtium flowers looks spectacular and tastes marvellous.

You can now buy both flowers and leaves in the salad sections of some chain stores.

PILAF

 Pilaf, a high adaptable dish from the Middle East, is basically any dish of grains with added spices, herbs and vegetables, and any mixture of grains and pulses. It is a very useful summer salad dish; it never fails to please luncheon guests. You can make it from a mixture of tabbouleh (bulgar wheat or cracked wheat) with lentils or mung beans, fresh green peas and masses of chopped parsley, chives and mint. The cold salads should be dressed with oil and lemon or lime. This pilaf is made from buckwheat, which is not a cereal at all but belongs to the same family as sorrel and rhubarb. Buckwheat's other name is Saracen grass because the Crusaders brought it back into Europe. Buckwheat must be cooked before it is used.

SUMMER PILAF
(SERVES FOUR)

8 OZ/225 G NEW TURNIPS
8 OZ/225 G FRENCH BEANS
4 OZ/120 G MANGE-TOUTS
3 CLOVES GARLIC, CRUSHED
2 TABLESPOONS OLIVE OIL
6 OZ/170 G BUCKWHEAT
SEA SALT AND FRESHLY GROUND BLACK PEPPER
GENEROUS HANDFUL OF PARSLEY, CHERVIL OR CHIVES, FINELY CHOPPED

METHOD

Trim the vegetables, quarter the turnips, halve the beans, leave the mange-touts whole. Simmer the turnips in boiling water for 5 minutes, the French beans for 3 and the mange-touts for only 1 minute. Heat the olive oil and stir in the crushed garlic, simmer for a moment to flavour the oil, drain the vegetables thoroughly and toss them into the oil. Place the buckwheat in a pan, cover with cold water to come 1 inch/2.5 cm above the buckwheat. Bring to the boil and simmer for 10 minutes, when the buckwheat should have absorbed all the water. Throw in the vegetables and mix thoroughly, season and add the fresh herbs. Serve warm.

MILLET PILAF

Pulses and grains contain complementary protein; amino acids that one lacks are supplied by the other, creating a whole equal to meat or soya.

4 OZ/120 G BORLOTTI BEANS, SOAKED OVERNIGHT
2 OZ/50 G LARGE BROWN LENTILS
6 OZ/170 G MILLET
4 TABLESPOONS OLIVE OIL
1 TEASPOON EACH CUMIN AND CORIANDER, CRUSHED
1 TEASPOON ASAFOETIDA, GROUND
2 ONIONS, FINELY CHOPPED
5 CLOVES GARLIC, SLICED
4 OZ/120 G MUSHROOMS, SLICED
2 RED PEPPERS, DESEEDED AND CHOPPED
1 TABLESPOON SOY SAUCE
SEA SALT AND FRESHLY GROUND BLACK PEPPER
1 LARGE BUNCH PARSLEY, MINT AND CHIVES, FINELY CHOPPED
JUICE FROM 1 LEMON

METHOD

Cook the beans, lentils and millet separately. The beans should be plunged in boiling water and cooked for 45 minutes, or until just tender. The millet and the lentils need 10 minutes boiling – no longer. Drain and combine all three – keep warm. Heat the olive oil in a pan, add the spices and then all the vegetables, stir and gently sauté for about 10 minutes. Add the soy and seasoning. Combine cooked vegetables with the pulses and grains. Stir in herbs and lemon juice just before serving.

PORTUGAL
THE MARKET

 At the Quarteira market, some twenty miles from Faro in the Algarve, the tourists buy food for their self-catering holidays. A stall selling sheepskin slippers and plastic flowers mixed in with sweet potato seedlings stands next to a table spread with purslane and vine cuttings; beneath it a sack of snails, antennae erect, doing the fast crawl to freedom. As well as lettuces, tomatoes, cucumbers and fennel, there are melons, almonds, chick peas and olives, pumpkins and slabs of withered salt cod. Proud black-robed Romanies sweep past balancing a cage of chattering ducklings upon their heads.

It is a scene from Goya – not much changes in the Iberian peninsula. Only the puce-fleshed British in their M & S shorts stand out, looking like boiled prawns jutting from a vegetable stew.

The fish markets are always alive with slimy movement; bizarre, unlovely creatures from the deep sluggishly expire while vendors prod and slap. Squeezing past waving spider crabs, the British squeal and pout with distaste. Octopus and squid, hake, bass, bream and grouper lie amid mounds of mussels and clams. There are baby monkfish, no bigger than a dab, and anchovies the size of mackerel. Like prawns, these fish are omnivorous and a shoal, locust-like, cuts a swath through the ocean.

But the British rarely buy – they prefer a chicken or pork loin from the meat market.

The clams are poached in white wine, garlic and chillies, chopped coriander being added at the last minute. Local sausages are cooked at the table in a pool of grappa that is set alight, laid across a terracotta rack.

P O T A T O E S

When I was a child, new potatoes boiled with a sprig of mint made the spuds taste delicately of the herb, but nowadays, although new recipes still advise you to boil potatoes with a few mint leaves or a sprig or two, and people still obey, I never seem to taste a minty spud. Dedicated for some years to regaining those pleasures of boyhood, I once made a kind of mint stew, boiling up several plants in a saucepan of water, throwing out the bedraggled vegetation and then adding the potatoes. The water was sludge green, but it did not make the slightest difference to the flavour of the potatoes.

There is a charming little book, *A Multitude of Mints*, published by the Herb Society and compiled by Guy Cooper and Gordon Taylor with a preface by Elizabeth David, which gives recipes for mint sorbets, mint juleps, mint teas and other delights, but it does not shed any light on how we can infuse a new potato with the taste of mint.

I suspect that strains of potato resistant to fungus are also resistant to the taste of mint. It may be that the new potato we all used to eat is not grown any more and that what is now grown refuses to absorb the mint flavour in the boiling water. That said, there are ways of having your new potatoes mint-flavoured. The obvious one is to serve the potatoes with mint butter, but always attempt to find ways of cutting down on butter. You can also toss the hot potatoes in a tablespoon of olive oil and about three tablespoons of finely chopped mint; or make a sauce of chopped mint and yoghurt. Or you can bake the potatoes in a roasting bag with a tablespoon of olive oil and chopped mint. Shake the bag well so that the potatoes are covered in the oil. Bake in a hot oven for thirty minutes. If the potatoes are large they can be baked in their skins, and when cooked, split and the insides mixed with chopped mint, yoghurt or curd cheese, then put back into the oven or placed under a hot grill to brown. But I must confess I am not overkeen on the flavour of yoghurt and potato; I mention them here because I know these sauces have their following.

Try to use mint freshly picked. The herb slowly looses its pungency the longer it is out of the ground. Chop it finely just before using it, for it is the oil in the leaves which has the flavour and aroma. For full strength the herb should be picked just before it flowers, generally in July, but I pick mint from the minute the first few leaves appear in the spring. Spearmint, *Mentha viridis*, is our common garden mint and is the one mostly used in cooking. But I prefer *Mentha rotundifolia*, called applemint, which is a tall vigorous plant. It makes the best mint sauces, for the leaves are rather thick and velvety. I have seven other mints growing in the garden, most of them too pungent for cooking, but wonderful to chew to cleanse the breath, or for making tea.

Be generous with the amount of mint you use in cooking. Cookery books always refer to a handful of chopped mint, but in the recipes below I have recommended 2 oz/50 g: that is roughly three handfuls.

One of the best salads is a potato salad with a mint-flavoured mayonnaise, but the following sauce is not so rich. It can be used for other salads, and is an excellent sauce with plain boiled new potatoes.

MINT SALAD SAUCE

2 OZ/50 G FRESH MINT, CHOPPED
JUICE FROM 1 LEMON
2 TABLESPOONS WINE OR CIDER VINEGAR
5 TABLESPOONS OLIVE OIL
10 TABLESPOONS SUNFLOWER OIL
2 OZ/150 G PARMESAN CHEESE, FRESHLY GRATED

METHOD

Mix all the ingredients thoroughly by hand or in the liquidiser. Leave for 24 hours before using. This amount makes just over ½ pint/175 ml, and the sauce will keep in a closed jar in a refrigerator.

POTATO MINT CROQUETTES

1 LB/450 G POTATOES
2 OZ/50 G FRESH MINT, CHOPPED
4 OZ/100 G CURD OR RICOTTA CHEESE
PINCH OF SEA SALT
1 EGG
SUNFLOWER OIL FOR FRYING

METHOD

Boil the potatoes, and skin them. Put them through a food mill and while still warm add the mint, the cheese and the salt. When cool fold in the beaten egg. Chill in the refrigerator for a few hours or overnight to make it easier to handle. Roll pieces of the mixture the size of a golf ball first in flour, then in beaten egg and finally in breadcrumbs. Fry in sunflower oil until brown and crisp on the outside.

POTATOES BAKED IN MINT STOCK

4 LARGE POTATOES
2 OZ/50 G FRESH MINT, CHOPPED
PINCH OF SEA SALT
¾ PINT/400 ML WATER
I GLASS OF DRY WHITE WINE
2 EGG YOLKS

METHOD

Scrub the skins of the potatoes, slice them into quarters, and prick the skins. Take a large casserole dish, put the chopped mint and salt into it, and pour on the boiling water. Fit the potatoes in, pour the wine over, put the lid on and bake in a preheated oven at 375F/190C/gas mark 5 for 1 hour. Then take the dish from the oven and drain the sauce off into a mixing bowl that has the two egg yolks in it. Stir together so that the sauce thickens. Place potatoes in a serving dish. Pour the sauce over and sprinkle with a little more chopped mint.

GRATIN JURASSIEN

2 LB/I KG POTATOES
2 OZ/50 G BUTTER
SEA SALT AND FRESHLY GROUND BLACK PEPPER
½ LB/225 G GRATED GRUYÈRE CHEESE
I PINT/600 ML SINGLE CREAM

METHOD

Peel and slice the potatoes thinly, either on a mandoline or in a food processor or just with a sharp knife. They should be the size and thickness of a 10 pence piece. Dump them in cold water and leave them for ½ hour. Drain and rinse with cold water, which gets rid of a lot of the starch, then pat them dry between two clean towels.

Butter a shallow, fireproof dish. Place a layer of potatoes on the dish, dot them with butter and seasoning, then sprinkle over some of the grated Gruyère cheese. Continue to do this with several layers of potatoes, dotting with the butter, the grated cheese and salt and pepper. Pour the cream over the top and place the dish in a preheated oven at 300F/150C/gas mark 2 for 2½ hours. Test after 2 hours by putting a knife in the centre – if it slips in then the potatoes are done. Gratins need slow cooking at a low heat.

SALADE ANGEVINE

3 TABLESPOONS WALNUT OIL
2 TEASPOONS LEMON JUICE
SEA SALT AND FRESHLY GROUND BLACK PEPPER
I LB/450 G COOKED FLAGEOLET BEANS
I LB/450 G COOKED FRENCH BEANS
I LB/450 G NEW POTATOES, STEAMED OR BOILED

METHOD

Mix the walnut oil, lemon juice, salt and pepper together in a large salad bowl. Drain the flageolets well and add them to the bowl, stir so that they are covered in the oil and lemon juice. Cut the French beans into 1 inch/ 2–3 cm lengths and add those to the flageolets. Cut the potatoes up to fairly small dice and finally add these. Give the whole salad a good stir before serving.

MOROCCAN POTATO CASSEROLE

2 LB/900 G POTATOES
6 FL OZ/170 ML VEGETABLE OIL
3 GREEN PEPPERS, DESEEDED AND SLICED
10 CLOVES OF GARLIC, CHOPPED
2 TEASPOONS GROUND CUMIN
2 TEASPOONS GROUND CORIANDER
1½ PINTS/850 ML WATER
ZEST AND JUICE FROM ONE LEMON
SEA SALT AND FRESHLY GROUND BLACK PEPPER

METHOD

Peel and quarter the potatoes. Heat the oil in a heavy saucepan and add the sliced peppers, garlic, cumin and coriander. Fry for a moment to flavour the oil, then take away from the heat and add the water, the zest and juice from the lemon, the potatoes and seasoning. Bring back to the heat and simmer until the potatoes are tender. Drain before serving.

SOLYANKA
(SERVES SIX)

4 MEDIUM POTATOES (PEELED)
8 OZ/225 G COTTAGE CHEESE
5 FL OZ/150 ML SOUR CREAM
5 FL OZ/150 ML YOGHURT
1 SMALL WHITE OR SAVOY CABBAGE (SLICED)
2 LARGE ONIONS, CHOPPED
2 OZ/50 G BUTTER
1½ TEASPOONS SEA SALT
½ TEASPOON GROUND CARAWAY SEED
½ TEASPOON DILL WEED
GENEROUS AMOUNT OF FRESHLY GROUND BLACK PEPPER
1 TEASPOON PAPRIKA
2 TABLESPOONS SUNFLOWER SEED

METHOD

Chop the potatoes and boil them. Drain well, then mash and add the cottage cheese, sour cream and yoghurt. Meanwhile, sauté the cabbage and onion in butter, add salt, caraway seeds and dill weed. Sauté for 5 minutes, then combine with the potato mixture and add everything else except sunflower seeds and paprika. Taste and check seasoning.

Butter an oven dish and spread the mixture into it. Sprinkle the top with paprika and sunflower seeds. Bake in a preheated oven at 375F/190C/ gas mark 5 for 25 minutes.

GOURMET POTATO SALAD
(SERVES SIX)

A salad made with new waxy potatoes is one of the great summer dishes. Make this dish with a variety like Pink Fir Apple, Kipfler, Aura, Ratte or Maris Peer. This is my luxurious version.

> I TABLESPOON RED WINE VINEGAR
> I TABLESPOON TOASTED SESAME OIL
> 2 TABLESPOONS OLIVE OIL
> 2 CLOVES GARLIC, CRUSHED
> SEA SALT AND FRESHLY GROUND BLACK PEPPER
> 2 RED ONIONS, SLICED THINLY
> 2½ LB/1100 G NEW SMALL POTATOES
> 6 SPRING ONIONS WITH THE GREEN TOPS, SLICED
> GENEROUS HANDFUL OF PARSLEY, CHOPPED FINELY
> 3 TABLESPOONS HOME-MADE MAYONNAISE, SOUR CREAM OR GREEK
>   YOGHURT

METHOD

Have ready the wine vinegar, oils, garlic and seasoning made up into a dressing in a large bowl. Stir in the sliced red onion rings and leave them to marinade while the potatoes are cooking.

Boil the potatoes in their skins until just tender. Slice the potatoes while warm and add them to the vinaigrette and onions. Mix thoroughly and let the warm spuds soak up the flavour. When cool, add the spring onions, parsley and mayonnaise or alternatives. Mix again and serve.

PRESS TRIPS
A CALIFORNIAN EXPERIENCE

On the Pan Am flight to San Francisco and back they played the first two acts of *Rigoletto* and the last two of *Carmen*, though the whole of both operas was advertised.

When I asked why, the answer came, full of casual and somehow sublime indifference. 'I guess somebody just goofed.' It set the tone for the whole trip.

I was among a party of food writers who were to tour the Californian raisin industry. A telex had been sent to our hosts informing them I ate no meat. Pan Am gave me boiled vegetables standing in half an inch of hot water, one of the most disgusting meals I have ever been offered. Quite unexpectedly, finding even palatable food was a major problem on this trip.

Raisins come from the Thompson seedless grape and these are grown in the San Joaquin Valley, just 50 miles wide but 240 miles long. Fresno, the centre of the valley, is an hour's flight from San Francisco. The valley is a flat expanse of baked earth between two mountain ranges which in August and September can reach 100F/38C and over. A perfect climate for drying out bunches of grapes, which are placed on brown sheets of paper beneath the vines and in three weeks become raisins. Not so perfect for a bunch of dehydrated British food writers moving within an ever-changing itinerary, where a fresh glass of lemonade or natural grape juice is unheard of. One name on the itinerary remained a constant mystery – Fudrucker's. Who or what was Fudrucker's? All would be explained, said the PR, on the night.

On TV in Fresno I am promised impulse body sprays, 200 feet of plastic wrap, crispy fried burritos and sizzlean strips of sweet regular premium beef. I am promised high calcium recipes for the prime of life and gourmet chicken. Ah yes, they sell a battery unit chicken wing with the same slick expertise they give to a car. There is Hawaiian style (with pineapple chunks), Danish style (with dried dill), Californian style (with orange juice), Greek style (with mozzarella), Irish style (with potatoes), Creole style (with green pepper), oriental style (with soy sauce).

On the day we fly to Fresno we spend a fascinating two hours with

Tom Payne who is in charge of research and development of the raisin. Each year they have a surplus, some of the raisins go to the Third World, the rest into animal feed.

Tom Payne was turning the raisins into raisin juice and adding them to various products; being high in fructose they were a natural sweetener and much of the juice went into wholemeal bread which made the loaves rise quicker and taste good. There was also a wholemeal and raisin pasta, which sounds awful but which was one of the best tagliatelles I have ever tasted. There was a range of other health products which contained raisin purées or juice, all of which were to be sent to me immediately. They have not yet arrived. I guess somebody just goofed.

The Thompson seedless grape was brought to California by a Yorkshireman, William Thompson, in 1872. In four years he had a modest harvest of 500 bunches. By the 1850s the Thompson seedless was beginning to overrun the whole of the San Joaquin Valley. It now accounts for ninety per cent of the raisin production. Four pounds of grapes gives one pound of raisins. In August the grapes are picked by hand. The labour comes from the south across the border, for each plantation suddenly needs thousands of workers for the next six weeks. A recent film, El Norte, movingly tells the story of a brother and a sister who travel to the promised land that we were now in. The squalor of their tragedy made a further irony out of the yearly raisin glut. In the industry of food there is no logic and little humanity. Which brings me back to Fudrucker's.

We arrived at 7.30 in the evening at the door of Fudrucker's, which turned out to be a butcher's. The windows showed serried ranks of beef carcasses dripping blood upon the floor. But no, this was not a butcher's, but a restaurant. It was a hamburger joint and our PR explained that they thought we should experience how the average American ate. I felt I knew how the average American ate and declined. My dutiful group of foodies tucked into hamburgers and chips while I fumed and eventually burst into a diatribe on the link between junk food and disease. My group considered this was an ungentlemanly outburst and though the PR admitted that they had a telex saying I did not eat meat, the connection between the telex and the meal at Fudrucker's was never made. I guess somebody just goofed.

In Fresno we had several lectures on healthy foods, until, in our gentle British way, we pointed out that we did not make mistakes like serving pasta pudding swimming in demerara sugar and covered in desiccated coconut. I had expected the intelligence, experience and wit of New York to be elsewhere in the States. What we found was not only an enthusiasm for a huge range of appalling junk foods, but an insularity and smugness about the subject. The hamburger in its plastic bun was all part of the American Dream and way of life, and you must be a commie to criticise it.

The raisin, one of the most natural foods around, for it is sultanas that are dipped in sulphur to preserve them, sits uneasily in the centre of this experience. Raisins are seventy per cent fructose but also rich in minerals and B vitamins; they could be a good source of energy in a meatless diet. If you add raisins to other foods you tend to get something resembling a cake or a fruit loaf. But mashing them by a food processor into a purée or a juice before adding them is another technique. The raisin flavour is absorbed by the yeast dough in the bread and it permeates in a pleasant and subliminal way. I wanted to try the purée mixed with vegetables and cereals in pies, tarts and rissoles, mixing it with tomatoes, aubergines and carrots, flavouring it with garlic, onion, herbs and spices. A supply of raisins was promised for these experiments, but they have never turned up. I guess somebody just goofed.

PROVENCE

Provence has many foods, regional dishes and ways of cooking. There is, of course, the extensive use of garlic; that coupled with the rich thickness of the olive oil makes for a heady mayonnaise and various sauces. There is tapenade, a purée of black olives, capers, anchovies or tuna fish, Dijon mustard and olive oil. Pistou, which is similar to Italian pesto, but omits the pine nuts, has given its name to a soup almost as popular as the gazpacho of Spain and, in my opinion, is far superior.

Provence has also given its name to a mixture of herbs, which, when growing in the real Provence of the mountains of the Var, exude a powerful aroma so that a mountain walk smells like the corridors of Culpeper. The herbs are mostly thyme, rosemary and oregano. We associate them with the cooking of meat, probably barbecued lamb, but in Provence they have been used successfully with fish.

The Provençal cuisine is not subtle or delicate; the flavours are strong and have an impact on the palate which can be as surprisingly abrasive as a fiery curry. Tapenade is not liked by some, yet spread on bread or croûtes (pieces of French bread dipped in oil and made crisp in an oven) it harmonises perfectly in a land full of harsh extremes, where the mistral blows, Van Gogh goes mad and either the sun burns blazingly or it pelts with unceasing, thunderous rain.

Perhaps Provence is known most of all for its bouillabaisse, its fish stew flavoured with onion, fennel, saffron and Pernod. It has in it a huge variety of Mediterranean fish – John Dory, red mullet, whiting, bass, perch, mackerel, eel and monkfish. It is served in two bowls, the soup in one, the fish in another, and is eaten with croûtes and a sauce rouille. I confess it is the sauce I like best of all. It is basically a mayonnaise made hot with ground red chilli peppers – some people use cayenne. Others also add a spoonful of tomato purée; this helps the colour but can ruin the flavour.

But there are other great dishes that should be known and enjoyed. In vain, I searched for aigo boulido, a garlic and sage soup; socca, which is a chick pea flour crêpe (the crêpe I ate was Breton and made from buckwheat flour); an omelette made from Swiss chard called troucha; bagna caouda, an anchovy and butter sauce for the crudités; fougasse, a salty flat bread made from olive oil. Nor did I find one of the great dishes of the world, the brandade, a purée of salt cod which should be soufflé-like in texture, achieved by beating hot olive oil and milk into the poached fish. It is flavoured, of course, with garlic.

But good Provençal cooking is unobtainable on the millionaire coastal strip of the Côte d'Azur. What an irony that the rich who can so easily pay for the best without noticing it are unable to enjoy it because they are too ignorant to know what it is. Instead, what they are given at mad prices is that token International Français foie gras, followed by underdone duck breasts in a pool of blackcurrant sauce.

Beneath the excesses of the jet set, the Côte d'Azur has become tawdry and vulgar, geared to affluent tourism with the French fries coming out of a commercial packet. The only memorable meals I had were in the mountains where local produce was cooked imaginatively.

Steamed artichokes picked when very young, asparagus and courgettes with their flowers were served in a beurre blanc sauce.

Take 4 or 5 shallots, chop them finely, place in a saucepan with 3 tablespoons of white wine vinegar and 3 of dry white wine, heat and simmer until the shallots are soft and the liquid has reduced to very little, then start adding 6 oz/175 g of butter an ounce at a time and whisk over a low heat until the butter is soft but not melted. It should look like thick cream. At first the sauce just tends to turn into melted butter – that's because the flame is too high. If it does, you can cheat by adding a spoonful of thick cream.

Soupe au Pistou

4 OZ/125 G DRIED HARICOT BEANS, SOAKED AND DRAINED
3½ PINTS/2 LITRES WATER
3 MEDIUM CARROTS, DICED
3 MEDIUM POTATOES, DICED
3 MEDIUM COURGETTES, CHOPPED
2 LEEKS, CHOPPED
1 LB/500 G TOMATOES, PEELED
4 OZ/125 G GREEN FRENCH BEANS, CHOPPED
4 OZ/125 G SHELLED GREEN PEAS
BOUQUET GARNI
2½ OZ/75 G SMALL NOODLES
SEA SALT AND FRESHLY GROUND BLACK PEPPER

METHOD

Boil the beans in the water for 1 hour, add the vegetables and the bouquet garni and simmer for another 45 minutes. You may need a little more water. Add the noodles and cook for a further 10 minutes. Taste and season; discard the bouquet garni. Take the soup from the heat and put it in a serving dish. Now add the pistou sauce, stirring it into the soup. Serve and have a bowl of freshly grated Parmesan on the table to sprinkle over the soup.

Pistou Sauce

3 FL OZ/80 ML OLIVE OIL
20 BASIL LEAVES
3 CLOVES GARLIC, CRUSHED
SEA SALT AND FRESHLY GROUND BLACK PEPPER
4 OZ/125 G PARMESAN CHEESE, FRESHLY GRATED

METHOD

In a blender pour the oil over the basil and garlic. Whizz, shredding the leaves into a thin green purée; add the seasoning and cheese, so that it is a thick sauce. Splendid with pasta.

Pipérade

Pipérade is one of the very first dishes I ever learnt to cook; it needs slow cooking so its heady aroma of oil, garlic and peppers permeates the house. It is usually made from green peppers, and is a very simple light supper or starter to a meal. It can be eaten warm or cold. There are such good red, orange and yellow peppers around that classic recipes like this one can take on a new look.

Red Pipérade
(Serves four to six)

3 TABLESPOONS GOOD OLIVE OIL

4 OR 5 RED AND ORANGE PEPPERS, DESEEDED AND CHOPPED

6 CLOVES GARLIC, SLICED

2 ONIONS, SLICED

I LB/450 G TOMATOES, PEELED

SEA SALT AND FRESHLY GROUND BLACK PEPPER

4 EGGS, BEATEN

Method

Heat the olive oil in a shallow pan and sauté the peppers, garlic and onions gently for about 20 minutes, stirring occasionally. Chop the peeled tomatoes and add them, continuing to cook for another 10 minutes, or until the mixture has become a rough purée. Season. Then pour in the eggs and scramble the mixture until the eggs are cooked.

PUMPKINS

Pumpkins are worth more than disembowelling and making Halloween masks out of. In fact, they make one of the very best soups that exists – golden, creamy and, in this recipe, with an added flavour of ginger.

GINGER PUMPKIN SOUP

3 TABLESPOONS OLIVE OIL
I OZ/25 G BUTTER
I OZ/25 G ROOT GINGER, PEELED AND GRATED
3 CLOVES GARLIC, CRUSHED
I LB/450 G PUMPKIN FLESH, CUBED
2½ PINTS/1.5 LITRES VEGETABLE STOCK
SEA SALT AND FRESHLY GROUND BLACK PEPPER

METHOD

Heat the oil and butter together in a large saucepan. Sauté the ginger and garlic in it for a moment, then add the cubed pumpkin.

Continue to cook for a few minutes more, so that the pumpkin soaks up the flavours, then add the stock and simmer for 15 minutes. Allow to cool, then blend to a smooth purée. Season to taste and reheat gently before serving.

Purées

Old, favourite or classic recipes have to be adjusted to new nutritional requirements. I have found over the last few years that the NACNE (National Advisory Committee on Nutrition Education) dictates on lower saturated fat are a challenge that can end, with a bit of luck, in recreating recipes into something vastly superior to the old ones.

For example, for most dishes which needed cream sauces you can substitute vegetables puréed in skimmed milk, and, I believe, make them better. Summer is a good time for experimenting, for these sauces only work when the vegetables are fresh. In other words, one of the best purées can be made from fresh peas cooked with a few green pods. A purée made from frozen peas would be a pathetic affair, though it might be worth trying with the specially developed peas in pod – tubbier than mange-touts – which Birds Eye are now marketing as 'jacket peas'.

The carbohydrate in the mature (but not old and floury) fresh pea thickens the mixture and gives it body and flavour. The colour is a most exhilarating grass-green, and, used as part of a filling for a pancake, or in the centre of a lasagne or moussaka, it gives enormous zest to the look of a dish.

Making the purée is simplicity itself. Pod 1½ lb/700 g fresh peas. Simmer them in a little water with a few of the pods which have been trimmed of their fibrous sides. When tender, drain thoroughly and add ½ pint/275 ml skimmed milk, then blend the lot. Season to taste.

A thicker purée for some dishes can be made using a ½ pint/150 ml of vegetable stock instead of the skimmed milk. Young broad beans can be used instead of the fresh peas, but the colour of the purée – a sludge green perfect for army manoeuvres – is a bit depressing.

Another summer vegetable that will oblige is tiny courgettes. But steam them, for their high water content thins a purée and makes it more suitable for soup. Mange-tout peas make a slightly sweet purée which is delicious cold as a sauce for a first course, poured around a vegetable mould or terrine. French and runner beans make rather grainy purées, but the flavour is so good the slightly rough texture is of no importance.

For the rest of the year, onions are a great standby but purées made from them tend to be too sweet, so use onions that are small and sharp in flavour. Shallots, of course, make purées which have become part of classic cooking. Brussels sprouts make a delicious purée, but cabbage tends to be too fibrous. To get a smooth purée, it would have to be overcooked and this changes the flavour into that nauseating thing we all recollect from childhood.

The other staple sauce we all used to use was the ubiquitous 'mornay' – cheese sauce high in fat and often as thick as a wet dumpling. The trick with a cheese sauce is to use a very small amount of a highly flavoured mature cheese, or use a vegetable purée with a little added Parmesan. Or make a sauce out of a hard, low-fat cheese of good flavour. I am particularly fond of the mature Gouda you can now buy which tastes a little like a good pecorino and is perfect for adding, finely grated, to pasta.

Vegetable variations of lasagne or cannelloni or moussaka – which is technically similar, for the aubergine is merely used instead of the pasta sheets – can improve on many meat versions because a mixture of vegetables, coated in various differently flavoured sauces, stimulates both the palate and the digestion. For example, the centre of a lasagne may contain slices of broccoli and courgette, still with bite in them, coated in a fresh pea sauce. Then, over the top of the pasta, pour a sauce made from shallots and the matured Gouda.

Cannelloni could have a filling of lightly cooked broad beans in a courgette sauce coated in a purée of fennel slightly flavoured with Parmesan. While moussaka, turning its back on the traditional tomato, could have in its centre a filling of sliced cabbage, walnuts and coriander and, to top it, a sauce made with a soft, low-fat cheese given bite with a flavouring of ground and whole green peppercorns.

Do not forget, either, that the blue cheeses make superb sauces and, though most are high in fat, just a little cheese will flavour the sauce beautifully.

Another product we tend to dismiss is a fruit sauce combined with a vegetable dish. Long accustomed to adding a sharp lightness for game and meat, we have thrown out the fruit with the flesh. Yet Middle and Far Eastern dishes combine fruit and vegetable intriguingly. Cauliflower, for example, can be coated with a plum or apricot sauce and makes a good side dish. A gooseberry purée contrasts nicely with diced, steamed parsnips or turnip. But if serving these as a side vegetable, be cautious in the amount of sauce you pour. Never drown a vegetable; merely place a little of the sauce at the side or around the edge.

None of these dishes could be made without the blender or liquidiser for reducing a cooked vegetable to a smooth purée in a matter of seconds. I do believe this machine, much more than the food processor, has revolutionised cooking, making possible all kinds of variations and new dishes. It is now an easy matter to make low-fat dishes of subtle quality with a pleasing combination of unexpected flavours.

R I S O T T O
Baked in the Oven Vegetable Risotto • Walnut Risotto
Real Risotto Risi e Bisi

R O Q U E F O R T
Wholemeal Pastry • Roquefort Quiche

R O U L A D E S
Roulade d'Épinards • Roulade de Poivre Vert

R U S S I A
Blinis • Bortsch

R I S O T T O
B A K E D I N T H E O V E N

In winter we need food to warm us through, so we gravitate naturally to thick soups and stews, to potato and pasta dishes, bulky food to fill us up. It's also food that might thicken the waistline – although food high in carbohydrates is not fattening, so long as large amounts of fat are not eaten with it.

The risotto is the perfect dish, made as it is with olive oil. The butter stirred in at the last moment (which is *de rigueur* in Italy) can be left out if you wish, but a couple of ounces of butter in a large dish, which will feed four to six, is not going to hurt anyone, unless you are on a strict low-fat diet.

Traditionally, the risotto is cooked on top of the stove, but after the initial cooking, I always put mine in the oven, and can then forget it for forty-five minutes.

Before serving, stir in the butter and the Parmesan. More Parmesan is added at the table. Always add to the stock a glass of either dry white wine or vermouth; or, with root vegetables and aubergines, a good glass of strong red helps the flavour no end.

The Italian risotto is not often made with red meat. Eaten as a first course, it is more likely to be made with tomatoes, mushrooms, spinach, shellfish or chicken. It is worth while experimenting with various vegetable and spice combinations, and possibly turning towards the East for more inspiration. Try grated ginger root with green peppers, for example, or a chopped green chilli with mushrooms and onions. Both combinations will give you a hot, spicy risotto reminiscent of Indonesia rather than India.

It is almost worth cooking more than you need, because leftover risotto is a delight in itself. The simplest way of reviving it is to heat olive oil and garlic in a frying pan or wok, tip in the rice mixture and stir-fry for a few minutes, until the oil is absorbed and the rice hot. You can also reheat it by steaming or by putting it back into the oven for re-baking, although that tends to dry it out.

One of the nicest ways, though, is an Italian dish called suppli.

Allow two beaten eggs to about 12 oz/350 g of leftover risotto. Mix in the eggs and take a spoonful of the mixture and place it in the palm of your hand, lay a slice of Bel Paese or mozzarella over the top, and then cover the cheese with another spoonful of risotto, so that the cheese is enclosed in a ball the size of a small orange. Roll the balls in breadcrumbs and fry them in hot oil, turning them over so that they are browned on all sides. The cheese will have melted inside. If you have a large batch to do, they can be kept warm in the oven.

VEGETABLE RISOTTO

I LARGE AUBERGINE
2 COURGETTES
2–3 TABLESPOONS GOOD OLIVE OIL
2 SLICED ONIONS
5 LARGE CLOVES OF GARLIC, CRUSHED
SEA SALT AND FRESHLY GROUND BLACK PEPPER
10 OZ/275 G RICE
I GLASS WHITE WINE OR VERMOUTH
1½ PINTS/900 ML BOILING WATER
2 OZ/50 G BUTTER
4 OZ/100 G PARMESAN CHEESE, FRESHLY GRATED

METHOD

Slice and cube the unpeeled aubergine into small pieces. Cut the courgettes into four lengthways, then cube each piece. Heat the oil in a heavy pan with a close-fitting lid (that can also go into the oven) and sauté the aubergines, courgettes, onions and garlic for 3 to 4 minutes, or until they are just about to go soft and have released some of their juices. Season generously and then add the rice and go on stirring for another moment or two, so that the rice begins to absorb the flavours.

Take the pan away from the heat and add the wine, then the boiling water. Stir vigorously to make sure nothing has stuck to the bottom. Place in a preheated oven at 350F/180C/gas mark 4 for 45 minutes.

Let it rest for ½ hour, and then reheat briefly before serving and stir in the butter and grated Parmesan cheese.

Walnut Risotto

4 OZ/100 G DRIED CHESTNUTS
I SMALL SLICED CABBAGE
I SLICED ONION
3 CLOVES GARLIC, CRUSHED
2 TABLESPOONS OLIVE OIL
10 OZ/275 G RICE
4 OZ/100 G CHOPPED WALNUTS
SALT AND PEPPER
2 OZ/50 G BUTTER
3 OZ/75 G PARMESAN CHEESE, FRESHLY GRATED

METHOD

Soak the chestnuts overnight in water. Boil them in the same water with a pinch of salt for about 1 hour, or until they are soft. Take off any of the brown skin that may be still clinging in their crevices. Allow to cool, then blend the water and the chestnuts as if you were making soup.

Sauté the cabbage, onion and garlic in the olive oil until just soft; add the rice and stir it around until it becomes translucent. Make up the chestnut stock to 1½ pints/900 ml by adding water. Add this to the rice and stir in the walnuts. Bring to the boil, taste for seasoning then place the risotto in a preheated oven at 350F/180C/gas mark 4 and bake for 40 to 45 minutes.

Let it rest away from direct heat, then add the butter and Parmesan before serving.

Real Risotto

 The above recipes do not specify the type of rice; in fact I used Patna rice, for when baked in the oven, the risotto came out well flavoured but dry, the way I preferred it. Yet, as everyone knows, this is not real risotto. Real risotto has to be made from arborio rice and the end result is creamy and slightly liquid. It has to be made on top of the stove and can be cooked for anything from ten to twenty minutes. The finest risotto I ever ate was in Venice and it is the simplest, risi e bisi. It was creamy and had the texture of velvet with the spring peas clearly singing through like the voice of a boy soprano.

Risi e Bisi

3 TABLESPOONS OLIVE OIL

I LARGE ONION, CHOPPED

2 LB/900 G FRESH PEAS, PODDED

6 OZ/170 G ARBORIO RICE

10 FL OZ/280 ML VEGETABLE STOCK

SEA SALT AND FRESHLY GROUND BLACK PEPPER

2 OZ/50 G PARMESAN CHEESE, FRESHLY GRATED

CHOPPED PARSLEY

Method

Heat the oil in a pan and throw in the onion, let it simmer until it is soft, then add the peas and the rice together, stir and simmer, to allow the rice to soak up some of the flavour, but only for a moment. Now add the vegetable stock, bring to the boil and let it simmer for 10 minutes or until the rice is done. Season then stir in the Parmesan and some chopped parsley.

R

ROQUEFORT

 Roquefort is wickedly expensive; but as the cheese is so pungently strong and delicious, you need very little if you are going to cook with it. The quiche below requires only 6 oz/175 g and as it will easily feed six that is not too harsh on the pocket.

Roquefort has been eaten since Roman times. It was the favourite cheese of Charlemagne. It is cured naturally in the caves of Combalou and has been protected by government charters since the thirteenth century.

It was, of course, the first authentic blue cheese. It is made from the milk of an especially handsome-looking sheep, and the cheese should have a moist buttery texture and taste rich and salty. Do not buy from a cheese that looks dry and where the blue veining is not even from the centre to the edge.

As the Roquefort filling is on the rich side, I decided the classic shortcrust pastry made from butter would be far too sickly. Hence the pastry case recipe below is made from wholemeal flour and sunflower oil. I usually suspect that such pastry may be too brittle and heavy, but I found this crust the perfect foil for the high-living gamy filling.

Wholemeal Pastry
(Amounts for one quiche)

8 OZ/225 G WHOLEMEAL FLOUR

I TEASPOON BAKING POWDER

3 TABLESPOONS SUNFLOWER OIL

3 TABLESPOONS COLD WATER

Method

Mix the flour and baking powder together, and then the oil and water. Stir the liquid in and mix quickly into a paste. Wrap the pastry ball in foil or cling film and refrigerate for an hour or a day. If the paste is too crumbly to roll out, smear it on to the cooking dish with the palm or fingers into the shape and size you want. Bake blind in a preheated oven at 425F/220C/gas mark 7 for 10 minutes.

Roquefort Quiche

I BUNCH OF PARSLEY

I BUNCH OF SPRING ONIONS

6 OZ/175 G ROQUEFORT CHEESE

3 OZ/85 G CURD CHEESE

3 OZ/85 G COTTAGE CHEESE

3 TABLESPOONS YOGHURT

2 EGG WHITES

I EGG

Method

Chop the parsley and onions. Mix all the ingredients together in a bowl and season with a little freshly ground pepper. Smooth the mixture over the cooked pastry case and bake in a preheated oven at 425F/220C/gas mark 7 for 25 to 30 minutes. Allow the quiche to settle once it is out of the oven for a further 5 minutes before serving.

R O U L A D E S

 A roulade is a roll. Almost anything – meat, fish, eggs and vegetables – that can be stuffed and then rolled becomes a roulade. A beef olive is essentially a roulade de boeuf. A Swiss roll is also a roulade and there are various party foods, like smoked salmon rolled with brown bread and butter, that are called roulades. The dish lends itself to cold buffets and summer luncheons because roulades look so attractive.

You will need a Swiss roll tin, or you can improvise and use greaseproof paper to make a shallow baking tin shape, which can then be used on a baking sheet. The size you need is about 12 x 9 inches/30 x 23 cm and both the tin or baking sheet and the paper must be well greased before cooking.

The two roulades here may seem a bit of a song and dance. A roulade de porc, where the loin is boned, then stuffed, rolled and roasted, is child's play compared with the gymnastic ploys with the greaseproof paper necessary here. But once you have mastered the knack of turning the roulade upside down (so that the cooked top in the oven becomes the outside of the roll) and avoided the temptation to over-fill it (so that it cannot roll neatly) and made sure that the roulade is pliable enough to roll without being so soft that it breaks – then you will have accomplished another small art of the kitchen.

It will not hurt the first roulade to be made completely out of spinach if you have no sorrel. You will find the green peppercorns give the second roulade a hot smoky taste, which may not endear itself to some palates. If so, leave them out and double the amount of olives.

R O U L A D E D ' É P I N A R D S

For the roulade
14 OZ/400 G SPINACH LEAVES
7 OZ/200 G SORREL LEAVES
I TABLESPOON PLAIN FLOUR

4 EGGS, SEPARATED

4 OZ/100 G DOUBLE GLOUCESTER OR SAGE DERBY CHEESE, GRATED

SEA SALT AND FRESHLY GROUND BLACK PEPPER

2 TABLESPOONS PARMESAN CHEESE, GRATED

For the filling

14 FL OZ/150 ML MILK INFUSED WITH BAY LEAVES, SHALLOT OR GARLIC,
   AND 5 PEPPERCORNS

1½ OZ/40 G BUTTER

1 TABLESPOON FLOUR

A GENEROUS HANDFUL EACH OF FINELY CHOPPED PARSLEY AND MINT

8 OZ/200 G RICOTTA CHEESE

METHOD

Tear the spinach and sorrel leaves away from their stalks. Discard the stalks. Wash the leaves, drain them and shake off all the excess water. Then cram them into a saucepan, place a tight-fitting lid on and cook over a low heat for 5 minutes, stirring once or twice. When soft and reduced to a purée, drain them in a sieve, gently squeezing out the liquid. Return to a dry pan and add the flour, stirring over a modest heat. Let the flour cook and thicken the purée a little.

Divide the yolks from the whites and when the purée is cool, stir in the yolks and the grated double Gloucester (or sage Derby) cheese, beating and mixing the mixture well. Season. Whip the whites of eggs until stiff and fold them into the purée.

Grease the Swiss roll tin and butter or oil the greaseproof paper laid over the tin. Make sure that it is really well oiled, because bits of charred paper sticking to the dish can be a disaster. Preheat the oven to 425F/220C/gas mark 7. Spread the purée over the prepared tin and place in the oven for 15 to 20 minutes, or until it is crisp at the edges and bouncy in the centre. Stick a knife in the middle and if it comes out clean the roulade is cooked through.

To make the filling, infuse the milk with a couple of bay leaves, some sliced shallots or crushed garlic and the peppercorns by adding them to the milk, heating it and then allowing it to stand in a warm place for 1 hour. Remove the herbs before adding the milk to the butter and flour which have been melted and mixed to a roux.

Chop the parsley and mint finely and add them to the ricotta cheese. Mix well, add to the sauce and stir, allowing it to heat but not to boil. Keep warm while you take out the cooked roulade. Have a fresh piece of greaseproof paper ready sprinkled with the grated Parmesan. Lift the paper at one end with the roulade upon it, so that it flops over on to the Parmesan paper and then peel off the paper it has cooked on. Smooth the filling over the roulade, but not right to the edges. Then, lifting the paper beneath, roll the roulade. Once the first section is tucked under it will roll easily. Serve at once.

R O U L A D E D E P O I V R E V E R T

For the roulade
1 OZ/25 G TIN GREEN PEPPERCORNS
7 OZ/200 G STRONG FLAVOURED HARD CHEESE (SUCH AS WENSLEYDALE, LANCASHIRE OR DOUBLE GLOUCESTER)
4 EGGS, SEPARATED
3 TABLESPOONS YOGHURT
12 BLACK OLIVES, STONED AND CHOPPED
2 TABLESPOONS PARMESAN CHEESE, GRATED

For the filling
11 OZ/300 G LEEKS
1 TABLESPOON OLIVE OIL
GENEROUS BUNCH OF PARSLEY
7 OZ/200 G RICOTTA OR LOW-FAT CHEESE
SEA SALT AND FRESHLY GROUND BLACK PEPPER

M E T H O D

Drain the peppercorns from their brine and add them to the grated cheese, egg yolks, yoghurt and chopped olives. Mix well. Whip the whites until stiff and fold them into the mixture. Preheat the oven to 425F/220C/gas mark 7 and continue as for the roulade d'épinards.

Meanwhile, chop the leeks very finely and cook them in the olive oil in a closed pan for about 5 minutes or until they are soft. Chop the parsley and mix it into the ricotta, add this to the softened leeks. Season and keep warm.

Take the roulade out of the oven and follow the instructions above.
Both roulades are superb cold with salad if there is any left over.

RUSSIA

The old Russian cooking is kept alive by the émigrés scattered over the globe, though I doubt whether any Russian will experience now the sumptuous banquets of pre-Revolutionary days when, like Melba, you could be forgiven for mistaking the appetisers for the main meal. It is said she stuffed herself on them and then could not eat the banquet.

I am told that the better class of émigré with White Russian pedigree, living as far afield as Australia, can provide an impressive cold table. Salted herring, boiled potatoes with dill, salted cucumber, smoked fish, radishes, sauerkraut, marinated mushrooms and fish, home-made sausages and liver paste. *The Russian Cookbook* by Nina Nicolaieff and Nancy Phelan, published by Papermac, celebrates Russian émigré cooking in great style. From this book I learned how to cook blinis and shall be addicted to them for evermore.

Blinis and bortsch are the two inherently Russian recipes which we value in the West, but what of that glutinous, ochre-yellow poultice of pap that bears the name of Russian salad. How sad that this soggy lump of diced vegetables always comes out of a tin. Does no one think it worth making at home? It can be good, if you make your own mayonnaise. If not, equal measures of olive oil, lemon juice and sour cream, in which the diced vegetables are tossed, is a pleasant second best.

Steam two large potatoes and two large carrots, and boil several beetroots. When cool, dice all the vegetables, slice a large onion and several pickled cucumbers; mix all the vegetables together in the mayonnaise or sour cream dressing.

Blinis are a yeast pancake. They are the most delicious of all pancakes, just beating, to my mind, the paper-thin buckwheat Breton galette. Blinis are rich but very light. The traditional way to enjoy them is with caviare and sour cream; but no one can afford to eat real caviare any longer. Danish lumpfish roe masked with plenty of sour cream goes down a treat, though.

But these blinis can be eaten with anything. Butter and jam, lemon juice and sugar, peanut butter or tahini, cream cheese and onion salad, honey and nuts. I ate mine with leek purée, croutons, and grated Parmesan.

B LINIS
(MAKES TWELVE)

> 1 OZ/25 G DRIED YEAST
> ½ PINT/275 ML LUKEWARM WATER
> 3 EGGS
> 1 TEASPOON SALT
> 1 TABLESPOON SUGAR
> ¾ PINT/400 ML HOT MILK
> BUTTER FOR FRYING

M ETHOD

In a large bowl dissolve the yeast in a little of the warm water. Separate the egg yolks from the whites. Add the rest of the water, the yolks, salt and sugar to the yeast and mix into the flour.

Beat the egg whites stiff and add them to the mixture, folding them in as you would a soufflé. Cover the bowl with a clean towel and leave in a warm place to rise for 2 or 3 hours. The mixture should double in bulk in that time.

Boil the milk and pour it into the dough while the milk is still hot. Mix well. Cover the bowl again and leave for at least 1 hour without touching it. It can be left overnight and no harm will occur. The surface of the dough should be pitted with tiny air bubbles.

Heat a frying pan and melt half a teaspoon of butter in it. With a ladle take about half a cup of dough from around the sides of the bowl, so that the mixture is left undisturbed. Pour from the ladle into the pan and cook on one side until there are more tiny holes in the surface, then place a small piece of butter in the centre of the pancake and turn it over, and cook for a moment more. Keep warm in the oven while you make the next one.

BORTSCH

1 LB/450 G RAW BEETROOTS
2 LARGE ONIONS, SLICED
2 LARGE CARROTS, SLICED
2 CELERY HEARTS, SLICED
1 TURNIP, SLICED
1 PARSNIP, SLICED
2 TABLESPOONS OLIVE OIL
1 OZ/25 G BUTTER
SEA SALT AND FRESHLY GROUND BLACK PEPPER
4 PINTS/2.3 LITRES BOILING WATER
2 BAY LEAVES
JUICE FROM 1 LEMON
SOUR CREAM OR YOGHURT

METHOD

Peel the beetroots and cut them into small dice. Add them to the other sliced vegetables in a large saucepan with the olive oil and butter, add a pinch of salt and sauté them over a low heat for 10 minutes. Add the boiling water and bay leaves and let the pan simmer for about 2 hours or until all the vegetables are tender. Add the lemon juice and a little black pepper, and let the soup cool. Take out the bay leaves and blend the soup into a purée. If it is too thick, add a little vegetable stock.

Sometimes, because of the type of beetroot used, the colour may have turned into a dismal reddish brown and not that vibrant cardinal purple that is the delight of this soup. If so, grate another raw beetroot, put it into a muslin bag, and leave it in the soup for a few hours. It not only improves the colour but also the flavour. Discard the muslin bag before serving the soup!

Serve the soup with the yoghurt or sour cream in a separate bowl.

SALAD
Honey Vinaigrette • Sour Cream Dressing • Spiced Salad Mould
Winter Salads Fennel, Orange and Ginger Salad • Green Pepper Salad •
Cauliflower and Green Sauce

SEA SALT
A Visit to Maldon

SEA VEGETABLES

SICILY
Pepperoni in Tortiera

SPAIN
How it Grows Produce for Our Stores
The Real Paella
The Cooking the Tourists Hardly Ever See Black Olive Purée • Mojete
The Tastes of Spain
Good Spanish Cooking

SPINACH
Spinach and Derby Cheese Salad • Spinach and Avocado Salad • Catalan
Spinach • Cannelloni Stuffed with Spinach and Almonds

SPROUTING SEEDS
The Greatest Nutritional Value in the Smallest Particle Sprouting Salad

STORES
Spiced Vegetable Stew • Spinach Croquettes • Potato Latkes
Stores When Snowbound

STUFFING VEGETABLES
Stuffed Lettuce Roll • Stuffed Spinach Rolls • Stuffed Chinese Leaf

S A L A D

Yehudi Menuhin once said that he would eat anything and enjoy it if he knew it was good for him – even if it was pretty disgusting. In my view this is being a martyr to the puritan ethic, and I refuse to go along with it. I consider that food can be of high gourmet quality and be healthy nosh as well. Take raw vegetables. We ought to eat more of them and yet how boring and bland they can seem. Yet this is only true if you keep within the tiny straitjacket of the British salad.

Alternatively, we could explore every rare and obscure vegetable we come across in the market, by nibbling a bit of leaf and stem (that is, after buying them, of course); and if you have a garden, however small, do not waste the space by growing the vegetables you can easily buy from the shops. Start growing ones that hardly ever appear here at all.

The woman who has done more to bring our attention to the world riches in salad vegetables since John Evelyn in his *Discourse of Sallets* is Joy Larkcom. She and her husband have a market garden in Suffolk crammed with the crunchiest stalks, stems and feathery leaves, which you munch as you peruse.

She has written a magnificent book, *The Salad Garden* (Windward). It has colour photographs by Roger Phillips who is the Norman Parkinson of spring greens. Phillips can make a manure heap look like a Magritte, and turn the humble carrot into an exotic lily, by merely managing to capture the object's precise truth.

There are chapters on planning the garden and plant raising and such economic practices as cutting the plant and leaving it to resprout – something Ms Larkcom says you can do two or three times.

But the real excitement of this book – enough to bring a hot flush to green fingers and a tingle of anticipation to the palate – are the chapters on these more obscure salad vegetables. What thrills me is their beauty, not only when growing – as splendid as shrubs in the herbaceous border – but in a mixed salad. They equal a flower arrangement any day, and flowers, of course, are often added, to be eaten with the leaves.

There are the oriental brassicas, pak choi or Chinese cabbages and Japanese spinach mustard greens, which have feathery fronds and peppery flavours. Some have cream stalks, purple leaves and yellow flowers and every bit can be eaten. There are the spinaches and the chards, sorrel and good King Henry, all of them strong in vitamins and minerals.

The milder flavoured leaves are lambs' lettuce or corn salad, so beloved of the nouvelle cuisine, where a clump of it rests on the side of the plate. It romps away in the garden seeding itself, but makes tidy clumps so it has the appearance of being tended.

Sharper flavoured leaves are coriander, fenugreek, land cress and shungiku, which is a chrysanthemum, and my own favourite, Mediterranean rocket. I love its sharp, hot, spicy flavour and will chop it small using it on the plate as a green bed for stuffed vegetables or leeks vinaigrette. Ms Larkcom was told by a Belgian salad grower that rocket was considered an aphrodisiac and medieval laws decreed that none was to be grown in the monastery garden. But it survived into the Renaissance so obviously it was the monkish equivalent of marijuana.

Joy Larkcom makes up bunches of mixed salad leaves, called 'saladini', which she sells on a small scale to restaurants and wholefood shops. Salads in restaurants are often a dire experience, so would imaginative and enterprising chefs contact Ms Larkcom at Montrose Farm, near Diss, Norfolk?

Honey Vinaigrette

YOLK OF 1 HARD–BOILED EGG
1 TABLESPOON RASPBERRY (OR OTHER FRUIT) VINEGAR
3 TABLESPOONS OLIVE OIL
1 TEASPOON SINGLE CREAM OR YOGHURT
1 TEASPOON HONEY

Method

Pound the egg yolk. Add the vinegar. Then, stirring all the time, add the oil, drop by drop at first, then in a thin stream once the mixture emulsifies. Add the cream or yoghurt and honey.

Sour Cream Dressing

Method

Mix ½ pint/300 ml sour cream with 1 teaspoon each of fresh fennel and chopped mint (yoghurt can be substituted for the sour cream and dill leaves for the fennel).

Spiced Salad Mould

- 1 LB/450 G CARROTS
- 1 SMALL SAVOY OR WHITE CABBAGE
- 2 LARGE ONIONS
- 1 TEASPOON SEA SALT
- 1 TEASPOON CURRY POWDER
- 1 TEASPOON GARAM MASALA
- 2 TEASPOONS HONEY
- 1 TABLESPOON ROSE WATER
- 1 TABLESPOON WHOLE SEED MUSTARD

Method

Finely grate carrots, cabbage and onions, mix in a bowl, sprinkle with sea salt, cover and leave for a day. Squeeze out all moisture from vegetables with your hands or through a sieve. When compacted and fairly dry, add other ingredients, mix thoroughly. Press into individual moulds (makes about six) and leave in a cool place for another day. To serve, unmould on a plate.

WINTER SALADS

An unpleasant side effect of the winter is that blown-out stuffed feeling which comes from a high consumption of fatty carbohydrates. The best antidote, apart from fasting, is light and refreshing salads. But in the winter lettuces are expensive and imported, and our own home-grown vegetables tend all to be the root variety. However, good and enticing salads can be made from turnips, swedes and parsnips (as well as the usual beetroot) if the vegetables are fresh and young. Grate them, blanch them, marinate for a day, then toss them in a well-flavoured oil and vinegar dressing with some crushed nuts. A variety of salads as a first course is a good way to begin a meal. They please the palate, look as appealing as a bowl of flowers, stimulate the gastric juices and do not blow you out for the next course.

A savoy cabbage, grated, then blanched, drained and dressed is good alone or mixed with grated carrot and onion. The salad can be dressed with oil and vinegar or yoghurt and sour cream. You can add a touch of honey and a pinch of garam masala or curry powder to the dressing for a spiced salad.

Really to get the most out of winter salads, you have to invest in a few unusual oils and vinegars. Explore Indian, Chinese and wholefood stores and delicatessens. Buy walnut, hazelnut and sesame oil. They are expensive, but you need very little; a teaspoon of walnut oil can be mixed with olive oil and it will flavour the whole salad beautifully. A bottle will probably last for a year.

As to vinegars – these are even more varied. There is the queen of the nouvelle cuisine, raspberry vinegar (though the pink peppercorn to flavour a sauce seems to be edging the vinegar out of its top league status). Then there is umbeshi, made from a salted Japanese plum. This vinegar is astringent as well as salty. A mixture of raspberry and umbeshi in the same dressing gives a slight twinge of sweet and sour and is particularly good with raw grated beetroot. No guest will analyse the fusion of flavours there, though I have a friend whose palate is so discriminating that he can list five or six different ingredients in a sauce and dressing and get them right.

There is brown rice vinegar and sweet brown rice vinegar. Both have a good flavour and are high in protein. There is apple cider vinegar and there are all the herb vinegars. Again, the latter are expensive and it is best to make your own in the summer. Tarragon vinegar in a dressing on a crisp lettuce is an excellent combination. In Chinese stores you will find other vinegars still: a black bean vinegar which is sweet, thick and rather pungent, sometimes necessary when the salad needs a good kick in it.

If you must have a lettuce salad, then jolly up the green leaves with radicchio, the red-leaved chicory which is imported now from Italy. I am pleased to say that I have successfully grown it in my garden. Brilliantly beautiful in its crimson, scarlet and purple shades, each leaf is a work of art, and if there was a climbing variety I would grow them on a trellis and around the front door.

Try mixing fruit with the vegetables. We are used to putting some grated cooking apple into a cabbage salad, and apple, whether it is a good eating variety like russet or the sharp cooker, goes well sliced and marinated with turnip or daikon, the long white radish that you now find in the markets. There are other large radishes around now too. They can all be sliced thinly, marinated or not, then mixed with onion or endive.

Do not ignore dried fruit either. Plump Turkish apricots need not be soaked before they are sliced thinly and added to a grated beetroot salad, though beetroot because it bleeds purple makes a mess of everything added to it. Sliced apricot and turnip salad looks more appealing because it preserves the apricot colour.

Salad and brine pickles go well together too, especially for a simple light lunch of various cheeses. Sliced pickled cucumbers, onions, cauliflower and cabbage, whether red or white, mixed with finely sliced fresh cabbage or cauliflower is an arresting combination.

And do not dismiss the sprouting seeds, mung beans, alfalfa and fenugreek, which make simple salads rich in minerals: all they need is a tiny squeeze of lemon, oil and a little seasoning. They should be served in a bowl on their own.

I am also keen on the warm salad. That is vegetables which have been steamed so that they are just al dente, then poured into a bowl and tossed in a vinaigrette. Broccoli and calabrese are both good and so are cauliflower and cabbage, and some of the root vegetables like carrot and turnip. The important point is to catch the vegetable when it still has plenty of bite in it.

Two vegetables which we never think of eating raw as a salad are the Brussels sprout and the leek, yet both are particularly good if they are sliced razor thin. The sprout has that nutty flavour which can be destroyed in cooking and the leek is astringently tart yet also delicate at the same time, a most satisfactory combination. Here are other ideas to try out throughout the winter.

Fennel, Orange and Ginger Salad

2 OZ/50 G PIECE GINGER ROOT
2 TABLESPOONS OLIVE OIL
1 TEASPOON CIDER VINEGAR
SEA SALT AND FRESHLY GROUND BLACK PEPPER
2 OR 3 FENNEL
JUICE FROM 1 LEMON
2 PEELED ORANGES

Method

Make the ginger dressing a day before, or better still make some up and store it in a bottle. It will keep for months. Peel and grate the ginger root into the oil, vinegar and seasoning. Discard the fibrous leaves of the fennel, cut across in thin rings, dip the rings in lemon juice, cut the orange across in circles, and arrange on a platter, interleaving fennel and orange. Pour over the ginger vinaigrette, but be careful not to allow the particles of ginger root on to the salad.

GREEN PEPPER SALAD

4 GREEN PEPPERS
2 ONIONS
I CLOVE GARLIC, CRUSHED
I TEASPOON CRUSHED CORIANDER SEEDS
2 TABLESPOONS SAUCE VINAIGRETTE

METHOD

Slice the peppers and onions very thinly – the thinner the slices the more pronounced the flavour – discarding the inner seeds and pith in the peppers. Blanch with boiling water and leave for a few minutes. Drain well. Add the crushed garlic and coriander seeds to the vinaigrette. Place onion and pepper in a bowl and pour the sauce over it. Toss well.

CAULIFLOWER AND GREEN SAUCE

I LARGE CAULIFLOWER, CUT INTO FLORETS
4 TABLESPOONS GREEN SAUCE (SEE BELOW)

For the sauce
5 FL OZ/150 ML OLIVE OIL
2 TEASPOONS WINE VINEGAR
6 OZ/175 G CAPERS
3 CLOVES GARLIC, CRUSHED
HANDFUL OF CHOPPED PARSLEY
SEA SALT AND FRESHLY GROUND BLACK PEPPER

METHOD

Blanch the florets for a few minutes. In a bowl, mix all the sauce ingredients well together. The sauce should be thick and chunky. Let it stand for 1 to 2 hours before using it.

SEA SALT
A VISIT TO MALDON

There is enough salt in the sea to cover the world's land masses to a depth of 115 feet; the average concentration of salt in sea water is ¾ oz per pint, while the Dead Sea has 4 oz per pint.

In our own islands a substantial amount of this salt has clung to the coastline, estuaries and inlets of Essex. Maldon at the top of the estuary of the Blackwater, across fifteen miles of salt marshes, has been at the centre of English salt-making since Roman times. The Domesday survey of 1085 lists forty-five salt pans in the area. The 'red hills' of Essex mark the spot where earthenware vessels were broken, the technique then being that you filled terracotta pots with sea water, then boiled the water away, leaving the salt crystals. But you had to break the pots to get to the salt.

Today Maldon Salt, a small family business, carries on these traditions while exporting all over the world. In the Middle Ages leaden pans for boiling the salt water were used; lead poisoning must have been an unknown hazard; now steel is used. But the ideal weather conditions remain the same: no rain, because fresh water dilutes the sea water; sun, so that the water evaporates from the marshes leaving the salt crystals; and a high tide so that the water sweeps across the marshes collecting the salt left behind.

When these conditions occur at Maldon, they collect the water from the middle level and pump it through filters into storage tanks. When the vats are full, the water is heated to boiling point and left to simmer. The pyramid-shaped salt crystals form on the surface and begin to cling to one another in rafts which, when heavy enough, slowly sink to the bottom.

When the level of sea water has reached the level of the salt, the heat is turned off and the crystals scooped to the side and left to drain and dry out completely before being packaged.

Sea salt is not just sodium chloride. A process as simple as this also produces magnesium chloride and sulphate, potassium sulphate, calcium carbonate, and potassium and sodium bromides. A high intake of sodium chloride alone has been implicated as a contributory factor in high blood pressure.

Our daily intake of salt varies enormously from 1,600 mg to more than 5 grams. This seems low: I have seen people sprinkling that amount over their food before even tasting it. But it is now thought that high blood pressure could be caused by a low intake of two other salts, potassium and calcium.

I first ate Maldon sea salt thirty years ago, loving the beauty of the crystals, which require no salt mill to grind them. In those days it was the only salt seen on the tables of connoisseurs. And it still is, if they have salt at all. For me its feel and taste on the palate render it far superior to any other.

SEA VEGETABLES

Seaweeds are still looked upon with suspicion, though everyone plumps for the seaweed in a Chinese restaurant. As this is finely shredded wind-dried spring greens, deep fried then sprinkled with brown sugar and monosodium glutamate – no wonder. But it does not further the cause of the true seaweeds – or, as the food producers like to call them, sea vegetables, which they feel confers greater gastronomic dignity.

Whatever the name, they are the most primitive plants still eaten, all of them a form of algae. Commercially they have become of much importance for they are a source of alginate, used as stabilisers in the food industry to keep the pig fat in ice cream in suspension, or in a range of custard mixes, blancmange powders, instant mousses and re-formed meat pieces.

Until recently the seaweed found in health shops has been imported from Japan. They have been eating the stuff for centuries.

They are grouped into green, red and brown types; we are used to seeing the browns on our beaches as they are the most common in northern seas. The most famous is kelp. Many of the most noted gastronomic seaweeds come from the red group: laver, dulse and carrageen.

The Japanese use a form of laver, called nori, to wrap sushi in. On these shores the Welsh have made it famous as laver bread. Bobby Freeman, in her book *First Catch Your Peacock*, quotes from Mrs Maria Rundell, writing in 1808:

> After the laver has been very well washed first in seawater, then in fresh, and wrung quite dry, it should be put in a pan with seawater, and if liked a little vinegar, and then simmered for several hours. The drained pulp can be kept for weeks, and it is in that state that it is sold as Laver 'Bread'.

Mrs Rundell continues with the way to make laver sauce: 'Set some of it in a dish with a bit of butter and the squeeze of a Seville orange, stir it till hot. It is eaten with roast meat, and is a great cleanser of the blood.' Bobby Freeman adds how good the sauce is with Welsh lamb.

You can now buy laver bread in tins, made by Colin Pressdee of

The Welsh Barrow, Llandeilo. It is sold at many health food shops and delicatessens.

Clokie's Scottish Sea Vegetables is a source of excellent quality. The range includes many not available before – sugar ware, finger ware, dabberlocks, grockle, as well as dulse and purple nori. Recipes are printed on the packets, but you cannot go far wrong with my own favourite method: stir-frying with garlic, chilli and ginger, so that they become crisp. All seaweeds have to be soaked in a little water for a few minutes. Pat dry.

A more involved recipe uses the Japanese nori sheets moistened in soy sauce and water, equal amounts of each; they will shrink a little but become pliable. These sheets can then be laid in individual moulds and a stuffing gently pressed down. I often use a mixture of diced cooked potato, onion, fresh herbs and diced avocado bound with mayonnaise or sour cream, but any stuffing you like to create will do. The moulds are then refrigerated for a day; they will unmould easily. As a first course they look and taste sensational – the nori is black and becomes polished like ebony.

SICILY

 Sicily I have known for almost thirty years now. The industrial zones, whose soaring chimneys dwarf the most powerful temple dedicated to Zeus, are latecomers and pollute the eye as much as the effluent does the fish. But, as Eric Newby says in *On the Shores of the Mediterranean*, one can so easily become a prophet of doom and an ecological bore. So, on a recent trip, I closed my eyes to the landscape mutations and wondered how the food had changed.

On my first visit to Messina in the late fifties, I ate at the cheapest trattoria, run by three ancient sisters, their wizened faces borrowed from time, who served nothing but spaghetti with either tomato or meat sauce. We named them the Harpies.

'Let us go to the Harpies,' we used to say, as if it had just appeared in *The Good Food Guide*. A litre of vino bianco cost something like sixpence. We ate our spaghetti with chopped raw garlic and either butter or olive oil. The Harpies served us with stony expressions and the wine almost erased the tedium of the meal. For the rest of the day I ate fruit.

Always fascinated by low dives and the trattorias which most people eat in, when they eat out, I explored them this time every day for lunch. As I was a guest of Island Sun, I had been booked into a choice of luxury hotels so ate dinner in ritzy splendour. The contrast was absorbing.

Take the Villa Igiea, a huge baroque palace surrounded by the docks in the bay of Palermo, a David Hockney oasis with palm trees and swimming pool and a view of white cruisers crossing the still, blue sea. Its dinning-room was designed perhaps for a ball which might have taken place in Lampedusa's *The Leopard*. The food bore a striking similarity to grand hotel food thirty years ago. The antipasto came from an hors-d'oeuvre trolley of vegetables and fish embalmed in a thick coating of what appeared to be carboxymethyl cellulose but which they referred to as mayonnaise.

Contrast it with the antipasto at a trattoria in a back alley in Trapani where there were broad beans and artichoke hearts, freshly stewed, thin slices of baked aubergine with a circle of melted mozzarella and pieces of bread baked with oil, garlic and oregano. A dish of quality – and all these trattorias served vegetable antipasto.

In Taormina, on the sea's edge at the Villa Sant'Andrea, amidst a scented garden of datura and jasmine, they treated a fillet of swordfish as a motorway café might, rolling it and stuffing it with Paxo. Ugh! While at a trattoria in Monreale, the swordfish was justly respected; it was grilled for two minutes, basted with oil and lemon.

At the same trattoria, I ate a minestrone that would never have appeared in any recipe book for it was made from the vegetables at hand – a few fresh broad beans, peas and sliced spinach, a vegetable stock and some pasta shells. The beans had given the stock their deep, dark brown taste and it replenished the parts, as it were, other soups could not reach.

Throughout the interior of the island, Greek ruins are poised upon hills in a landscape which, in the spring, was rife with flowering acanthus, euphorbia and mimosa, wild garlic and anemones. It is easy to find sites like Palazzolo Acriede where you may be alone as a tourist. There you will find a small 600-seat Greek theatre and another next to it that seems made for tiny tots, but which was a council chamber.

The town below has many trattorias and, in finding them, you stroll through some of the finest rococo architecture in Sicily. Explore and eat cheaply. I was particularly delighted to rediscover some dishes I had borrowed for my book *Mediterranean Vegetarian Cooking* (Thorsons). This way with peppers is particularly good.

PEPPERONI IN TORTIERA

1 EACH GREEN, YELLOW AND RED PEPPERS
3 CLOVES GARLIC, CRUSHED
1 TABLESPOON EACH CHOPPED MINT AND PARSLEY
3 TABLESPOONS WHOLEMEAL BREADCRUMBS
5 TABLESPOONS OLIVE OIL
SEA SALT AND FRESHLY GROUND BLACK PEPPER
1 TABLESPOON LEMON JUICE
6 BLACK OLIVES, STONED AND SLICED

METHOD

Burn and blister the peppers under a hot grill or over a flame. Scrape the skin away. Slice the flesh and discard the core. Lay the strips in a shallow dish.

Add the crushed garlic and herbs to the breadcrumbs with 2 tablespoons of oil, then the seasoning and lemon juice. Pour this over the peppers. Scatter the chopped olives over the top, pour the rest of the oil over that and bake in a 400F/200C/gas mark 6 oven for about 10 to 12 minutes. Serve hot or warm.

S P A I N
H o w   i t   G r o w s   P r o d u c e   f o r   O u r   S t o r e s

 Much of the fresh produce sold at our large supermarket chains is Spanish in origin, so it was music to the ears of a small group of British food writers to hear a farmer, Don José Gandia, recently praise British supermarkets.

He claimed they set standards far more exacting on the farmer for flavour and excellence than the French market. José Gandia was at a conference of fruit farmers recently in France and was brave enough to inform them of this impression. This was an incitement to riot if not a declaration of war.

Luckily, the French chairman of the conference is married to an Englishwoman and he stepped in to say he agreed. More uproar! How could the British be better at anything to do with food? However, although the French admitted the produce in the British supermarkets might be of greater quality than theirs, they insisted they scored more Brownie points because they demanded their lemons unwaxed while we did not care.

At José Gandia's farm at La Rinconada, south of Seville, acres of peach and nectarine trees spread away to the distant horizon. It was like Eden; to pick a ripe fruit, sink one's teeth into the sun-warmed skin and rediscover the first impact of peach juice upon the tongue is one of life's most sensual pleasures. A buyer from Marks & Spencer has suddenly discovered white peaches and was astounded at the superiority of their flavour over the yellow fruit. Thirty years ago, I recall, the white peach was 'U' while the yellow was definitely 'non-U'. White peaches appeared on the table at upper-class dinner parties but it was an appalling *faux pas* for others to be seen lurking in the fruit bowl.

There was also a particularly trendy dessert which starred for a short time. Just before dinner, allowing one white peach per person, you pricked it all over with a fork, placed it in a goblet and poured champagne to cover. You served these, topping up the glasses with more bubbly, and, as the guests chattered, they toyed with their disintegrating peach while sipping the champagne which had taken on some of the perfume of the fruit.

They are doing extensive research on the flavour of fruit at La Rinconada, for José Gandia is convinced it is flavour the British consumer wants. He also told us that five to ten per cent of the fruit on sale has gone over its peak period and the public throw away twenty to thirty per cent of the fruit that they buy. He grows 150 different varieties of peach and nectarines each year in his search for the perfect fruit. One variety will last for ten years before a new one takes over.

From the minute La Rinconada decides on a new variety, it takes a further two or three years before it reaches the market. On the controversial matter of chemical pesticides, La Rinconada was keen to inform us that their policy was to keep the use of them to the minimum and all information on the amount and type of pesticides used is passed on to the retailers. They say their objective is to be totally free of pesticides altogether and to control the pests by the use of other parasites. Their buyers can see at any stage what the pesticide treatments are. As a method of pest control their research also covers genetic engineering.

Further up the Costa Blanca they grow loquats (nisperos). The loquat trees are just ten to fifteen feet tall and are thickly hung with burnished yellow fruits like pieces of Mycenaean bronze and gold jewellery. The fruits are perfectly ripe when they show minute brown flecks, a fact which goes against their commercial acceptance but their flavour is astonishing, an intense fusion of tartness and sweetness. The darker the amber colour, the sweeter the flesh. Alas, the Spanish food industry does little with this miracle fruit other than can it in syrup. I suggested that, like apricots, they dry the loquats in the sun.

East of Murcia near the Campo de Cartagena, José Antonio Canovas supplies honeydew and galia melons to Sainsbury's. We toured the melons and his five different methods of cultivation. Sainsbury's prefer the traditional one, maintaining there is a slight improvement of flavour. In the previous two years, while we had torrid early spring weather, Spain had rain and cold winds and the melons growing outside in the fields suffer unless they are well wrapped in their polythene sheeting. Once the Spanish summer drought sets in, the roots of the melons have gone down far enough to reach the water below the subsoil. To avoid the damage caused by bad weather conditions, some of Don Canovas' production then uses hydroponic methods where the melons are protected by polythene houses and grow out of water and nutrients instead of soil. He made the point that British shoppers choose their melons by pressing the fruit for softness, especially the ends, and were all choosing over-ripe fruit. He suggested they choose by colour instead and then the fruit will be ripe but not over-soft.

There is a pimenton factory at Espinardo, on the outskirts of Murcia. Here they make sweet and hot paprika as well as a small amount of smoked paprika which is used by the Spanish meat industry for chorizo, a type of sausage. Half of the Spanish pepper industry goes to make pimenton and, for the sweet variety, they use the small round pepper, *Capsicum annuum* Negral, which are dried in ovens at a temperature between 149 and 158F/65 and 68C.

The quality of the pimenton is determined by whether just the red flesh is used or whether the seeds and stem are also ground up. The factory has been in the same Albarracin family since 1854 and family pride in the product is illustrated by Juan José Albarracin's enthusiasm for his best-quality paprika which uses only pepper flesh and is of a brilliant fiery scarlet. He claimed that much of paprika made in Hungary contains the stem and seeds which give it a brown hue. The browner the paprika the lower the quality. Once the peppers are dried they are ground between two stones, with the powder then placed in a humidifier so that some moistness is added, enabling it to run or sprinkle from containers.

One of our missions on this Spanish visit was to look at the growing and marketing of young garlic. In our spring it is sometimes seen in markets, imported generally from Brittany, and is young garlic of crystalline whiteness with thick stems still moist with the cloves being just discernible. The flavour is, if anything, stronger than if it is dried at a later stage. This young garlic is harvested in April or early May, but in Spain they use garlic at an even earlier stage, when they are no larger than spring onions. It is then that you can use all the green leaves in cooking, a particularly delicious flavour. However, though we visited one of the largest garlic growers east of Cordoba, Don Antonio Quesada, he claimed that no such garlic was grown in Spain. When we counterclaimed that we had seen it in the market at Seville, he said it must have been a different species grown at La Mancha.

We looked at his 150-hectare field with both purple and white garlic, producing about 1,500 tonnes a year, and resigned ourselves to the mystery. But the very next day we discovered the very young garlic in the market in Alicante. The stall-owner told us that it grew profusely in the Alicante area and was used extensively in their dishes in early spring. She told us that with chopped peppers, using all of the green garlic leaves as well as the white bulb, they would sauté it in olive oil and use it as a sauce with sardines, or with parsley over clams, or with the young asparagus finely chopped in scrambled eggs.

We tried this last dish and it was a triumph of flavours. This very young garlic is seldom imported here as the green leaves quickly droop and fade. But you can easily grow it yourself: plant the cloves in October or November as usual, but harvest in March rather than waiting until July or August.

THE REAL PAELLA

 The paella the tourist generally eats is an upstart dish. Paella dishes were born in the Albufera, a natural lagoon near the town of Valencia where the rice is still cultivated and where the local catch or crop was cooked with the rice: snails, broad beans, eels, perhaps rosemary. Later a little chicken and rabbit were added.

For 900 years rice dishes have been part of Iberian cuisine; vigorous, even fierce, in texture and range of taste, yet subtle in its complex fusion of flavours.

For example, there is the way the sofrito is put together with an intensely flavoured fish fumet. For the fumet, rock fish – baby hake, eels, crabs and rascasse living in shallow waters – are used, and added to a rich sofrito of olive oil, garlic, onion, tomato and nora or nyora, a round sweet pepper the colour of dried blood, one of those peppers that hang in clusters in the markets. The sofrito is cooked slowly so that the flavours fuse and the whole mixture is simmered for three hours.

The scents from this fish stew bring a feline fan club, their whiskers pressed to the bars of the kitchen window, waiting to be fed fish debris. Bomba, a short-grained rice from the area of the Pega, chosen to hold the moisture, is added to olive oil and garlic before the stock is poured over. The rice intensifies all the flavours, and is called arroz abanda (rice separate). The whole is a staple food of farmers and fishermen.

This kind of cooking appears both simple and direct, yet hides discordant flavours. Mira Cielo (looking at heaven), for example, is a dish of red peppers, roasted and marinated in oil and garlic with slivers of dry roasted salt cod. Dry roasting – a la plancha – is cooking on the hot plate without oil.

Another dish, pericana, owed much of its singularity to this method of cooking. It has only three ingredients, garlic, salt cod ('the fish of the mountains') and dried pimentos, the long red sweet peppers which are also used ground up as a pepper. The salt cod is soaked, drained, skinned and boned, then placed flat on the hot plate with about thirty fat cloves of garlic. They are turned after two or three minutes and are modestly charred.

The dried red peppers are plunged in very hot olive oil and deep fried for about one minute, then drained. They puff up and become brittle, so are easily crumbled. (I had always made the mistake before of soaking these before cooking and wondered why they did little for a dish.)

The garlic and cod are then finely chopped – the food processor is never used nor did I see one in any of the kitchens I visited. The pimento is crumbled and the three ingredients are combined in measures of two-thirds pimento to one-third garlic and cod. Oil is poured over them and the mixture is eaten with bread as part of tapas.

This dish was eaten at Venta del Pilar above Alicante, an eighteenth-century coaching inn with deep stone-arched dining-rooms. Here they also made borreta, a traditional soup eaten on Christmas Eve. Olive oil is heated in a large pan and to it is added a couple of heads of chopped garlic, salt cod, monkfish and squid, the broken up dried sweet peppers and some chopped potatoes with pimento powder. All is sautéed for a few minutes before some strong fish fumet is added.

Grandmother Maria's hake (merluza a la abulela Maria) is also an interesting combination; the centre is stuffed with minced pork, spiced with parsley, cloves, cinnamon, lemon zest and black pepper, while bajoques farcides – a stuffed red pepper – is filled with a mixture of onion, garlic, tomato, red pepper, ham and rice, then steamed over a bed of fresh tomatoes. Another coaching inn high up above Valencia at Bunol, Venta L'Home, cooks olleta, a thick vegetable and game stew. The intensity of flavour again is astonishing. But consider the range of vegetables that go with this dish: turnips, parsnips, broad beans, red kidney beans, leeks, carrots, chick peas, gourd, cardoon and celery. There are also five kinds of sausage and various parts of pig and lamb.

One of the most interesting Valencian chefs with his own restaurant is Noberto Jorge, whose establishment is fifty kilometres behind Alicante. He has created some thirty dishes which revolve around the Mediterranean tradition of preserving the roe and flesh of tuna by salting and pressing. Hueva is the roe, which he calls tuna caviare. He uses it with other ingredients as a stuffing in crêpes or with a soufflé. Sometimes his ideas seem to run ahead of his cooking, ending in dishes which are not successful.

A colleague of Noberto's told him: 'You are not salmon and trout class but a sardine man', getting to the nub of real Spanish cooking, its complete lack of pretension. It is traditional and peasant. It marries, in the most dramatic manner, fish, game and vegetables and it has a dense complexity unlike anything else in Europe.

S

The Cooking the Tourists Hardly Ever See

Spain's cuisine has been for too long in the shadow of France and Italy.

Food connoisseurs have shunned Spain, but any country that can come up with thirty different ways of making gazpacho and at least twelve different versions of garlic soup earns my respect and curiosity. The path to good food is not just paved with paella or leaden tortilla; a relief to me, as paella always struck me as trying to please too many palates for too much of the time.

The best Spanish cooking derives from its regions: each has its own traditions, dialect, food, wine and often cheeses which are unknown outside the area. Alas, the cheeses are never exported.

Spanish history is part of the richness of their cooking. The Romans introduced garlic and the olive tree; the Arabs, spices like nutmeg, saffron, black pepper and the fruits – bitter oranges, lemons and dates. Later, Spain brought back from the New World cocoa, tomatoes, potatoes, peppers and the avocado.

It is the cooking which fuses Arab and European traditions that I find most rewarding. A haricot bean purée flavoured with cumin and chilli. A tomato sauce with bitter marmalade. Red peppers stuffed with rice and smoked cheeses.

Their fish cooking is probably the most adventurous. Cod in a garlic, vegetable and lobster sauce might strike one as a little bizarre, yet it is a wonderful amalgam of the plain, the rich and the exotic. Perhaps one of the simplest dishes of all is the most delicious, cooked in both Portugal and Spain and often eaten as tapas, those enticing hors-d'oeuvres in which Spain like Greece excels: gambas al ajillo. These are shrimps cooked with masses of garlic and a dried red chilli in olive oil. Best to marinate everything in the oil for several hours before cooking it, then mop up all the hot oil with good bread.

An even more succulent version of the dish is to use the largest Mediterranean prawns you can buy, allow three for each person, shell, then squeeze the juice from the heads into a ramekin dish. Add three peeled cloves of garlic and one dried red chilli to each dish. Cover with good extra

241

virgin olive oil, then bake in a preheated oven at 425F/220C/gas mark 7 for ten minutes. The oil should have bubbled. Soak the oil up with bread after eating the prawns, but do remember not to consume the chilli – guests have been known to gag.

Not only can we not think of Spanish cooking without olive oil, but the olive itself tends to play a prominent part. There is that plump green oval which the Spaniards call aceituna de la reina – olive of the queen. So perfect and rotund is this green jewel she looks more like a grand duchess. They are picked by hand and placed with care into baskets which are slung from the back on a leather halter. I disappeared up a flimsy ladder and into the silver leaves of an olive tree and picked a few myself. They do not come easily from their stalks for they are still unripe, and it is a labour needing patience as well as balance. If the olive is bruised in the harvesting it is discarded.

The smaller olives which are often stuffed are called manzanilla. Machines stone them, then a girl feeds a strange tangerine ribbon into another machine with teeth spinning on a wheel. The ribbon is pimento paste. It tastes of nothing except filtered sea water. The machine bites off tiny portions of paste and stuffs them into the olives, then it throws the filled olive on to a mini-escalator and they tumble down to the packers.

I found the cocktail olive rather disconcerting, and prefer to consider the black olive. Saturnine black in taste, too, wonderful as a purée in a tart or the purée eaten plain with fromage frais. A black olive purée served within half a ripe avocado can also be good; decorated with green olives it looks appealing, though I would resist those stuffed with pimento paste.

Around Seville, in the olive industry, they are fond of using the green olive in their cooking, but more often than not, the olives seemed to be scattered as garnish and not used for their flavour. I think it wise to be cautious about the green olive, for its strong acidity might well strike a lethal blow to a dish. When I tried a Piperada Sevillana the sixteen manzanilla olives were unleashed upon the palate with all the subtlety of a rock band in the Wigmore Hall.

In fact, good regional cooking eschews the olive. They are part of tapas, that is all. It was only in the northern areas near Pamplona and Zaragoza that I found that dark olive purée eaten as it is in Provence, but here made with bitter oranges instead of lemon juice.

BLACK OLIVE PURÉE

8 OZ/225 G BLACK OLIVES
JUICE FROM 2 BITTER ORANGES
2 CLOVES GARLIC, CRUSHED
½ TEASPOON CRUSHED CORIANDER
½ TEASPOON FRESHLY GROUND BLACK PEPPER

METHOD

Stone the olives and place them in a blender with all the other ingredients. If the mixture is not smooth and needs more liquid add enough olive oil to make a thick purée.

MOJETE

4 LARGE POTATOES
4 CRUSHED CLOVES OF GARLIC
I BAY LEAF
½ TEASPOON PAPRIKA
4 TABLESPOONS OLIVE OIL
SEA SALT AND FRESHLY GROUND BLACK PEPPER
4 EGGS

METHOD

This is an egg and potato casserole from the district of La Mancha. It is a simple supper dish for 3 to 4 people. Peel and slice the potatoes into the size of a 50 pence piece. Place in a shallow earthenware dish with the garlic, bay leaf, paprika and oil. Bake in the oven at 400F/200C/gas mark 6 for 1 hour or until the potatoes are tender and the top is slightly crisp. Season them. Then break the eggs over the top and place back in the oven for a few minutes or until the whites are cooked and the yolks unset.

THE TASTES OF SPAIN

In the Cathedral at Santo Domingo de la Calzada, if minded to bend the knee in awe and piety, you are likely to be deafened by a cock crowing. On turning around you are just as likely to see a rampant white cockerel chasing a hen around a gilded cage built into the cathedral walls. Cock and hen stay there throughout the year, except for a few winter months when it is too cold.

The legend behind their existence tells of a man – innocent of the crime he has been hung for – returning to life while he is still hanging from the rope. The crowd run to the Mayor who is dining off two roast chickens. 'Nonsense,' the Mayor cries, stabbing a chicken breast, 'it is as likely that these birds will get off the plate and run from the table,' whereupon they did, miraculously growing feathers and squawking loudly. The murals in the cathedral paint the scene in all its comedy and horror.

On first discovering these birds in the house of God, I cackled as loudly as they did. Yet there was something still British enough in me to also reflect on how inappropriate it was. But this mixture of opposites is the kernel of Spain, which often hits you with a sense of disbelief and astonishment.

Fancy a casserole of fish in meat or chicken stock? Well, I didn't, as it happened, nor did I care for the idea of a goat's foot with clams, or goose giblet soup with saffron and conger eel. But I am picking out the more electrifying combinations because they illustrate an explosive imagination at work which I find heartening and fascinating. Give me this dedication to trying out flavours and unlikely combinations any day, rather than the old-hat British conformity of prawn cocktail doused in commercial pink sauce.

Some combinations we are used to. I am not too sympathetic to the idea of cooking dried beans with smoked meat or serving petits pois with bacon because you are destroying the natural flavour of the vegetables and swamping it with smoked meat. But I was intrigued by the mixture of clams or mussels with vegetables. One lunchtime, in the town of Castel-horra, there were three dishes of clams with haricot beans, artichoke hearts and petits pois, which worked as the flavour of the clams was just as delicate as that of the vegetables.

But the most stunning fusion of flavours and one which I have now used at home is to cook fish in either an artichoke or asparagus stock rather than fish fumet.

There are endless fish dishes cooked with vegetables and though the most famous Basque combination is with tomatoes – or a sauce made from tomatoes, onions and red peppers which is served with the salt cod – there is also another Basque sauce which crops up constantly – salsa verde, as in almejas en salsa verde. The almejas are tiny clams which make as wonderful a soup as we make using mussels in a moules marinière. But hake too is cooked in the green sauce, which is made from parsley, peas, garlic and oil and sometimes flour and sherry.

The Iberian peninsula is amazingly rich in fish recipes. There is not only a large variety of seafood but also an enthusiasm for using large amounts of garlic, onion, chilli pepper and olive oil with the fish. We use tabasco with oysters, so why not hot chillies with fried hake?

I saw freshly caught lobsters, crayfish, prawns, crabs and shrimps, mussels and clams, spider crabs, angler fish, hake, sea eels and sardines, octopus, squid, black grouper and sole. They make wonderful fish soups and casseroles. It is often difficult to tell the difference, or when a soup becomes a casserole. Possibly it comes down to how large the portions of fish are – if chunky cutlets then it is a casserole or a stew. There is the marmitako which is made from fresh tuna, potatoes, red peppers, onions, garlic and olive oil. Or the angulas de Cazuelita which is a stew of baby eels with garlic and chillies.

A steaming carzuela, the earthenware casserole, arrives at the table, filled with fish and vegetables, the fish cutlets adorned with clams, mussels, prawns and asparagus spears. There is nothing subtle about the flavours of the sauce itself. No French cook would be brave enough to serve a sauce so intensely redolent of the sea and the fruits of the earth.

Good Spanish cooking is untouched by sophistication. It stems from working homes, from the wives of farmers and fishermen, the dishes deriving from small scraps of meat and fish, dried or salted, and a great variety of vegetables and herbs. The cooking is often done over open fires and on a hot plate. Large prawns are brushed with oil, garlic and herbs, then thrown on to a plate and seared on each side, so that the shells become crisp, transparent and faintly brown.

But also there are foods which look appealing but have their drawbacks – like the tiny cooked crab which you eat whole, crunching up the shells and claws. I did this dutifully, watched over by a smiling patron, then managed to escape outside and spat the wretched bits out. Crab shell is not good for the teeth and bits of it seemed to be sinking back into the gums for the rest of the day. As I drove the elegant BMW 635CSi, lent to me for the trip, I was still spitting out crab shell and possibly hitting some potential admirers.

Good Spanish Cooking

The vivid contrasts that make up Spain pound the senses with the same hot blast the eyeball gets surveying the scorched plateau of the interior. The climate can change within minutes, the dialect and geography within miles, and each area has its own distinctive cooking.

I have recently driven through the Rioja area and the Basque country, avoiding after the first confrontation that foul coastal road between Santander and San Sebastian which is loaded with freight and poisonous with fumes.

Within the mountains and plateaus of the Cordillera the temperature gauge of the car registered 92F; there were eagles circling the sky in search of prey; near the Orduna, Basque pride had obliterated all road signs, replacing them with one word – España; wild roses, poppies and mimosa line the roads, the scent of rosemary and marjoram fill the air and another fragrance of crushed blackcurrant leaves that was unidentifiable but seemed as potent as Proust's madeleine.

The purpose of my visit was to search out good Spanish regional cuisine, avoiding the cooking for tourists, or the mock French which the Spaniards tend to think is the food we want. I was not disappointed. Once you search for them, new dishes and amalgams of unexpected flavours abound.

Abroad I rely on sniffing the air to see where the most delicious smells emanate from, but on this trip I was lucky to have an interpreter of beauty and charm who could make sense of a guidebook, *La Gula del Viajero* (published by Banco Exterior España), which never let us down.

In Spain the relationship between customer and waiter is of friendly equality. The waiter exists to give the customer a good meal. If, as happened, a Spaniard found the unlabelled vino tinto too cold, another bottle of the right temperature was immediately found. If the manchego cheese was too young, the diner would prefer to go without and the waiter sympathised. Then there was the waiter who told my companion not to have the vinaigrette sauce with the asparagus, for it was a vegetable of delicate flavour and only demanded oil and a suspicion of vinegar, and that is precisely what she had.

Another time we were hungry and had left all our money in the hotel. We went out into a tiny bar which also sold espadrilles, Persil and tourist trinkets, with only the equivalent of ten pence between us. The owner insisted on giving us two glasses of wine, bread and a saucer of boquerones and would not take a peseta. Boquerones are fresh raw anchovies, filleted and then marinated in wine vinegar, garlic, a little salt and water for a day and served with oil and chopped parsley. They are delicate and delicious. This kind man was amazed that we could not return to England and buy our own fresh anchovies and make them ourselves. I wish Spain would can or bottle them for the UK market.

I visited the asparagus fields and dug and cut white asparagus – though not with the quick precision of the Spaniard who went down the earth cloches digging and slicing all in one rapid movement. How, I wondered, did the man know in what spot in the earth mound the bleached spears were hidden? He pointed to the hairline cracks in the earth's surface, which showed that a spear was an inch or two below. The few spears that had grown above the earth and turned an English green were thrown away with disdain.

Ebro-Export is a group of companies that sell canned and bottled fruit and vegetables to the UK. The river Ebro winds through a verdant valley near these asparagus fields. It is as wide as the Thames at Westminster but was the only river I saw with water – the rest were each an expanse of stones with a few puddles.

Wine is produced near here in the Rioja province and at this time of year vegetables are at their best and most plentiful. There were fat nectarines, peaches, apricots, Swiss chard, artichokes, lettuce, huge tomatoes, mounds of glistening cherries in silken reds, green peppers, large scarlet chillies, runner and broad beans, petits pois.

They eat their vegetables as a first course and in this area they have a favourite dish, minestra verdura – mixed vegetables, which are a selection, all al dente, cooked in artichoke or asparagus stock. Spain is famous for hors-d'oeuvres – entre meses. They are rightly proud of these, and much Spanish ingenuity goes also into the tapas that you eat in the bars. In restaurants there can be up to fifteen small dishes; in cafés where the locals throng there can still be eight or ten, even if one is only green chillies eaten raw dipped in sea salt.

Some of these dishes may hold only a few slices of mortadella or salami but the famous sausage, chorizo, is a heady mixture of meat and garlic, spiced with paprika and chilli. Chorizo is also used extensively in cooking. Other saucers will hold slices of smoked hams, a few marinaded clams, stuffed baby squid in their own ink – chipirones en su tinta – flaked spider crab in hot sauce, stuffed peppers, chopped pimento, tomato and garlic, artichoke hearts fried in egg and breadcrumbs, prawns fried in garlic and hot chillies.

Twice I came across fungi of immeasurable beauty. Seta de cardo had been sliced down the stalk, its cap spread out in a fan shape, brushed with oil and grilled on a hot plate – a la plancha. The colour of the gills was tawny gold changing to blue. I was told by Ebro-Export that these are sometimes canned. Do more, I begged, and export them all to the UK. Perrichones were another fungi of exceptional flavour, sold in the markets and cooked in oil and served covered in a little scrambled egg.

Though Spanish food still lies beneath the tourist cloud of the package-tour paella, Spanish wine, for the aficionados at least, has begun to come into its own. It would seem like an obvious cliché to say that the wine complements this food, like the chorizo and beans, which is another favourite dish, but the wines I drank were a revelation.

The Paternina Banda Azul is available over here and is amazing value. It is especially good when opened and left to breathe for a few hours. It tastes like a superior Bordeaux which would cost four times the price. I was told that a 1928 Rioja had still not reached its peak. And when I drank a 1964 Rioja the waiter asked us to lower the glass to knee level and admire the 'brillo'. This was the translucent sheen of the colour, which was exquisite. How difficult it is to conceive of a wine waiter here enjoying the aesthetics with so much fervour.

SPINACH

SPINACH AND DERBY CHEESE SALAD

2 LB/1 KG FRESH SPINACH
6 OZ/150 G DERBY CHEESE
4 TABLESPOONS SALAD OIL
SEA SALT AND FRESHLY GROUND BLACK PEPPER
2 TABLESPOONS HOME-MADE MAYONNAISE DILUTED WITH A LITTLE
   FRESHLY BOILED WATER
WINE VINEGAR OR LEMON JUICE (OPTIONAL)

METHOD

Prepare and wash spinach. Blanch quickly in boiling salted water. Drain and refresh in cold water. Press between two plates to remove excessive moisture. Place in a wide bowl.

Using two forks to help separate the leaves, dress the spinach with the salad oil, salt and freshly ground black pepper. A little wine vinegar or lemon juice may be used to season the salad.

Place the spinach in a shallow serving dish. Cut the Derby cheese into cubes, mix with the mayonnaise and extra seasoning if necessary and spoon on top of the spinach. Serve lightly chilled.

SPINACH AND AVOCADO SALAD

½ LB/225 G VERY YOUNG SPINACH LEAVES
2 RIPE AVOCADOS
2 TABLESPOONS HAZELNUT OIL
1 DESSERT SPOON WINE VINEGAR
SEA SALT AND FRESHLY GROUND BLACK PEPPER
1 TABLESPOON SOUR CREAM
2 TABLESPOONS CHOPPED HAZELNUTS

METHOD

Wash spinach leaves, tear them from the stalks, drain and pat them dry. Peel and stone the avocados. In a large bowl mix the oil, vinegar, salt and pepper and sour cream together. Add the sliced avocados, then the spinach leaves. Turn the salad carefully in the dressing so as not to break the avocado slices. Sprinkle with the chopped hazelnuts and serve.

CATALAN SPINACH

  2 LB/900 G FRESH SPINACH LEAVES
  2 TABLESPOONS OLIVE OIL
  4 CLOVES GARLIC, CRUSHED
  2 TABLESPOONS PINE NUTS
  I TABLESPOON CURRANTS
  SEA SALT AND FRESHLY GROUND BLACK PEPPER
  2 OZ/50 G BUTTER
  4 SLICES OF BROWN BREAD

METHOD

Cook the spinach in a covered pan without water for about 10 minutes. When soft, drain any juices off, or steam them away by raising the heat and stirring the spinach at the same time so that it does not stick. Take from the heat and chop it coarsely with the edge of a wooden spoon.

Heat the olive oil in a pan and add 2 of the crushed cloves of garlic, the pine nuts and currants, cook for a few minutes, then add the spinach and stir well. Season and lower the heat. In another pan, melt the butter, add the rest of the garlic and fry the bread, cut diagonally, until the slices are crisp. Pour the spinach into a bowl and stick the fried bread around the rim. Serve.

CANNELLONI STUFFED WITH SPINACH AND ALMONDS

12–16 SHEETS OF CANNELLONI
2 LB/900 G FRESH SPINACH LEAF
2 OZ/55 G BUTTER
8 OZ/225 G GROUND ALMONDS
2 OZ/55 G BUTTER
2 TABLESPOONS DOUBLE CREAM
SEA SALT AND FRESHLY GROUND BLACK PEPPER
2 OZ/55 G GRUYÈRE CHEESE, GRATED
½ PINT/275 ML SINGLE CREAM
2 OZ/55 G PARMESAN CHEESE, GRATED

METHOD

Have a large saucepan full of boiling salted water. Cook the cannelloni sheets until they are just done, about 10 minutes. Slip them into a bowl of cold water with some oil in it so that they will not stick. Drain them on towels and kitchen paper. Meanwhile, take the leaves from the spinach stalks and use half the butter to cook the spinach over a very low heat. The spinach should have shrunk to less than half its bulk and be cooked through in 5 to 6 minutes. Let it cool, and drain off the excess liquid. Place the spinach in a bowl and chop it up small with a wooden spoon. Add the ground almonds, the rest of the butter, double cream, seasoning and the grated Gruyère. Mix well.

Take a cannelloni sheet and lay some of the mixture on it, roll it up and tuck in the ends. Continue for all the sheets. Butter a large, shallow ovenproof dish and lay the cannelloni rolls in it. Preheat oven to 300F/150C/gas mark 2.

Pour the single cream over the cannelloni, then sprinkle the grated Parmesan over the top. Put the dish in the oven to heat through and for the cheese to melt, about 20 minutes. Serve piping hot.

Sprouting Seeds
The Greatest Nutritional Value in the Smallest Particle

Spring is sooner recognised by plants than by men, a Chinese proverb claims, but inevitably the energy of spring becomes vividly apparent. It is a significant reminder of the fact that we too easily forget the nutritional value of the sprouting seed: 'The force that through the green fuse drives the flower' can be tipped into the salad bowl.

Bean and grain sprouts have been eaten in the East for five thousand years. In the winter months they were a source of vitamin C when no green vegetables were available. In 1768, Captain Cook used them on a three-year voyage as an antidote to scurvy, using a recipe for a drink made with sprouting barley seeds. That voyage was free of scurvy, at a time when it was common to lose half the crew from the disease. The government was not impressed, however, and used a far more expensive lemon cure for the affliction.

A seed is a dormant embryo waiting to be activated by warmth and water which will work on the seed's starch. Once the sprout begins to grow it contains vitamin C (ascorbic acid is always concentrated in rapidly growing tissue) and other vitamins and minerals appear soon after. Sprouts after five or six days' germination also contain vitamins from the B complex group, including B12 and vitamins E, G, K and U. Some vegetarians and health enthusiasts have made extravagant claims on the spectacular nutritional value of the sprouting seed: Harold McGee rather prosaically summarises the recent research done as proving the sprout has a nutritional value somewhere between the dry seed and the complete green vegetable.

Sprouting seeds are a major addition to the salad both in taste and texture. All sprouting seeds can also be stir-fried without losing their food value. Both grains and legumes can be sprouted. McGee comments that with legumes the sprouts do not produce flatulence as their dried selves would do when cooked. When purchasing seeds, buy the ones intended for sprouting, as seeds for planting may well have been treated with fungicides or insecticides. Always sprout whole seeds; do not attempt split peas or cracked wheat.

Various sprouting utensils are on sale in health and wholefood shops; they are basically perforated trays which drain to a bowl beneath. But a jar with a muslin or nylon net top held on by an elastic band will do the job as well. The seeds need to be rinsed twice a day with cold water. All the water is then drained away. You must rinse thoroughly: any water left at the bottom of the jar will pong, and the seeds will start to go mouldy. Seeds will sprout in the dark or light, but they will not like either a too cold temperature or direct sunlight. The ideal temperature for germination is 55–70F/13–21C. Once the seeds are sprouted you can keep them in the refrigerator in a covered container for a week. My favourite seed for sprouting is alfalfa, as I am fond of the flavour and the rather candy-floss texture in sandwiches. Experiment with others. Here is my list:

Alfalfa: has a higher protein content than beef or milk, has all the obscure vitamins like B12 plus K and U. It is this seed in particular which gave the 'miracle food' reputation to sprouting seeds. The Arabs called it 'Father of all Foods' and fed their horses on it. It is ready in about five days and needs only a daily rinse.

Aduki beans: this bean is popular in the East and was introduced into the West as an important component of the macrobiotic diet. Like alfalfa seed, it is high in protein, vitamins and minerals. When sprouted the flavour is slightly nutty.

Barley: it sprouts easily and is very high in vitamin C and the B complex group. Sprouts are eaten after three or four days.

Fenugreek: a good spicy flavour. Leave for five to six days when the sprouts are over an inch long. A medicinal herb. If cooked for too long in the stir-fry it will grow bitter.

Lentil: excellent in flavour and nutrition. Will be ready after five days.

Mung beans: these are the bean sprouts used in Chinese cooking. They will be ready in four days. Soak them first in plenty of water for twelve hours until the husks split. Then follow the jam-jar method. When ready, swill them around in plenty of cold water, so that the husks are removed. Excellent flavour of fresh garden peas.

Soya bean: being a complete protein, the bean has outstanding nutritional value. But it will need rinsing four or five times a day. It helps to soak them first like the mung above. They easily go mouldy when sprouting: some people believe it helps to rinse in tepid water. They will be ready to eat in three or four days. They are always eaten cooked, either steamed or stir-fried, as when raw the protein is made indigestible by the trypsin inhibitor which, in some degree, is in all legumes.

Wheat: these have a delicious flavour of maize and are easy to sprout. Eat them when they are about ½ inch/1 cm long.

Finally, to make Captain Cook's drink for healthy sailors you will need about 1 lb/450 g of barley sprouts, 2 pints/1.1 litres of boiling water and a tablespoon of honey. Place the sprouts, the honey and ½ pint/ 275 ml of water in a blender and liquidise to a mush. Add the rest of the water and leave for several hours. Strain before drinking. It can be reheated gently, but do not boil as it will destroy the vitamin C. Or add the juice from a couple of lemons, and it will make an excellent summer drink.

Sprouting Salad

Excellent for slimming, this salad has complementary protein and is more substantial than it seems.

I CLOVE GARLIC, CRUSHED

2 TABLESPOONS OLIVE OIL

I TEASPOON LEMON OR LIME JUICE

PINCH OF SEA SALT AND FRESHLY GROUND BLACK PEPPER

I SMALL ONION, FINELY SLICED

2 OZ/50 G SHELLED PISTACHIO NUTS

HANDFUL EACH OF ROCKET AND DANDELION LEAVES, OR A SMALL COS
   LETTUCE

4 OZ/120 G ALFALFA SPROUTS

4 OZ/120 G MUNG BEAN SPROUTS

Method

In a large bowl make a dressing with the garlic, oil, juice and seasoning and let the sliced onion soften in it for 1 hour. Add the nuts, leave for ½ hour. Add the sprouts and leaves and toss thoroughly.

STORES

At the beginning of 1983 I moved house three times; this is one article I wrote at that time of chaos.

It is somewhat weird for a cookery writer to be without a kitchen for any length of time, but such is my present state. At first I used other people's kitchens, but found strange anomalies that drove out all desire to cook. No sharp knives or pepper mill, spices so old and hard they could have been used as moth balls, herbs like sawdust and not a drop of virgin olive oil to be seen.

So I began carrying a kitchen survival kit in a grip on the back seat of the car: garlic presser, two sharp knives, a chopping board, a jar of Dijon mustard, paprika, sesame salt and a piece of ginger root.

I have now come to rest in a house, but there is still no kitchen, nor will there be for another month. I have two electric rings, but no oven or gas hob. All the electric gadgets have been left behind: no blenders or Magimix, no grinders or whisk. The crockery is stacked on the concrete floor. There is no refrigerator and the central heating turns the milk sour in a day.

There is one table which I found in bits in the yard and hammered together again. It holds a large jar of breakfast muesli and a range of products from Sunwheel Foods, like sesame oil, shoyu, red umeboshi vinegar (a Japanese product made from fermented plums), nori (a seaweed condiment of such deliciousness that a little on a piece of toast would make a high-class lunch – except, of course, I have no grill and so cannot make toast).

Also on the table are storage jars of coffee, flageolet beans and besan flour. This flour is made from chick peas and can be bought in all Indian shops. It is a smooth yellow flour, marvellous for a little thickening of soups and stews as it has a good flavour and low starch content. Small rissoles or croquettes rolled in this flour never taste floury or too heavy.

I have two saucepans, a wok, a frying pan and a wooden spoon. Being reduced to such simple utensils is a salutary exercise and one I am enjoying. For there are new challenges. When preparing a meal for friends, I must consider whether to use the ancient one-pot method or the wok and stir-fry. With just two rings, one ring takes the rice or pasta while the other deals with whatever method of cooking the vegetables I have chosen. Meals tend to be basic for what one is eschewing are all the finer points of cooking like the sauce which complements some poached delicacy.

I have been converted to the one-pot method out of necessity and it is interesting to discover the variations. Its tradition must be almost as old as cooking by fire itself. Some of the dishes, like boiled beef and carrots, are still firm favourites. If you do not have to cook the meat, long slow cooking is not essential, though any stew with dried beans should have a good two hours' simmering.

A spiced vegetable stew will stand or fall by the spices and flavourings you use. Always start by frying the chopped vegetables in a good olive oil and ground spices, turning and slightly searing the pieces. Then add the water or stock. Always finish the cooking by tasting the juices and then adding other flavours until you have achieved something which delights the palate and warms the tum.

SPICED VEGETABLE STEW

4 GREEN PEPPERS
4 LARGE ONIONS
3 LARGE POTATOES
3 TABLESPOONS BESAN OR STRONG WHITE BREAD FLOUR
3 TABLESPOONS OLIVE OIL
I TEASPOON EACH OF GROUND CUMIN AND CORIANDER
I GREEN CHILLI (OPTIONAL)
I LARGE CAULIFLOWER
2 TABLESPOONS GREEN PEPPERCORNS
I TABLESPOON OF SHOYU OR NATURAL FERMENTED SOY SAUCE
SEA SALT AND FRESHLY GROUND BLACK PEPPER

METHOD

Coarsely chop the peppers, onions and potatoes and toss them in the flour. In a large saucepan heat the olive oil. Add the cumin and coriander. Sauté the pieces of vegetable in the oil, moving them around so that they do not stick. Add the deseeded chopped green chilli, if you want the stew to be extra hot. Pour in enough water to cover all the vegetables and let them simmer until the potatoes are just done. Break up the cauliflower into sprigs, add them and simmer for another 4 or 5 minutes. Finally add the green peppercorns and soy sauce. Stir and taste for flavour.

SPINACH CROQUETTES

2 LB/1 KG SPINACH
1 EGG
2 TABLESPOONS BESAN FLOUR OR STRONG WHITE BREAD FLOUR
2 OZ/50 G PARMESAN CHEESE, GRATED
2 OZ/50 G SAGE DERBY
FRESH BREADCRUMBS
OLIVE OIL FOR FRYING

METHOD

Wash the spinach, chop it coarsely, let it drain and then shake it as dry as possible. Put it into a saucepan with the lid firmly on over a low heat and let it cook in its own juice – about 5 minutes. Take the lid away, stir and let the juice evaporate. Turn the spinach out into a bowl and chop it into smaller pieces with the edge of a wooden spoon. After it has cooled, add the egg, flour and cheeses. Season with a little salt and pepper. Take a spoonful of the mixture, roll in breadcrumbs and then fry in hot olive oil.

POTATO LATKES

1 LB/450 G POTATOES
2 LARGE ONIONS
2 BEATEN EGGS
2 TABLESPOONS FINE MATZO MEAL
1/2 TEASPOON BAKING POWDER
SEA SALT AND FRESHLY GROUND BLACK PEPPER
SUNFLOWER OIL FOR FRYING

METHOD

Peel and grate the potatoes into a bowl, grate the onions and mix them into the potatoes. Add the eggs, matzo meal, baking powder and seasoning. Heat some sunflower oil in a pan and drop spoonfuls of the mixture into the oil. Fry until golden brown on both sides.

STORES WHEN SNOWBOUND

For two winters running I was snowed in for a few days. At the time I feel equivocal about this. One part of me enjoys the experience of being cut off from the rest of the world (even the Telecom lines crackled ominously as if tapped or about to snap), finding a challenge in looking at the food and wine stores and assessing how long they will last. (My anxiety about wine stocks is hysterical.)

The point about stores is that the foods you need most for health and well-being, like fresh vegetables and fruit, do not keep and a diet of just carbohydrates is an unexciting prospect. That is the lowering aspect of the challenge. For want of electricity I have no deep freeze, so the abundance of summer fruit and vegetables has to be eaten or given away. Hence, when the snow came, the small Calor gas refrigerator contained nothing but a carton of red grape juice, some soya milk, a packet of miso and several pounds of unsalted butter. Try making a meal out of that.

As usual the jars of pulses came into their own. Home-made baked beans, lentil soup and green flageolets are delicious once a week but not all on the same day. Root vegetables can also be cooked far more imaginatively (see the recipes for turnips on p. 275-6) but several of them eaten twice a day is depressing. There was no cabbage, no spring greens and no salad whatsoever. The nearest shop was a three-mile walk through the snow and unlikely to have any vegetables except in packets or tins.

The one food that I missed more than anything was the lemon. The sharpness of its juice and the aroma of its oil in the zest seemed like the most desirable perfume. I could have done with a Seville orange instead, and either fruit would have turned any of those rather stodgy vegetables into a delectable dish.

STUFFING VEGETABLES

'Life is too short to stuff a mushroom,' Shirley Conran once said. But I disagree. Mushrooms and much else can be stuffed as fast as you can skim *Lace*. If you allow five minutes to make the stuffing, another five for filling six or eight large mushrooms and ten minutes for baking them in a hot oven, you have done a splendid first course in twenty minutes and Superwoman has egg on her face.

Any of the stuffings below can be used for mushrooms and the recipe is child's play. Take out the stalk, fill with the stuffing, place on a baking sheet and cook in an oven at 400F/200C/gas mark 6 for ten minutes. Do not overcook the mushrooms so that they are flabby. Let them have a little crispness and still retain some of their raw flavour.

Ricotta cheese is invaluable for stuffing vegetables. It is much used in Italian cooking, and its smooth creamy texture amalgamates well with vegetable purées and fresh herbs. It is especially useful for stuffing leaves.

We are used to dolmades, those little parcels made from vine leaves. But other leaves can be used – cabbage, lettuce, spinach, Swiss chard and Chinese leaf. Some can be eaten raw and others have to be cooked. When cooking these little parcels, use either uncooked rice, breadcrumbs or both in the stuffing, to absorb the juices. A mixture of both is often best, for a balance has to be achieved between shape and flavour in your parcel.

Chinese leaf is one of the dullest of green vegetables unless stir-fried and tossed in black bean and chilli sauce – and then it is merely the excuse to have the sauce. But because it is bland it can take a spicy stuffing and stands up well in the parcel service, as stout as a good cabbage leaf. Spinach and Swiss chard are both more tender, and will not need as much cooking. Spinach if picked young can be used raw.

All the leaves need blanching first. Choose undamaged leaves and lay them in a bowl, pour boiling water over them and leave them for a few minutes. Take them out and drain them by hanging them over the side of a colander. Sometimes the ragged edges of lettuce and spinach leaves get too sodden for use, so simply tidy the leaf by cutting the ragged edges away. Also remove any crisp part of the stalk that is not pliable. The leaf must roll without bursting. The first two recipes are for a cold first course, though the spinach can also be baked for ten minutes and eaten hot or warm. Stuffing quantities given are for about ten leaf rolls.

STUFFED LETTUCE ROLL

I ICEBERG LETTUCE (ALLOW 2 LEAVES FOR EACH PERSON)
FLESH FROM I AVOCADO
6 OZ/170 G RICOTTA CHEESE
2 OZ/55 G CELERY, FINELY CHOPPED
2 CLOVES GARLIC, CRUSHED
HANDFUL OF CHOPPED PARSLEY
SEA SALT AND FRESHLY GROUND BLACK PEPPER

METHOD

Blanch the lettuce leaves, drain them and tidy them up. Make the stuffing by mashing the avocado flesh into a purée and adding the rest of the ingredients. Put a generous tablespoon of the stuffing in the first quarter of the lettuce leaf at the stem end and wrap the leaf up, tucking in the sides as you go. Roll in more finely chopped parsley and arrange on a serving dish.

STUFFED SPINACH ROLLS

SPINACH (ALLOW 2 LEAVES, PICKED YOUNG, FOR EACH PERSON)
6 OZ/170 G RICOTTA CHEESE
2 SHALLOTS, FINELY CHOPPED
2 CLOVES GARLIC, CRUSHED
2 TABLESPOONS GREEK YOGHURT
2 TABLESPOONS BREADCRUMBS
HANDFUL OF CHOPPED PARSLEY
SEA SALT AND FRESHLY GROUND BLACK PEPPER
I TABLESPOON GROUND WALNUTS

METHOD

Blanch the spinach leaves and drain them. Make the stuffing by mixing everything together. Taste for seasoning. Cut away any stalk which is not pliable. Place a generous tablespoon of the stuffing almost at the end of the leaf and roll, tucking in the ends as you go. Arrange on a serving dish and sprinkle with the ground walnuts.

STUFFED CHINESE LEAF

CHINESE LEAVES (ALLOW 2 LEAVES FOR EACH PERSON)
1 OZ/25 G BUTTER
1 MEDIUM ONION, SLICED
4 OZ/115 G MUSHROOMS, CHOPPED
5 OZ/140 G SPINACH, CHOPPED
½ TEASPOON SALT
FRESHLY GROUND BLACK PEPPER
1 TABLESPOON SESAME AND PEANUT PASTE
1½ TABLESPOONS BREADCRUMBS
2 TABLESPOONS UNCOOKED PATNA RICE

METHOD

Look for a Chinese leaf which has not had its top shorn to disguise its age. Cut the leaves from the base. Blanch them by pouring boiling water on the ends and then slowly submerging the whole leaf. Leave the thick ends in for at least 5 minutes. Drain them.

Make the stuffing; melt the butter in a saucepan, add the sliced onion, the mushrooms, the chopped spinach, the salt and pepper. Let it simmer for 10 minutes. Pour contents into a blender, add the sesame and peanut paste and the breadcrumbs. Blend to a thick purée. Stir in the Patna rice. Take each leaf and cut the base of the white stalk away in a deep V shape (all the stem that is, which will not bend), leaving the green leaf either side. Turn the leaf upside down, place stuffing at the end of the leaf and roll it in the above manner. Place in a buttered oven dish, dot with a little more butter and bake in a preheated oven at 400F/200C/gas mark 6 for 25 minutes.

The stuffing you make reflects your own personal taste. This one has a suspicion of nuttiness, but is not overpowering. The spinach and mushroom flavours are still dominant.

TABBOULEH
Tabbouleh • Tabbouleh and Lentil Salad

TAHINI
Spiced Tahini Sauce

TARRAGON
Tarragon and Lemon Sauce

TOFU – MIRACLE FOOD

TOMATOES
Chilled Tomato and Red Pepper Soup • Tomato, Caper and Mozzarella
Salad

TRUFFLES
The Black Treasure of Valencia

TURNIPS
Turnips with Ginger • Turnips with Walnuts • Turnips with Garlic and
Parsley

TABBOULEH

Tabbouleh is the name of the cold salad made from the grain, bulgar wheat, or cracked wheat.

TABBOULEH

> 5 OZ/125 G BULGAR WHEAT
> 1 GENEROUS BUNCH EACH OF PARSLEY AND MINT
> 1 BUNCH OF SPRING ONIONS
> 3 FL OZ/75 ML OLIVE OIL
> JUICE FROM 1 LEMON
> 2 OR 3 COARSELY CHOPPED TOMATOES
> SEA SALT AND FRESHLY GROUND BLACK PEPPER
> 1 LETTUCE HEART

METHOD

Pour the wheat into a bowl and cover by a good inch with cold water. Leave for 2 hours or more until it has soaked up all the water. Place in a sieve and squeeze it down to get rid of excess water. Chop the parsley, mint and onions as fine as you can, put the bulgar wheat into a large bowl, stir in the herbs, oil, lemon juice and tomatoes. Taste and season.

To serve, have the heart of a good lettuce and arrange the leaves in a circle on a large platter. Pile the tabbouleh in the centre.

Tabbouleh and Lentil Salad

This is a delicious summer salad which is also highly nutritious as the proteins complement each other. Use any freshly chopped herbs, such as chives and basil, though the mint is traditional.

6 OZ/170 G BULGAR WHEAT
6 OZ/170 G BROWN LENTILS
6 OZ/170 G COOKED PEAS
JUICE AND ZEST FROM 2 LEMONS
5 FL OZ/150 ML OLIVE OIL
2 TABLESPOONS TOASTED SESAME OIL (AVAILABLE FROM CHINESE STORES)
3 CLOVES GARLIC, CRUSHED
1 BUNCH SPRING ONIONS, FINELY CHOPPED
GENEROUS HANDFUL OF FRESH MINT, FINELY CHOPPED
GENEROUS HANDFUL OF FRESH PARSLEY, FINELY CHOPPED
SEA SALT AND FRESHLY GROUND BLACK PEPPER

Method

Soak the bulgar in cold water for 20 minutes. Then place it in a colander or sieve and press out all the water. Meanwhile, cook the lentils in plenty of boiling water for 10 minutes, strain and reserve. Add the lentils and the peas to the soaked bulgar, with the rest of the ingredients.

Mix thoroughly, and leave for 2 hours to soak up all the flavours. It may need more lemon.

TAHINI

 Tahini is a paste made out of sesame seeds, ubiquitous all over the Middle East. It is, of course, highly nutritious, but it is also wonderfully delicious and has a hundred uses as a sauce and flavouring. Sometimes recipes tell you to add lemon juice – do not worry that the effect is first of all to turn the tahini into a thick gunge; continue with either the lemon juice or the water and it will turn into a creamy sauce. The recipe below is for a sauce from Lebanon to serve with fish or with crudités.

SPICED TAHINI SAUCE

3 CLOVES GARLIC, CHOPPED
2 RED CHILLIES, BROKEN UP
GENEROUS HANDFUL OF PARSLEY
GENEROUS HANDFUL OF MINT
ZEST AND JUICE FROM 2 LEMONS
6 FL OZ/170 ML TAHINI
WATER
SEA SALT AND FRESHLY GROUND BLACK PEPPER

METHOD

Place the garlic, chillies, herbs, lemon zest and juice in a food processor. Blend to a green gunge, add the tahini, mix thoroughly, then add enough water to make a smooth sauce. Add the seasoning to taste.

Tarragon

Tarragon is the herb we mostly associate with fish. In the summer when the green shoots of tarragon appear on the plant immediately prior to flowering it is a good thing to pluck them and place in a bottle of white wine vinegar, two or three shoots to half a pint/275 ml, leave for a week and then take them out and you will have a strong tarragon vinegar to flavour dishes and sauces. The sauce below, however, uses the actual herb finely chopped, and is delicious with white fish or smoked haddock.

Tarragon and Lemon Sauce

1 OZ/25 G BUTTER
1 TABLESPOON PLAIN FLOUR
ZEST AND JUICE FROM 1 LEMON
½ PINT/275 ML STRONG VEGETABLE STOCK
3 TABLESPOONS FINELY CHOPPED TARRAGON
PINCH OF SEA SALT
PLENTY OF FRESHLY GROUND BLACK PEPPER

Method

Melt the butter, add the flour and make a roux, cook for second or two then add the zest, lemon juice and stock, stirring to make a smooth sauce. Add the tarragon and cook over a low heat for 2 or 3 minutes. Add the seasoning, if the sauce needs it.

TOFU – MIRACLE FOOD

Tofu is soya bean curd. There are now many brands on sale, though in flavour there is little difference. Its protein value is a high as chicken, and as it is rich in lysine, an essential amino acid which most grains lack, it acts as a complementary protein. (Baked beans and wholemeal toast is the classic example of this interaction between two foods which boosts the protein of each.)

Soya complements grains in particular, so stir-fried tofu and vegetables with a grain like rice, millet, buckwheat or couscous is a sound meal, richer than it would seem. A tofu mixture in a sandwich or pitta bread is a perfect combination.

High-protein foods are often also high in saturated fat and cholesterol, but tofu is very low. It is also a fine food for babies and young children as it is an excellent source of calcium. Because of its bland taste, it can be flavoured delicately or strongly.

Tofu is like a blank sheet of paper on which you write – though when you begin cooking with it, you might think you only have invisible ink. For tofu is notoriously reluctant to soak up flavours, unless you use it as a pudding and mash it up for use like fromage frais or quark.

A few years ago, you could only obtain here two kinds of tofu: vacuum-packed packets of Morinaga silken tofu from Japan, which could be stored outside the refrigerator; or the home-made tofu bought at Chinese stores. The Morinaga is very soft and, for stir-frying, must be drained and left for a day. But it can be used at once for puddings, when you need a smooth, thick sauce. Both can still be easily purchased.

But there are now many more tofus in the cool stores of every wholefood shop. Another fairly soft tofu from Japan is made by Kikkoman, who also make high-class soy sauce. Cauldron Foods now make a smoked tofu which is particularly good if used as part of a first course or as a stir-fry ingredient.

The classic Eastern method with tofu is to drain it, cube it and then marinate in soy sauce with grated ginger root and chopped spring onion. But other flavourings can be used as a dipping sauce, a combination of miso and tahini, or wasabi (Japanese horseradish) and tomato, or chilli and onion. Squares of tofu in a kebab can also be pleasant, mixed with peppers, mushrooms and onion, placed for a few minutes under a hot grill and then eaten with a peanut or sesame sauce. Before cooking the tofu, do marinate it in a mixture which is fairly pungent if you want it to taste of anything. Lightly score the cubes diagonally and make sure the marinade soaks in.

Lime juice with zest and grated ginger is good but a tandoori paste will give you a fiery kebab which goes well with peppers and mushrooms. You can, with the scoring method, also rub dry ingredients into the tofu, like spices and herbs or various mixtures of powdered paprika, ginger and garam masala.

If the tofu cubes are going to be lightly fried, then they can be rolled in breadcrumbs which themselves can be flavoured. Or the tofu can be dipped into a batter and that, of course, can be flavoured as well. We are too used to batter as a bland covering to a tasty food; in the case of tofu, you reverse the process.

Perhaps tofu is most easily used as an ingredient in puddings. It can be used in cheesecake and ice cream, or blended with soft fruits and used as a fool, though in all cases I would use equal quantities of tofu to curd cheese, cream or smetana. This cuts down the saturated fat intake.

Tofu has a clean and elegant aspect and I particularly like using smoked tofu as part of a first course. Sliced thinly and used with sliced avocado and a fruit, like mango or pawpaw, fanned out over leaves with a lime vinaigrette, it is most refreshing.

Because smoked tofu in particular can be cut and shaped, it can be used in layers, with purées or moulds. Recently, I cooked small ramekins of fresh peas and unmoulded them on to a circle of smoked tofu, then garnished the plates with a few chive stalks. Another time, I sandwiched small circles of tofu with a beetroot jelly and a carrot purée so it was like individual layered cakes and ringed it around with a green herb sauce.

Once you start cooking with tofu, new ideas will occur to you. The definitive book on the subject has long been *The Book of Tofu* by William Shurtleff and Akiko Aoyagi (Autumn Press). But Leah Leneman's *The International Tofu Cooker Book* (Routledge & Kegan Paul) is also full of recipe ideas.

TOMATOES

 The problem for many years has been how to find a well-flavoured tomato. The small cherry-sized fruits often have more flavour and far higher acidity. Growing your own is not always the answer, for many varieties sold to gardeners turn out to be bland or insipid. Is it due completely to climate? When living in the Mediterranean I grew tomatoes as full of flavour as the ones I could buy in the market.

When plenty of home-grown tomatoes are around, it is time to make the simplest soup and one of the most exquisite there is. I cannot understand recipes that tell you to peel and deseed the tomato. Does anyone ever deseed a tomato? And I am certain that much of the flavour of the tomato lies in the skin and green stalk.

Place 2 lb/900 g of tomatoes in the skins and with their stalks in a saucepan, add a pinch of salt, put the lid firmly on, place over a low flame and forget about it for 10 minutes. The tomatoes will cook in their own juices. To help them and to stop the risk of them burning or sticking to the pan, you can puncture the tomatoes or cut them into quarters, but I have never found it necessary. Let the tomatoes cook, then pop them into a blender and liquidise; sieve them, discard the debris.

What you now have is a tomato soup that can be reheated and eaten with chopped basil or pesto. But the soup is even better chilled and enjoyed just as it is.

This easily made purée is also a basic tomato sauce which can be used on other vegetables (see chilled marrow soup, p. 140-1.)

Adding red peppers, stock and red wine to the mixture gives a little kick to the flavour and darkens the colour.

CHILLED TOMATO AND RED PEPPER SOUP (SERVES FOUR)

2 LB/900 G TOMATOES
2 RED PEPPERS
½ PINT/280 ML VEGETABLE STOCK
½ PINT/280 ML RED WINE
SEA SALT AND FRESHLY GROUND BLACK PEPPER
A FEW BASIL LEAVES

METHOD

Chop the tomatoes, slice and deseed the pepper, put them into a pan with the stock, red wine and seasoning, bring to the boil and simmer for 10 minutes. Leave to cool, then pour into a blender and liquidise. Place in a sieve and strain the soup. Throw away the seeds and skin. Chill in a refrigerator for 1 hour. Chop the basil leaves and float them on the soup as garnish.

TOMATO, CAPER AND MOZZARELLA SALAD

A tomato and mozzarella salad is a simple and classic Italian dish which, I think, can be greatly sharpened by the addition of anchovies or capers.

1 LB/450 G SMALL TOMATOES, SLICED
1 TABLESPOON CAPERS
6 OZ/170 G PACKET FRESH MOZZARELLA CHEESE
5–6 LARGE BASIL LEAVES, SHREDDED
FRESHLY GROUND BLACK PEPPER
2–3 TABLESPOONS OLIVE OIL

METHOD

Arrange the slices of tomato over a large platter. Slice the mozzarella thinly and insert the slices between the tomatoes, and sprinkle the capers over them.

Scatter the basil leaves over the top. Give the dish several grinds with the black pepper mill, then dress with the oil just before serving.

TRUFFLES
THE BLACK TREASURE OF VALENCIA

Morella is a walled medieval town in the northernmost part of Valencia. It was an important fortress in the Peninsular War, then one of the last towns to be subjugated by Franco and renowned again recently for harvesting the black truffle.

Fifteen years ago, Morellanos, if they thought of truffles at all, associated them with chocolate. But they observed a Catalan group who arrived one day in a van. Inside the van were some bicycles and on each bicycle there was a box which contained a dog.

The Catalans said they were hunters and carrying their guns, accompanied by their dogs, they disappeared into the forests of scrub oak which cover the mountains and hills around Morella. In the evening, the Catalans returned and vanished into the rooms of their hotel.

The Morellanos were somewhat puzzled by these hunters who brought back no kill. They were bewildered further by the incredible aromas emanating from the Catalans' rooms. Such enigmatic aromas within the narrow cobbled streets of Morella were hard to pin down, but the lush perfumes deepened day by day.

Eventually the smells drove out the truth from the Catalans and they confessed that their game thrived a foot underground among the roots of the evergreen oak. In the heated discussion which followed a compromise was achieved with the Catalans selling the Morellanos their dogs. The price was so steep it was never disclosed.

Shrewdly the Catalans still run the Spanish truffle market, buying the Morellanos' harvest and selling it again. After a day's travel a Morella truffle can easily become Gallic and end up in a Périgord market, just like a Hungarian goose liver, some say.

There is a mystique about the truffle which has made it rare and valuable. Its flavour is elusive and the group of food writers who inspected the Morella truffles were first given a sopa Morellana, a game soup with choux pasta pieces (bunuelos), where the truffle deepened the gamy flavour of the stock, and then a thick Spanish omelette which had chunks of truffle in it like a cake stuffed with dried fruit. The texture, I found, was slightly crisp and woody, the flavour milder than an oyster mushroom and nowhere near as delicious as a slice of puffball fried in butter. The following day, the Morellanos cooked a buffet spread in our honour and went to town boning and stuffing lambs, pigs, chickens and rabbits and then boiling them to dingy rags. It was a sad and flavourless feast.

I am reserving judgement on the Morella truffle for I returned with three. One I have pickled in brandy at their suggestion. A little brandy is then used in the cooking which carries the flavour of the truffle. The second truffle I have buried in a jar of rice. The third truffle is at the centre of a bowl of free-range eggs. Let us see if the truffle dissipates its fragrance as the myth has always claimed. For the Morella truffles are far from cheap; depending upon supply and the way the market goes they cost from 10,000 pesetas per kilo to 50,000 (£50–£250). Yet in the boqueia in Barcelona they are bought eagerly by your Spanish housewife whenever she is lucky enough to find them.

But then a Spaniard's attention to the quality of food might astonish a British housewife. A premium is paid for quality and freshness. Take fish, and how it is caught. Fish caught on a line costs two-thirds more than fish caught in a trawl net, for fish in a net, they say, becomes drowned and waterlogged. Or take the pata negra de Salamanca or jabugo, which is a leg of cured ham. Free-range pigs have longer legs and cost eight times as much as a pig bred on a farm.

As factory farming is unknown in Spain (the farm pigs have a field to themselves) the distinction becomes even more discriminating. Whether a pig has been on a diet of acorns and chestnuts is another decisive factor, for the Spaniards say the fragrance is there within the meat after it had been cured for a year. These salted pressed hams are also made out of goat and, more surprisingly, bull. Their hefty thighs are sliced with reverence, the carmine-coloured scraps smelt like a cigar, then rolled on the tongue.

'It is the difference between a Mercedes and a Fiat,' said Angelo, qualifying the free-range or farm pig. He has his own restaurant with his wife Nina (a self-taught but brilliant cook) at Grao-Castellon, where the cooking strives to take all the good hearty peasant dishes and, by adapting them slightly, turn them expertly into a variation of nouvelle cuisine.

Some dishes strike me as ill-conceived. For example, small squares of veal (the veal is again free-range and is not fed on a liquid milk diet to induce white meat) in a cabrales sauce (cabrales is a blue mountain cheese from Santander) seemed unnecessary, for cheese and slices of meat are a rich and unnatural fusion.

But when the cooking stuck closely to the original Spanish tradition it was judiciously refined. A revuelto de cigalas, scrambled eggs cooked with scampi and tomato in a bain-marie, tasted intensely of the sea because the cigalas were freshly caught. While the merluza pil-pil was shown to us at the table.

This method is unique to Spain and is basic to Basque cuisine. The sauce is a marriage of olive oil, garlic and the gelatine from the hake skin. The sauce can only work with a fish, or a part of the fish with a high gelatine content (the cheeks of the hake – kokotxas – are often used). They are laid skinside down in a tian, or earthenware dish, which has a little oil and freshly puréed garlic in it. The dish is placed over a flame and cooked slightly, then taken off the flame and while still warm the dish is gently turned and shaken, until the sauce suddenly emulsifies.

It is a gentle fusion of temperature and movement, often as temperamental as mayonnaise. Whatever my own personal feeling, Nina and Angelo prove, nevertheless, that the new Spanish cooking can travel the world and be respected as both distinct and distinguished.

Turnips

The French rightly consider navets a vegetable distinguished enough to have trouble and imagination spent upon them. We tend to dismiss the young spring turnips and just buy the large winter ones, treating them in the usual cursory manner of parboiling and roasting or else just mashing them boiled, when they become a tasteless watery slush. The larger turnips have a bit part to play in winter soups and stews, but it is the young spring turnips we need for the recipes below.

Turnips with Ginger

2 LB/910 G TURNIPS
2 OZ/55 G BUTTER
2 OZ/55 G GRATED GINGER ROOT
JUICE AND ZEST OF 1 LEMON
1 TABLESPOON HONEY
SEA SALT AND FRESHLY GROUND BLACK PEPPER

Method

Trim and halve the turnips, steam or boil them in a little salted water for 4 to 5 minutes. Drain them well, melt the butter in a pan, add the grated ginger root and fry for 1 or 2 minutes, then add the rest of the ingredients. Place the turnips in the sauce and turn them over, letting them cook for a few more minutes.

TURNIPS WITH WALNUTS

2 LB/910 G TURNIPS
3 TABLESPOONS WALNUT OIL
2 OZ/55 G BROKEN WALNUTS
JUICE AND ZEST OF 1 SEVILLE ORANGE
SEA SALT AND FRESHLY GROUND BLACK PEPPER
2 TABLESPOONS PARMESAN CHEESE, FRESHLY GRATED

METHOD

Trim and halve the turnips and cook as above. Cook the walnuts in the oil for a few minutes, add the zest and orange juice, the well-drained turnips and the seasoning. Cook for a few moments, turning them over in the oil, then sprinkle them with the Parmesan and place under a hot grill for a moment or two.

The small purple-shaded turnips are delicious and worth taking more trouble with than just boiling.

TURNIPS WITH GARLIC AND PARSLEY

1½ LB/675 G SMALL TURNIPS
1 HEAD OF GARLIC
3 TABLESPOONS BREADCRUMBS
3 TABLESPOONS OLIVE OIL
GENEROUS HANDFUL OF PARSLEY, FINELY CHOPPED

METHOD

Trim and halve the turnips, boil in a little salted water for 3 minutes, then drain. Slice the cloves of garlic, and fry with the turnips until both have just turned golden brown. Mix the breadcrumbs and parsley together, sprinkle over the top and place the pan under a hot grill so that the surface browns a little.

VEGETABLES

New Vegetables Stir-Fried Paksoi • Steamed Garter Beans

A VEGETARIAN IN THE FAMILY

VEGETABLES
NEW VEGETABLES

It seems that we have all heard of aubergines, peppers and courgettes. But only three-quarters of us recognise fennel, artichokes and Chinese cabbage and only half of us have seen celeriac and salsify referred to, and we are not sure how to pronounce their names. Well, I never know how to pronounce anything and my restaurant French is Churchillian with a touch of Charles Boyer. So I know exactly how a veg like salsify can trip you up, for I once asked for a tin of satisfy. It is the artist's impression of words – if you say them with enough confidence, the other person thinks they are mispronouncing.

I give this advice because I cannot endure the thought of all us cooks feeling threatened by strange vegetables with awkward names. Only half us have heard of kohlrabi and I bet most of us think it is something to do with eye make-up. Surprisingly, mange-tout is the least known of all, when it is the pride of nouvelle cuisine and can also crop up in the Chinese take-away.

But I declare it is not our fault. What about Birds Eye freezing the mange-tout then? They are an easy crop to grow and far more tasty than that viridian-dyed sugar drop which has been the frozen food best-seller for the last decade. What about a dish of smoked aubergine, puréed and flavoured with garlic, coriander and cumin, as one of Marks & Spencer's new lines? Then, indeed, I imagine, frozen salsify would be a most satisfying vegetable to have in the freezer, while celeriac is infinitely nicer than celery. The whole root can be eaten, while with a bunch of celery most of the fibrous stalks are only good for stock, and even then the bits that are left can still lasso your teeth.

But the British have a passion for celery. It comprises one-quarter of the whole amount of vegetables consumed, excluding potatoes.

Our consumption of potatoes has fallen since 1975, while that of other root vegetables has increased slightly. All the frozen vegetables continue to sell well, which is why there is room for packaging the new ones.

More of us are now aware that fresh vegetables are good for us and a source of dietary fibre, the best source, and we are trying to eat more. We also, quite rightly, have worries about the processing of food and how it destroys necessary vitamins. These statistics come from a report by the KMS partnership for Bonduelle, who want to promote the more obscure vegetables in Britain but have found up to now the market sluggish and wary.

A few years ago an enterprising director of the Central Bureau of Dutch Auctions travelled around the world in search of new vegetables. The bureau planned to grow them in Holland and export them to western Europe. He returned with nearly 100 different seeds, plants, vegetables and flowers, many of which are now being grown in Holland and a few have become major crops. Some are exported to the UK.

I was invited to Holland to see plants growing, to watch the auction and, most fascinating of all, to look at the work going on at the Research and Experiment Station, which takes seeds grown in the tropics and tests them to see how they can be adapted to life in the temperate zones.

Holland is a major producer of peppers, including a new black variety, radishes, both scarlet and white, kohlrabi, Chinese leaves and beef tomatoes. It now grows garter beans (they can be a metre long) which are moist and without strings or fibre, radicchio, red lettuce and chicory, types of curly and straight endive, purslane – a fleshy herb eaten cooked there, but which can also be eaten raw in salads – and Japanese and Indian mustard greens, which can also be eaten cooked or raw. One of these, paksoi, looks a little like Swiss chard, but the leaves are less frilled, though the stalks are as white and can be eaten separate from the leaf.

At the research station they are experimenting with growing mediums and are keen on something they referred to as rockwool. This is a stone fibre spun from lava which holds water and nutrients, rather like those green porous blocks you stick cut flowers into. So keen are they on rockwool that I began to see it everywhere, stuck on the ceilings, climbing up the walls, and inside the red wax masquerading as Edam. But the great advantage of this woolly lava is that it avoids diseases of the soil.

They have another department which addresses itself to the problems of pests and diseases. Instead of using chemical sprays to rid the plants of bugs, they were placing other bugs upon the leaves to act as parasites on the disease-bugs: using, in fact, nature's way of keeping the healthy status quo.

The paksoi, giant mushrooms, garter beans, red oakleaf lettuce and radicchio are available in small amounts in wholesale markets all over the United Kingdom. But retailers are nervous of buying them because they fear that customer interest would be low. So you will probably need to pester your greengrocer, market stallholder or supermarket to stock them. Garter beans, for example, have been sold in Nine Elms, but only in small quantities and most often only to restaurants.

If you want to stimulate the taste buds and widen the experience of flavours you only have to ask.

STIR-FRIED PAKSOI

Cut the thick white stalks away from the leaves and slice them in 2 inch/ 5 cm lengths. Put a little walnut oil into a wok, add a little grated ginger root and some chopped garlic. Stir-fry the cut stalks for a few minutes, then add the leaves and continue to stir-fry for another 2 minutes, or until they have reduced their bulk by a third. Pour one-third of a cup of shoyu sauce over the greens and the same amount of dry sherry, raise the heat, and stir for another ½ minute so that the greens steam in the liquid. Serve at once.

STEAMED GARTER BEANS

Trim the ends and coil them like cooked spaghetti into a steamer. Steam for about 5 minutes. They should be al dente. Beans are splendid eaten plain – it all depends what you are eating them with – but they are also especially good with chopped fresh herbs. The classic French way is to eat broad beans with summer savory, but beans can also be enjoyed with a little fresh tomato sauce with some chopped shallot in it. Garter beans are generally cut into shorter lengths before cooking but there seems little point in breeding a vegetable as idiosyncratic as this one and serving it up so that it resembles a French or bobby bean.

A VEGETARIAN IN THE FAMILY

 Buying food for the family today can seem like entering a minefield. So much now can go wrong with food; sadly, the old sacred trust between the customer and the farmer, through the retailer, has become confused and muddled.

Over the years the most persistent enquiry I have had from *Guardian* readers is what to do when one member of the family becomes a vegetarian. They usually say the father of the household insists on eating meat for at least one meal every day and looks upon a meal without meat with grave suspicion. The biggest growth of vegetarians is in the age group twelve to twenty, and more and more families must be faced with this problem.

The first step for the cook of the household is to think of this as not being a problem at all. Easy to say, I know, for it seems to entail the preparation of two separate meals. But first, a word about nutritional concerns. Banish all worries about whether the child is getting adequate nutrition from such a diet; a balanced vegetarian diet is possibly a lot healthier than one heavily biased towards meat. We tend to eat too much protein, certainly too much animal protein, almost twice as much as we actually need. As there is no organ in the body for storing excess protein, the surplus is expelled in the urine. Americans, it is said, pass the most expensive urine in the world.

Until recently, too, protein from animals was thought superior to that from plants – they were even, misleadingly, termed first- and second-class proteins. Such entrenched opinions were largely the result of ignorance. Meat, eggs, milk and fish were familiar protein sources, whereas the varied vegetable protein foods – legumes (especially soya beans), nuts, whole grains, root vegetables and seeds – were less common in Western diets. Nowadays stores offer a great range of these foods from all around the world. Protein is a part of every cell in our bodies. It is always in a state of flux, being broken down and remade in the ceaseless work of repairing and building tissues, regulating body chemistry, and defending against infection. In digestion, the protein foods we eat are broken down into the twenty or so amino acids of which they are made. Eight of these amino acids (nine in children) are not produced by living tissue, but must be obtained in the diet. 'Complete' protein foods have a correct balance of these essential dietary amino acids, egg yolks being the standard example. Soya milk, tofu, miso and TVP (textured vegetable protein) are also complete – as are all dairy products.

But we can also obtain complete protein by combining two or more complementary protein sources in one meal – rice with beans or sesame seeds, for example, or beans with corn, barley or oats. Each supplies the amino acids the other may lack. The classic example always given us is beans on toast. If you ponder a moment on this mix of complementary proteins, you will see how naturally we use it in many of our favourite meals. A vegetable curry, for example, is served with rice and a lentil dal. We soak up hummus with pitta bread. We eat peanut butter sandwiches.

Think of the vegetarian in your midst positively, and respect the wisdom of their choice. It gives the cook an opportunity to widen the repertoire for the whole family. So the meals need not be so completely separate as you might think. In fact, it is often the meat eater who is out of step and it is the meat component of the meal which might have to be considered as a separate entity. Vegetables, rice, cereals and pasta can all be shared amongst the family happily.

It is easier now to cook simple nutritious vegetarian meals than it was, say, five years ago. There is a range of foods and ingredients on sale to help the vegetarian cook which are often of a higher quality than the ones on sale for the carnivore. I am thinking in particular of the stock cube. I have always been suspicious of meat and chicken stock cubes, knowing that they are derived from pulverised remnants and the unwanted day-old chicks. The vegetarian stock cubes, if you choose the low-salt variety, are now of excellent quality and flavour. It is a simple matter to make a thick winter vegetable soup using vegetables, pulses, pasta or added dumplings, a soup which could become a firm family favourite.

But you will probably find that to help the single vegetarian the store cupboard should be expanded with some new ingredients which the whole family will enjoy. For such a soup, for example, a good extra virgin olive oil and garlic would greatly improve the flavour of the finished dish.

Vegetarian cooking should never be dull. Vegetable flavours are superb in themselves when they are not overcooked, and fresh herbs and spices, sauces made from tomato, aubergine, carrot or low-fat sauces from quark or fromage frais will all add immeasurably to a dish.

V

For the hungry adolescent the three 'Ps' – potatoes, pasta and pizza – are essential fodder. Baked potatoes are always a firm favourite, and they need not always be served with butter. Cottage cheese can be used, and you can stuff the potato with a mixture of different vegetables moistened by a sauce and flashed under the grill. But there are also other potato dishes. All the great classic French gratin dishes like dauphinoise and lyonnaise can have variations.

Gratin dishes involve slicing the potatoes thinly, washing the pieces in cold water to remove the starch and placing them in a shallow buttered earthenware dish. The potatoes are layered with various other ingredients in between, with the addition of cream, a sauce or stock. They are then baked slowly for two hours. The top should be crisp and brown and the underneath moist and succulent. Lyonnaise is where the potatoes are interleaved with onion but various additions could be carrot, celeriac, turnip and parsnip. Or there is the Irish dish, colcannon, where the potatoes are mashed and mixed with butter, leeks and spring onions – a curiously satisfying dish.

There are many new flavoured pastas available which only take a few minutes to cook, and a sauce can easily be made from a tin of tomatoes with a little added oregano, garlic or onion. But it does not take much more time to make a baked pasta dish using a cheese sauce baked over the cooked pasta, then baked in the oven with a final flash under the grill to make sure the top is brown and bubbling. Pizzas are also easy to make; all sorts of toppings can be smeared on the dough and baked quickly in the oven.

Rice is another great staple, and risotto rice is now freely available. This makes a creamy risotto within ten to twelve minutes and it is a simple matter to chop a few vegetables and mushrooms, cook them in olive oil until they are soft, then throw in the rice, add a little stock and leave it to cook for ten minutes.

There are, of course, already plenty of meat substitutes – Tivall, Quorn and TVP – and I am sure there will be new ones. But the range of vegetables is wide, and the world's cuisine full of limitless ways of cooking and serving them, so there should be no need for substitutes. Besides, sustaining life on vegetables means that one is more likely to eat in season from fresh produce – always a boon.

WATERCRESS
Watercress Soup • Watercress and Leek Soup

WORCESTERSHIRE SAUCE
How the West Was Won

WATERCRESS

This slightly peppery green-leafed plant grows in shallow streams and is commercially grown in tanks of clear running water. Its flavour is sharp and it makes marvellous soups.

The first recipe makes a light and refreshing soup good hot or chilled.

WATERCRESS SOUP

I LARGE BUNCH WATERCRESS
2 PINTS/I LITRE SEASONED VEGETABLE STOCK
5 FL OZ/I 50 ML SINGLE CREAM OR SMETANA

METHOD

Reserve a few of the smaller leaves for garnish. Cut off the stalks, chop them and then simmer them in the stock for 10 minutes. Drain, discarding the stalks and reserving the stock. Now simmer the top leaves for 3 minutes. Cool a little, then blend the stock and leaves. Reheat gently adding the cream or smetana. Throw in the garnish and serve.

WATERCRESS AND LEEK SOUP

½ OZ/I 5 G BUTTER
I LB/450 G LEEKS, CHOPPED
I LB/450 G POTATOES, CHOPPED
I ½ PINTS/840 ML VEGETABLE STOCK
I BUNCH WATERCRESS, CHOPPED
½ PINT/280 ML MILK
SEA SALT AND FRESHLY GROUND BLACK PEPPER

METHOD

Melt the butter in a pan and throw in the leeks and potatoes, sauté for a moment then add the vegetable stock, bring to the boil and simmer for 20 minutes. Blend half of the soup and return to the pan. Mix the watercress with the milk and blend the two together. Add to the soup. Gently reheat and season to taste.

WORCESTERSHIRE SAUCE
HOW THE WEST WAS WON

In the saga of how the Wild West was won the name of Lea & Perrins is never mentioned. That it played a largely unsung part, up to now, I have no doubt, for the makers of Worcestershire Sauce rose to prominence and riches in the last half of the nineteenth century, helped enormously, they say, by the expansion of the States.

The story goes that as vast chunks of land west of the Mississippi were wrested from the Indians, the conquerors dosed their food liberally with the sauce to make it palatable. This sheds a new light on a scorched earth policy. Later in the century, as wagon trains rolled over the Oregon–California Trail, the habit had caught on and buffalo steak was not the same without its Worcester.

The British were more circumspect. Colonel Kenney-Herbert in 1885 considered Worcestershire Sauce 'too powerful an agent to be entrusted to the hands of the native cook'.

Looking at the figures it would seem that America still consumes large amounts of it; every year they get through thirty dozen five-ounce bottles per thousand people. Australia leads the world at the rate of forty-six dozen per thousand. We lag a little behind at twenty dozen.

But it actually works out as a minute amount of sauce per person per year, only 1.2 fl oz/30 ml in our case, which is roughly what I pour into my own mix of Bloody Mary, turning it the colour of mud.

There is no doubt that the sauce is pre-eminent among all commercial bottled sauces (its only rival in my kitchen is good-quality soy), so I was eager to see the factory in Worcester itself. They take great pride in their product and, though the ingredients are now on the label of the bottle, the recipe with the ratio of the amounts is closely guarded.

Lea & Perrins are almost fussily concerned with the quality of their ingredients and buy from all over the world. Shallots come from Holland and anchovies from the Mediterranean, the garlic, tomatoes, red wine and sherry from Spain. Tamarind, fenugreek and cumin come from India, chillies and cloves from Madagascar and molasses from the West Indies.

These ingredients are placed in malt vinegar for three years in casks which hold seventy-five litres. One of the most interesting facts is that the ingredients are left whole; great heads of garlic with their stem and papery leaves lie in the vinegar macerating for this length of time. As the acetic acid leaches out all the flavour, they very slowly disintegrate.

The anchovies are salted in layers and after three years are perfectly edible and delicious. I plunged my hand into a barrel and ate one and all it needed was a piece of hot toast and strong Indian tea to wash it down. The shallots are spiked before immersion and are crushable between the fingers within twenty-nine months. After three years the contents are poured from the casks into huge maturation tanks, holding 33,000 litres, then the dried red chillies are added and the liquid is very gently mixed for only fifteen minutes each day while it is left for one month. Then a pump is used to percolate air through the tanks, but only for a few minutes each day for the next two months.

The next stage is the rotary sieve which separates the solids from the liquid; from each tank 26,000 litres of concentrated sauce is recovered. The vegetable debris, smelling powerfully of fish guts and spices, is too acid to use for manure and is thrown away as land fill.

Samples of the liquid are now taken to the chemist, who will test for acidity, specific gravity and suspension of solids. The concentrate is then reblended and sieved once again to remove the very tiny fibres left from the tamarind. Finally it is skimmed to remove the oil. They are proud that the bottles bear no expiry date and they claim that the sauce can only improve with time. A 100-year-old sauce was tasted and said to resemble old port. It was in 1823 that Mr Perrins of Evesham met Mr Lee of Worcester and they opened their first chemist's shop. It sold, among other products, dandelion coffee, live leeches for bleeding and gentlemen's trusses.

Much of its trade was to the Far East and India, where quinine and Dr Chloris's chlorodine were major essentials in the medical box. So it was not in the least unexpected when in 1835 Lord Sandys – a former governor of Bengal – brought his old Indian recipe to the chemist's shop to be made up.

Out of curiosity, Lee & Perrins made a large enough batch for themselves to try, but thought it so disgusting they closed the cask and forgot they had it for another two years. Then, discovering the cask while stocktaking, they had another taste and were so delighted that the sauce was marketed that year and sold nearly 2,000 bottles.

In 1854, within seventeen years, the amount had shot up to 36,000 bottles and the Wild West boom was yet to come.

YOGA
A Gourmet Vegetarian Weekend

Y O G A
A G O U R M E T V E G E T A R I A N W E E K E N D

Recently I attended the second Gourmet Vegetarian Weekend at the Yoga for Health Foundation at Ickwell Bury in Bedfordshire. I confess that I found the names of the two patrons irresistible – La Duchessa Simonetta Colonna de Cesaro and the Princess Helena Moutafian; for a moment I felt I might be attending a play by Jean Anouilh. But I was also intrigued as to how good the gourmet vegetarian food might be and how it would fuse with yoga philosophy, for I have an abiding fascination for that enigmatic relationship between sensuality and metaphysics.

The Yoga Centre is run by its director, Howard Kent, who strongly believes that gurus are bad for you. His reasoning is pragmatic enough. If you have a leader you follow, instead of doing it yourself and being self-reliant. Kent, though, is obviously made of guru material. Last winter in the depths of February he trotted out into the snow in a loincloth wearing a wet towel over his shoulders in an exercise to show the power of the mind over the physical state. He sat down to concentrate on heat and immersed himself in a tropical climate beneath a torrid sun. Within two and a quarter hours the wet towel was bone dry and he trotted back to work at his desk, disdaining the hot bath awaiting him. However, this weekend Howard Kent was in the States on a lecture tour, so there were no pyrotechnics of the mind so obviously displayed. Yet something stunning, unusual and energetic was at play within the group of guests which could not be ignored. Great flair and individuality had certainly touched the food, which was astonishingly good and liberal in its portions, considering the shoe-string budget they exist on, but what also deeply impressed me was the work the staff do with disabled people.

In the ten years after the Centre opened in April 1978 more than 2,000 disabled people stayed there, though these are still a minor portion of the guests: the weekend I was there ten of the thirty guests were disabled. Among the disabling diseases that benefit from the yoga are multiple sclerosis, muscular dystrophy, motor neurone disease, Parkinson's disease and others. When I was there the most striking guest was Kirstin, aged 32, who suffers from myosotis ossificans. In this disease the skeletal muscle turns to bone and the whole body slowly ossifies into hard chalk. Kirstin, already disabled at birth by rubella and twisted into a shape the mind finds awesome and troublesome to contemplate, looks after herself. She inches her path through the room and, with her yoga teacher, cheerfully goes through the exercises. The casual observer would say she is not moving at all, but the head or a foot moves a fraction of an inch to the right and then to the left, and her doctors back home have to agree that improvement has occurred, slight as it is, since she began coming to the Centre.

The holistic approach which views symptoms as products of mind, body, energy and spirit extends naturally to the food we place in our mouths, which is the fuel we exist by. No dead flesh and no junk ingredients. Not only does the food have to be pure, but Michelle, the young and lively cook, who has a natural passion for her art, has to produce food for particular diets – dairy- and gluten-free, low-yeast-mould, and macrobiotic are strict variations of the vegetarian, low-fat, low-sugar and low-salt recipes we ate with such gusto throughout the weekend.

For dinner on Friday we began with a spinach timbale surrounded by a garlic sauce which was, I am happy to say, highly generous with the garlic. A dish which would not have disgraced many a *Good Food Guide* restaurant. To intensify the sophistication, we followed this with a pineapple sorbet served in a hollowed out orange which was free of all ice crystals and full of flavour. As a main course we had pancakes stuffed with chilli beans and a selection of vegetables all cooked al dente. This was followed by a generous selection of puddings and cheese.

Having never done yoga before in my life, I found myself in the lotus position meditating at 6.45 the next morning. It lasted for fifteen minutes and I may have nodded off for part of that time. Then I threw myself into the swan, the cat and the cobra, all yoga positions and all deeply relaxing rather than exhausting. A further two hours of yoga exercises followed later that morning before the gourmet lunch, which was a huge spread of stuffed brioche with brie and plaited pastries filled with spiced vegetables, plus tarts, numerous salads of raw vegetables and dressings made with avocado, egg and herbs.

You are free, of course, to do whatever you like; you do not need to join in if you do not feel like it. You can walk the grounds – Ickwell Bury has an extensive walled garden rich with fruit, vegetables and flowers – or just sit and observe the wildlife which is attracted by the nature reserve also in the grounds. The Centre is open seven days a week, all the year round.

Kirstin returns for a month or two several times a year and the staff say she is the most cheerful of people. She was full of jokes when I spoke to her and was unembarrassed when I felt her back, which was as hard and as resistant to the touch as stone.

A weekend here, there can be little doubt, would lessen the manic stress of urban life. I was too moved by the vigour of the positive attitude among these disabled people to remember to enquire about who the patrons were, but I shall return especially for Michelle's tomato and garlic sauce and hope for a glimpse of La Duchessa while in the cobra position.

sour cream dressing, 223
salads, 221–2
apple and avocado, 32
apple and walnut, 17
artichoke and potato, 23
avocado and butter bean, 32
avocado and spinach, 33
avocado, grapefuit and purslane,
89–90
blue cheese apple, 16
broad bean and courgette, 47
carrot and apricot, 118
celeriac and egg, 64
chicory, orange and pistachio, 68
courgette, 165
fennel, orange and ginger, 226
gourmet potato, 194
green pepper, 227
Russian, 216
salade Angevine, 192
spiced salad mould, 223
spinach and avocado, 250
spinach and Derby cheese, 250
sprouting salad, 255
summer salad, 164
tabbouleh, 264
tabbouleh and lentil, 265
tomato, caper and mozzarella, 271
two pear, 35
warm calabrese, 61
winter salads, 224–6
salt, 228–9
sandwich roulade, 108–9
Saracen grass *see* buckwheat
sauces:
apple, 18
beurre blanc, 199
caper, 98–9
green, 227
mint salad, 190

mornay, 204
mustard and egg, 99
pesto, 43
pistou, 200
porcini, 12
spiced tahini, 266
tarragon and lemon, 267
Worcestershire, 286–7
sauerkraut, 53
sausages, Glamorgan, 85
sea salt, 228–9
sea vegetables, 230–1
seeds, sprouting, 253–5
semolina:
gnocchi di semolino, 171
sesame paste, 266
cauliflower in tahini sauce, 62
shallots:
beurre blanc sauce, 199
purée, 204
Sharon fruit, 126
shrimps:
gambas al ajillo, 241–2
Shrubland Hall, 116–17
Sicily, 232–3
smoked tofu, 269
solyanka, 193–4
sorrel:
roulade d'épinards, 213–15
soufflés:
asparagus, 28
white egg fungi, 150
soups:
bortsch, 218
broad bean, 47–8
chilled apple, 17
chilled marrow, 140–1
chilled tomato and red pepper, 271
courgette and parsley, 80
curried marrow, 140